THE V E

THE DRYDEN PRESS · 1944

ERAN

COMES BACK

WILLARD WALLER

This book has been manufactured in conformity with government regulations for saving paper. A lighter-weight paper substantially reduces the bulk of our books, and narrower margins provide more words to each page. Smaller, more compact books save paper, metal, and labor.

Acknowledgements

I wish to acknowledge indebtedness to Ann Rosenzweig and Ursula de Antonio for help in reading and digesting materials for this book, and to Stephen Brigham and George Kaplan for certain materials that they supplied. My colleagues at Columbia University have offered criticisms and suggestions, and the staff of the Columbia University Library has been extremely helpful. Donald S. Howard, Russell H. Kurtz, and Sigrid C. Holt, of the Russell Sage Foundation, have also given assistance. Morris Zelditch, Director of War Services, Family Welfare Association of America, and Donald Ambler, of The Dryden Press, have kindly read the manuscript and have contributed certain excellent suggestions. Stanley Burnshaw, of The Dryden Press, has given help which amounted literally to collaboration.

I wish to extend my thanks to all these, and to the authors and publishers who have permitted quotation of copyrighted materials. The illustration of the soldier on the jacket is used by permission of the United States Advertising Corporation, of Chicago.

I must, of course, assume the full responsibility for any errors in this book, as well as for the opinions expressed therein.

WILLARD WALLER

Barnard College
Columbia University

Contents

Prologue and Introduction

PART ONE ## The Civilian Is Made into a Professional Soldier

ENTR'ACTE: SOCIETY CHANGES WHILE THE SOLDIER IS AT WAR

PART TWO   *The Soldier-Turned-Veteran*
                       Comes Back to an
                           Alien Homeland

1. THE VETERAN IS BITTER— AND WITH REASON

2. MANY THINGS INTERFERE WITH THE VETERAN'S ADJUSTMENT

PART THREE   *Our Past Attempts — and Failures — to Help the Veteran*

PART FOUR   *Helping the Veteran to Adjust to Peacetime Living*

Epilogue

Prologue and Introduction

Prologue:
The Soldier's
Ancient Wrong

THE WISEST man the world has ever known was born as a result of the dirtiest double-cross in history. The victim of this betrayal was, of course, a soldier.

"And it came to pass, after the year was expired, at the time when kings go forth to battle, that David sent Joab, and his servants with him and all Israel; and they destroyed the children of Ammon, and besieged Rabbah. But David tarried still at Jerusalem.

"And it came to pass in an eveningtide, that David arose from off his bed, and walked upon the roof of the king's house; and from the roof he saw a woman washing herself; and the woman was very beautiful to look upon.

"And David sent and enquired after the woman. And one said, Is not this Bathsheba, the daughter of Eliam, the wife of Uriah the Hittite?

"And David sent messengers, and took her; and she came in unto him, and he lay with her; for she was purified of her uncleanness; and she returned unto her house.

"And the woman conceived, and sent and told David, and said, I am with child.

"And David sent to Joab, saying, Send me Uriah the Hittite. And Joab sent Uriah to David.

"And when Uriah was come unto him, David demanded of him how Joab did, and how the people did, and how the war prospered.

"And David said to Uriah, Go down to thy house, and wash thy feet. And Uriah departed out of the king's house, and there followed him a mess of meat from the king.

"But Uriah slept at the door of the king's house with all the servants of his lord, and went not down to his house.

"And when they had told David, saying, Uriah went not down

unto his house, David said unto Uriah, Camest thou not from thy journey? why then didst thou not go down unto thine house?

"And Uriah said unto David, The ark, and Israel, and Judah, abide in tents; and my lord Joab, and the servants of my lord, are encamped in the open fields; shall I then go into mine house, to eat and to drink, and to lie with my wife? as thou livest, and as thy soul livest, I will not do this thing.

"And David said to Uriah, Tarry here today also, and tomorrow I will let thee depart. So Uriah abode in Jerusalem that day, and the morrow.

"And when David had called him, he did eat and drink before him; and he made him drunk; and at even he went out to lie on his bed with the servants of his lord, but went not down to his house.

"And it came to pass in the morning, that David wrote a letter to Joab, and sent it by the hand of Uriah.

"And he wrote in the letter saying, Set ye Uriah in the fore front of the hottest battle, and retire ye from him, that he may be smitten, and die.

"And it came to pass, when Joab observed the city, that he assigned Uriah unto a place where he knew that valiant men were.

"And the men of the city went out, and fought with Joab; and there fell some of the people of the servants of David; and Uriah the Hittite died also.

"Then Joab sent and told David all the things concerning the war:

"And charged the messenger, saying, When thou has made an end of telling the matters of the war unto the king,

"And if so be the king's wrath arise, and he say unto thee, Wherefore approached ye so nigh unto the city when ye did fight: knew ye not that they would shoot from the wall?

"Who smote Abimelech the son of Jerubbesheth? did not a woman cast a piece of millstone upon him from the wall, that he died in Thebez? why went ye nigh the wall? then say thou, Thy servant Uriah the Hittite is dead also. . . .

"And the messenger said unto David, Surely the men prevailed against us, and came out unto us into the field, and we were upon them even unto the entering of the gate.

"And the shooters shot from off the wall upon thy servants; and some of the king's servants be dead, and thy servant Uriah the Hittite is dead also.

"Then David said unto the messenger, Thus shalt thou say unto Joab, Let not this thing displease thee, for the sword devoureth one as well as another; make thy battle more strong against the city, and overthrow it; and encourage thou him.

"And when the wife of Uriah heard that Uriah her husband was dead, she mourned for her husband.

"And when the mourning was past, David sent and fetched her to his house, and she became his wife, and bare him a son. But the thing that David had done displeased the Lord."

So died Uriah, the good soldier, because he would not taste pleasure while his comrades were in the field. While the ark and the soldiers of Israel were encamped in the fields, he would not lie with his wife. Good soldier, true comrade, front-line fighter, he died by treachery.

David was a good king. He has come down to us as the great man who slew his tens of thousands and dealt fairly with everybody except a few poor fools who fought for him and for the glory of Israel. *And some of the king's servants are dead, and thy servant Uriah the Hittite is dead also.* David was a wise king. When he wronged a man, he had that man killed. David had no veteran problem. But if Uriah the Hittite had survived, David would have had a veteran problem.

Uriah did not come home, but many millions of veterans have come home to confront those who have betrayed them in matters great and small. Veterans have written many a bloody page of history, and those pages have stood forever as a record of their days of anger. Many times has their blind, understandable fury changed the course of human events.

Introduction:
Veterans—Our Gravest
Social Problem

W HERE shall we begin the story of the veterans? Apparently
the memory of man runneth not to the time when veterans
were not. Should we begin with Odysseus, spoiler of cities,
who returned from Troy to make a counterrevolution in Ithaca?
With Aeneas, also a veteran, and a very dynamic agent in history?
Mythical characters, those, but as in the historical record fiction
slowly and ever imperfectly gives way to fact, we find the Cartha-
ginian veterans upon a blood-red page, and a few generations later
is Catiline, who led Sulla's pot-bellied veterans to honorable death in
his most dishonorable cause.

Everywhere in history are veterans, in every age and every nation.
There is enough in American experience with veterans to afford a
point of departure; and a "bearable" point at that, since the United
States has been fortunate in its veterans—fortunate indeed when
compared with other countries. On occasion we have mistreated
our returning soldiers, but they have usually been docile, and when
they were not they were content with small pensions. However, our
country has seen some disorders in which embattled veterans have
stood up to the authorities, demanding their rights. There has been
mutiny on the rolling hills of New Jersey. Rebellious veterans have
marched down the turnpike that leads through the fat lands of
Pennsylvania from Lancaster to Philadelphia. Congress has been
put in fear and forced to change its headquarters to another city.
The South has witnessed a secret and terrible counterrevolution.
Our armies have had their deserters and stragglers who have turned
into bushwackers and guerrillas.

Veterans and the War of Independence

At the end of our Revolutionary War, the morale of the American army sharply tumbled. Though dissatisfied with military life, the troops did not want to be demobilized without first receiving their pay. While in this uncertain and rebellious state, the troops at New-burgh (N. Y.) grew ominously restless. An anonymous letter was circulated in the camp, an excellent bit of writing in the "Hello Sucker" vein characteristic of soldiers at the end of a war. An excerpt:

> " ... If this then be your treatment while the swords you wear are necessary for the defence of America, what have you to expect from peace, when your voice shall sink and your strength dissipate by division; when those very swords, the instruments and companions of your glory, shall be taken from your sides, and no remaining mark of military distinction left but your wants, infirmities and scars? Can you then consent to be the only sufferers by this Revolution, and, retiring from the field, grow old in poverty, wretchedness, and contempt? Can you consent to wade through the vile mire of dependency, and owe the miserable remnant of that life of charity, which has hitherto been spent in honor? If you can, go, and carry with you the jest of tories and the scorn of whigs. Go, starve, and be forgotten! But if your spirits should revolt at this; if you have sense enough to discover, and spirit sufficient to oppose tyranny, under whatever garb it may assume, whether it be the plain coat of republicanism, or the splendid robe of royalty; if you have yet learned to discriminate between a people and a cause, between men and principles; awake, attend to your situation, and redress yourselves! If the present moment be lost, every future effort is in vain; and your threats then will be as empty as your entreaties now."

Go and carry with you the jests of the tories and the scorn of whigs. Go, starve, and be forgotten! It is easy to imagine the effect of such an incendiary piece of writing upon a group of rebellious, discontented veterans who were in want of everything and were convinced that their country intended to defraud them. It took the personality of Washington to soothe the soldiers into a less rebellious mood.

The news that the war had ended was in fact received sullenly by the soldiers. Washington and his officers even considered the possibility of suppressing the news temporarily, but their better judgment prevailed.[1] Like Cromwell's New Model Army, like the mercenaries of Carthage, Washington's soldiers wanted their money.

---

[1] For this fact and the material that immediately follows, see Varnum Lansing Collins, *The Continental Congress at Princeton*. The Princeton Library, 1908.

Insignificant though it was, their pay was all they had and without it they were reduced to beggary. When an attempt was made to furlough them without settling their accounts, it met with resistance.

The most serious outbreaks took place in Pennsylvania. Though the soldiers stationed at Philadelphia were mostly recruits who had served only five months and had done nothing more arduous than guard a few prisoners, among them were veterans of the famous mutiny of 1781. Meanwhile, eighty soldiers set out from Lancaster to demand justice from Congress. With the disaffected Philadelphia garrison they constituted a body of 250 to 300 fully armed troops. They menaced the Continental Congress, but laid hands on no one except President Boudinot, and that assault was very slight. Obliging civilians contributed to the excitement by furnishing the soldiers with liquor. Authorities were afraid to call out the militia—they would not dare unless the troops became violent.

Congress removed to Princeton and the mutiny died. A little later the soldiers were discharged, short-changed, and disgracefully swindled. They went, the jest of tories and the scorn of whigs. They went, starved, and were forgotten. In the fraud of which they were the victims were the germs of many evils to come in the next hundred and fifty years; pensions, tariffs ostensibly to pay the pensions, a Civil War partly because of the tariffs, then more pensions to pay more veterans and more tariffs, and an endless series of raids on the treasury. In the settlements following the Revolution was initiated America's traditional policy of paying on account of veterans' claims too much, too late, in the wrong way, and to the wrong persons.

The revolution was as much a civil as an international war, and it died hard. In the rhythmic interplay of revolution and counterrevolution that swept across the states after the war, discontented officers and soldiers played a great part. The officers had their organization (the Cincinnati), and there were men among them who would have been pleased to see monarchical institutions reestablished. There were radical risings, such as Shays' Rebellion, which was led by a former soldier of the Revolution, and was so fortunate in its outcome for the reactionaries that well-justified suspicions have arisen concerning its origins. After the Constitution had been adopted, the speculators who held the greater part of the veterans' dismissal-pay certificates reaped a rich reward when these were paid in full.

In time the political activities of Revolutionary veterans were directed into the more conventional channels of attempting to care for the disabled and to secure pensions for the men who needed them. But the mistreatment suffered by the soldiers at the end of the war furnished a moral justification for exactions on their part in later years. The belated and not very well considered attempts to redress these injustices supplied our precedents for handling the veterans of our other wars.

Confederate Veterans and the Ku Klux Klan

After the Civil War the soldiers of the Union furnished the dynamic element in the politics of the era of good stealing. Republicanism, Protectionism, and Pensionism became the objects of their emotional and political attachments. The Republican Party and the Grand Army of the Republic were their organizations that worked hand in hand for pensions and tariffs. The energies of the returned soldiers were thus allowed to come to expression without greatly disturbing the *status quo* in the North.

In the South, however, the veterans' bitterness had cruel work to do. The North had imposed a revolution upon the South. The veterans made a counterrevolution. After the war, the bottom rail was on top in southern society; the former rulers disfranchised; Negroes and carpetbaggers in the Federal and State offices. In the movements that restored the white race to its traditional supremacy, veterans apparently took the leading part. Typical of the agencies used for this counterrevolution was the Ku Klux Klan. When first organized in 1865 by six young veterans in Pulaski, Tennessee, the Klan was probably intended to be only a harmless social club.[2] The eery costume was first adopted for reasons of wholesome fun; its utility for terrorizing freedmen was discovered later. The Klan's announced purposes sounded innocent enough: "To protect the weak, innocent and defenseless from the indignities, wrongs, and outrage of the lawless, the violent, and the brutal; to relieve the injured and oppressed, especially the widows and orphans of ex-Confederate soldiers." When the Reconstruction Acts of 1867 were

---

[2] Claude G. Bowers, *The Tragic Era: The Revolution after Lincoln.* Houghton Mifflin, 1929, pp. 306 ff.

passed, and the vise was thus tightened on the South, the Klan became committed to the counterrevolution.

The now politically active Klan found its predestined leader in Nathan Bedford Forrest,[3] whom Sandburg calls "a born killer made for war." He was the perfect leader of the movement to restore white supremacy. A log-cabin boy, a former slave trader, an able business man, a killer a hundred times over but a godly man who prayed before he went into battle, he became a general known for his sudden and terrible forays and a soldier who knew how to make war support war. He had no moral scruples against slavery: "If we aint fightin' fer slavery then I'd like to know what we are fightin' fer." He was in charge when Negro troops were massacred at Fort Pillow, this first Grand Wizard who led the Klan in 1867.

The entire South was the "Invisible Empire" and the Grand Wizard the supreme head, and under him were lesser officers: Grand Dragons, Grand Titans, and Grand Cyclops. The Klansmen called each local chapter a "den" and themselves "regulators." Force and violence were part of their methods—though they were rarely if ever convicted of crime—but they preferred to rule by terror where they could. While their ritual and mumbo-jumbo helped greatly in subduing the ignorant and superstitious Negroes, without the driving force and organizing ability of such men as Forrest, the counterrevolution would certainly have failed.

After the formal dissolution of the Klan, other organizations took up the work of resistance to Reconstruction, but the methods, and in large part the leadership, remained the same; the men of the South continued to be led by former officers acting in their capacity as veterans. In South Carolina a red-shirted party swept Wade Hampton into power in one of the last acts of the drama of Reconstruction. In the end the old order was restored and the revolution was in vain; the Bourbons returned to power, having learned nothing and forgotten nothing.

German Veterans of World War I and Fascism

It remained for the First World War to release the dynamic force

---

[3] Eric William Sheppard, *Bedford Forrest, The Confederacy's Greatest Cavalryman.* London, Witherly, 1930. See also Carl Sandburg, *Abraham Lincoln, The War Years.* Harcourt Brace, 1939, Vol. III, pp. 36-44.

of veterans upon a global scale. Of the more than 63,000,000 men under arms, about 55,000,000 veterans came home.[4] Their impact upon Western civilization has been incalculably great. Russia was the first major power to feel it. As early as 1915, army deserters had become extremely troublesome; Warsaw restaurant keepers, for example, had orders to serve only soldiers whose papers were in order.[5] When the Revolution came, these deserters and mutinous soldiers played a mighty part. It is no mere coincidence, therefore, that the Soviet government has probably made more intelligent use of its veterans than any other great power.

Since 1918, veterans have furnished the dynamic of politics in nearly every major nation, and the world has reaped many a bitter fruit of veteran discontent. The effects in the United States, though disquieting to some, have been relatively benign. France was much more unfortunate; its veterans' societies carried on vicious wars against the liberties of the French people. But it was in Germany and in Italy that the veterans' anger became the principal organizing force in society.[6]

Like the men of our own South, the Germans of 1918 lost the war but kept their cause. For many Germans World War I never came to an end. In 1918 many of Germany's conscripted soldiers, and a section of the German people rose against the German army and overthrew it, but many persons primarily loyal to the German army never accepted defeat and continued an unceasing, if secret, war. Of 200,000 officers, 190,000 could find no military employment. They had to doff their uniforms but the army lived on in their hearts. They did what they could for the cause that they never regarded as lost. Thieves, perjurers, cut-throats, and midnight assassins, they killed and lied and stopped at nothing.

The methods of the counterrevolution were simple. Assassination. Conspiracy. Concealment of weapons. Organization of secret armies under one harmless name after another. Perversion of justice. Death to the inner enemies. Bloody revenge, utter implacable ruthlessness. The Civil War first, then the international war. But first Civil War

[4] Quincy Wright, *A Study of War*. U. of Chicago Press, 1942; Vol. I, Table 56, p. 664.

[5] Frank P. Chambers, *The War Behind the War, 1914-15*. Harcourt Brace, 1939, p. 119.

[6] An illuminating analysis of the counterrevolution in Germany has been furnished by Konrad Heiden, *Der Fuehrer, Hitler's Rise to Power*, Houghton Mifflin, 1944.

to weld the German people into a perfect instrument of warfare.

A young officer, Ernst Röhm, organized one secret army after another, changing titles frequently but keeping the nuclei intact. He sent out assassins and gave orders to corrupt judges who accordingly adjudged the conspirators not guilty. A fatherly officer beloved by his men and a homosexual murderer, Röhm never got the army out of his heart.

Not the great officers but the lesser ones carried on this struggle. Many of the captains and lieutenants had never learned any trade other than war, and war had been good to them. Having graduated from school early, they quickly became officers without going through the long grind of preparation and waiting for promotion. Their work was dangerous but exciting and the pay was good, especially for such young men. As officers, they were men of mark. When peace broke out, these men found no career, no bread.

These former officers struggled to win the proletariat. An obscure corporal showed them the way. Before the war, he had been an unsuccessful painter who did little pictures that were pasted on furniture. For years he was an inhabitant of a shelter for homeless men, literally, in American slang, a bum. Then he was a masochistic soldier who gloried in slaughter and hardship but never wanted a woman; a queer psychopathic soldier who never complained. After the war, he became a spy for the counterrevolution. With his loud harsh voice, he said things over and over until the veriest oaf could understand him. Before the war a bum, after the war a stool-pigeon and a finger-man, he was the lowest of the low. But he was shrewd, cunning, and intelligent, and he knew the way to the hearts of the German people.

With the help of some of the landowners and industrialists, with the assistance of the deluded proletariat, these veterans made the German counterrevolution. The civil war first, and after that the international war.

After the international war, what wars will come and who will make them? When this World War I group of veterans marches off the stage of history, who marches on to take their places?

We have chosen only a few of the thousands of stories of veterans which lie scattered over the pages of history. These few examples suffice, perhaps, to illustrate our central fact: *The veteran is, and always has been a problematic element in society, an unfortunate, misused, and pitiable man, and, like others whom society has mis-treated, a threat to existing institutions.*

Veterans: America's Gravest Social Problem

No one supposes, of course, that all veterans are alike. As an army is an expression of the national culture, so is the man who has served in that army. American veterans could never behave like German veterans; they could never become Storm Troopers, never be the hired bullies, thugs, and assassins of a stupid counterrevolution. They could never make war against their fellow-citizens. Or could they? Armies, while they vary somewhat with the national back-ground, are strangely alike, and there are striking similarities in the behavior of army-made men, of veterans, in all times and places. Perhaps if the American veterans of World War II return to a society similar to that of the Germany of 1918-1932 they too will raise up a Röhm and a Hitler.

The veteran who comes home is a social problem, and certainly the major social problem of the next few years. Not always but all too often he is a problem because of his misfortunes and his needs, because he is maimed, crippled, demented, destitute, cold and enhungered; these things he is, these wants he has, from no fault and no desire of his own but solely because of what we have done to him; only because we have used him as an instrument of national policy; because we have used him up, sacrificed him, wasted him. No man could have a better moral claim to the consideration of his fellows. And no man could have a better right to bitterness.

But the veteran, so justly entitled to move us to pity and to shame, can also put us in fear. Destitute he may be, friendless, without political guile, unskilled in the arts of peace; but weak he is not. That makes him a different kind of problem. That hand that does know how to earn its owner's bread knows how to take your bread, knows very well how to kill you, if need be, in the process. That eye that has looked at death will not quail at the sight of a policeman. *Unless and until he can be renaturalized into his native land, the veteran is a threat to society.*

We now face the return to civilian society of that one-tenth of the population which the other nine-tenths have used to fight a war. These men will return, if they are like other soldiers, in no easy and comfortable frame of mind; it will be difficult to find the equable, complacent, obedient boys we sent away in the bitter, anger-hard veterans who return. But we have made them what they are, we have used them for war and war has put its curse on them; they are our boys whom we delivered to Moloch; our finest and bravest, a whole generation of our men-children. We must somehow find the way to win them back.

The condition that faces us is nothing new to the United States. From colonial times to the present, our nation has always had a group of veterans, we have always had a veteran problem, and we have never known how to handle that problem. We have been in twelve major wars since the Revolution, according to Quincy Wright's count and have engaged in over 170 military campaigns; for such a peace-loving people, we do seem to have a lot of trouble![7] We have never made adequate provision for the veterans of those wars. The history of our policy toward the returned soldier is in fact so discouraging that one may well wonder whether we shall ever manage to combine intelligence and humanity in the treatment of the men we send to fight for us.

Our kind of democratic society is probably worse fitted than any other for handling veterans. An autocracy, caring nothing for its human materials, can use up a man and throw him away. A socialistic society that takes from each according to his abilities and gives to each according to his needs can use up a man and then care for him the rest of his life. But a democracy, a competitive democracy like ours, that cares about human values but expects every man to look out for himself, uses up a man and returns him to the competitive process, then belatedly recognizes the injustice of this procedure and makes lavish gestures of atonement in his direction which somehow never quite suffice to gather up the spilled milk or put Humpty-Dumpty together again.

Our traditional policy has been to neglect our veterans for a period of years after the end of a major war. During this period of neglect, uninjured veterans take up the broken threads of their lives as best they can, struggle against discouragements to compete successfully, force their way into economic, social, and political life, while the injured, the maimed, gassed, tubercular, and men-

[7] Wright, op. cit., Vol. I, pp. 636 ff. Wright counts as wars any hostilities which were legally defined as wars or which involved more than 50,000 troops.

tally unbalanced contrive to live by such little jobs as their conditions permit, learn to beg on the streets, and become paupers, steal and are sent to prison, or else just starve and are forgotten together with their widows and dependents. Then, after some years, the veterans suddenly emerge as a powerful political force. Still burning with resentment over their own wrongs, they see to it that ample provision is made for unfortunate veterans. But it is too late then to do justice, too late to help many who have died or been ruined beyond hope of reclamation.

We waste the golden years in which rehabilitation is possible, then spend billions in fruitless penance for wrongs that can never be undone. We allow the tuberculous veteran, ruined by war, to cough out his lungs in the county poor-house; then, years later, perhaps more than a hundred years later, we pay a pension to a woman who was not born until years after the end of the war, a woman who married a senescent veteran in anticipation of the benefits that would accrue to his widow. Our policy is to pay on account of veterans too much, too late, to the wrong person, in the wrong manner. We have spent many billions on veterans' claims, and most of it has been wasted. We have never spent enough at the right time, or spent it on the right persons.

What the times demand is a new art, the art of rehabilitation. We know how to turn the civilian into a soldier. History has taught us that all too well; tradition has given us marvellously adequate techniques. But we do not know how to turn the soldier into a civilian again. This is the art that we must perfect if we are ever to solve the problem of the veteran in our society. Such an art should begin with an attempt to understand the veteran and the veteran problem; particularly, it must begin with an understanding of the veteran's attitudes. We must learn what it is to have a rendez-vous with death and to live through it, to be, for a time, expendable, and then to be expendable no more. What happens when the expendable one returns? What attitudes does he bring with him? That is the principal task of this book: to present and to illuminate the veteran problem, and to explain the veteran's mental and emotional nature and the problems in the way of his readjustment in society.

In developing our theme, we shall analyze, in Part I, what being in the army does to a man, and how military experience molds him in such a way as to make him no longer fit for civilian life. An Entr'Acte then tells how society changes while the soldier is away, thus aggravating his problem of adjustment. Part II describes and attempts to explain the curious, corrosive bitterness that floods the veteran mind, and points out some of the difficulties that the veteran encounters in his attempts to adjust to peacetime living. Another Entr'Acte discusses the veteran as a political threat. Part III describes and evaluates past attempts to help veterans to adjust to civilian life. A third Entr'Acte tells of the present challenge of our returning veterans, while Part IV makes some suggestions concerning the manner in which we can and should meet the problem of the returning expendables of World War II.

The Civilian Is Made into a Professional Soldier

The Army Machine Annihilates the Soldier's Individual Will

A man who has once been a soldier can never be quite a civilian again. A military experience, especially in time of war, leaves a mark upon a man. If we are to understand the veteran, we must learn what he experiences as a soldier.

While military organizations differ in important respects, they have many characteristics in common. For the sake of simplicity, we may concentrate on the common elements and ignore the differences. By army, we shall mean any military organization; by soldier, every man under arms.[1]

And when we speak of the soldier, we mean the typical soldier, not any particular soldier or every soldier. Our generalizations apply to most soldiers in some degree and describe the reactions of many soldiers quite closely, but no one supposes that they apply to every man Jack of every army in the world. In all our thinking about man, we are forced to construct types. The economist knows that the economic man is not every man, and in fact is not any man, but he is what all men tend to be under certain circumstances. Not even the law of gravity can describe with accuracy anything that actually happens, although it describes very well what always tends to happen. Just so, the soldier of whom we shall speak is not any soldier in particular, but he is what all soldiers tend to be.

When we take a man and make him a soldier, we subject him to the conditioning processes of a peculiar environment, removing

---

[1] For the female veteran, some of our generalizations may not hold, although one of the most valuable autobiographies of World War I was written by one—Vera Brittain's *Testament of Youth*, an excellent document upon which we shall draw freely. While we disagree with Miss Brittain's recent stand on bombing, her personal history in World War I is valuable because of its presentation of the woman's eye view of war.

him from his accustomed world that has made him what he is. A human being is the creature and the creation of the society in which he lives; he has whatever habits his society permits and encourages him to have, no more and no less, and those habits are the man. Change the society and you change the man. The civilian-turned-soldier derives his distinguishing characteristics from the social environment of the army.

Perhaps more definitely than any other human social arrangement, the army is a social machine. It is a machine designed for violent action, which enables a million men to act with a single will; a machine so designed that it will not disintegrate under the impact of crisis or sudden disaster. It is a machine, and the men in it are the parts. In order to become a soldier, a man must shed some of his personal characteristics, and the army must ignore the rest. The parts of the machine must be interchangeable and standardized. They must be expendable, that is, if some men must die for the good of the whole, the leader must be free to give the order that sends them to their death.

The Army's Will Is the Only Will That Counts

The aim of an army is to impose its will upon the enemy. Before an army can succeed in this purpose, its leaders must first impose their will upon the men in their organization. They must mold the common soldiers and the officers into perfect instruments for expressing the will of the leader.

The essence of military action is cooperation according to design imposed from above. In order to achieve that cooperation, the army must partly annihilate and partly ignore the soldier's private will. And it must organize, plan, and execute an incredible amount of hard work in order that a few soldiers may fight for a short time.

The nation gives its young men over to the army by process of law, but they must give themselves too. In human affairs, there is no absolute compulsion, none that is not associated with some degree of consent. The recruit must submit himself to the army; he must take an oath. From then on he is held in the iron grip of military discipline. Military men understand this procedure. According to the European tradition, men must be got into the army by whatever means necessary, and then discipline will transform them into soldiers. There is an old saw that the army cannot make a man fight, but it can take him where the fighting is and he can use his own judgment.

Our present army is a drafted army, which means that its members gave a minimum of consent to military service. It may be that the draftee was anxious to evade service and tried hard to get out of it. Nevertheless, once he has joined the army—once he has, under some compulsion, consented to take the oath—he suddenly finds himself full of patriotism. Often he makes a virtue of necessity, and speaks and no doubt thinks as though his military career were a matter of his own free will. Nearly always, he comes to be contemptuous of civilians and 4Fs and all who are not doing their bit in uniform,—having by now forgotten his own confused feelings concerning military service. When the soldier becomes a veteran, he continues, as a matter of pride, to think of his military contribution as the result of an unforced choice.[2]

When the soldier has given himself over to the army, he discovers a world in which his private personality and his private will no longer count. No one says please to him any more, because to use that word as we do in civilian life would imply that he has it in his power to withhold the action he is ordered to undertake. He is part of a great machine in which the private has very little option and from which the self-will of the soldier must be systematically eradicated.[3]

He has few belongings, and those only of the simplest sort, practically all government issue. He has no privacy; all the actions that were once private must now be performed publicly. He eats, sleeps, bathes, upon order and very often by the numbers, all in

2 All this is said to explain the psychology of the soldier and the veteran and not to detract from his sacrifice. His sacrifice is just as great, and his claim upon society equally large, whether he chose freely or was in part coerced to join the colors. In fact, the draftee has in some ways a better claim upon our consideration than the man who voluntarily chose the military life.

3 As the soldier rises in the military hierarchy, he receives a wider choice of means to employ in attaining the end desired by the army. A source of strength in the present German army is said to be the encouragement of initiative in under officers by allowing them a choice of means. Our own army, while insisting upon conformity as to time and place, allows its under officers some scope for initiative. The definition of the sphere of responsibility is a difficult point of policy. There must be close coordination of action, but the initiative of the individual must not be completely crushed. Lee's policy was to leave tactical decisions to his general officers in charge of operations, and while it worked well with such men as Jackson, it did not always succeed. Some argue that this policy cost Lee the Battle of Gettysburg.

the full glare of pitiless publicity. He rarely hears his own given name. On Sunday morning he marches off to church with a thousand others, "whether he has a religion or not." If he offends the military law, his shortcomings are weighed in court with the mathematical impersonality of a Monroe Calculator.

The military machine follows the individual remorselessly, crushing out every resurgence of his private will against it. He can never excuse himself by saying, "I forgot," because drill-sergeants, understanding that a man can remember anything that he really wants to remember, treat every such forgetting as rebellion. In time the soldier ceases to be Samuel Jones of Main Street, Green-trees, and becomes Private Jones of the Army of the United States, whose one job, one goal, one mission in life is war. He is a very specialized kind of human being, a trained and disciplined killer,—indeed, a kind of weapon.

In order to settle all matters of authority and to avoid clashes of personality, the army has fashioned a minutely graded hierarchy in which everyone has a special place of his own. Orders come down from the top, all the way down, and they can never go up. Everybody is *under* orders; high and low alike are subordinated to the task at hand. The aim of military organization is to arrange things in such a manner that there can never be any doubt as to who has the right to order whom to do what. An attempt is also made to fix responsibility beyond argument. Succession to authority follows rigidly established lines.

Variations in uniform indicate exactly the place of each individual in the hierarchy. The corporal's authority is published by the stripes on his sleeve and extends to a certain group of men. The lieutenant's authority and responsibility extend much further. The relationships of the various levels of the hierarchy are embedded in such ceremonies as the salute, the use of the third person and of the word, "sir." These rituals are carefully depersonalized; one is taught to salute the uniform and not the man. Sometimes the soldier salutes the man as well as the uniform—which is all right—but he must never fail to accord the proper respects to the uniform because of his opinion of the man in it. When a William Saroyan salutes a Red Cross worker "because of the dignified expression on her face," a military tradition has been perverted. Good leadership, of course, in the army as anywhere else, can not depend too much upon such externals. Nevertheless it is almost true that the army ceremony not merely demarcates the relationship between leaders and led but in fact *is* the relationship.

Regimentation Makes the Recruit a Soldier

Along with this apparently superficial and ceremonial character of life goes great emphasis upon appearance. The soldier must care for his uniform; he must shine buttons endlessly; he must keep his shoes immaculate and his leggings straight. Strange as it may seem to the civilian this emphasis on appearance is a means of welding men into a harmonious well-disciplined whole. "Spit and polish" is a synonym for a certain kind of discipline which is more apt to flourish, naturally, in time of peace than in time of war, and is more appropriate in training than in combat. The same kind of care is lavished upon all parts of the soldier's equipment as well as his living quarters. At first these things come hard to the recruit, but after a while he learns the tricks of the trade—to let his shoes dry and then brush them, how to fold things and put them away, how to clean a rifle without completely disassembling it. Perhaps he comes to realize that there is no such thing as a regulation uniform, but only a collection of permitted deviations from a norm. When the recruit has been taught to conform in such matters, and has learned a technique of conforming, he has begun to be a soldier.

But the demands of group living involve even further regimentation. In an army a great many men must live together in a semi-communal social order. The satisfaction of the elementary needs of life and the laws of sanitation necessitate inflexible regulation of behavior. An army must spend a great deal of its energy in feeding and caring for itself. Even at best, it can provide only the simplest necessities for its members, hence the private soldier must simplify his needs. Furthermore, an army must be prepared to live in the field, and the soldier must learn how to take care of himself under field conditions, which means, among other things, that he must learn to transport himself and his equipment over long distances on his own motive power. The physical training and psychological conditioning of the soldier reflect these necessities.

For the primary military initiation of the civilian in uniform, the army allots about three months. In that period, the recruit becomes a soldier. He learns, in Pershing's phrase, to "shoot and to salute." He learns to take orders. He comes to accept discipline. His body hardens. He adjusts to the army culture, learns the names of things and the rules of the game, the techniques of getting by in the army. He becomes army-wise. After his first period of rebellion against the army, he ultimately becomes rather proud of the fact that he is a soldier. At the end of this training period, he is a soldier and knows how to take care of himself under army conditions. In many respects, the effects of this initial period of military training upon personality are distinctly favorable.

Unhappily, it is impossible to subordinate a human being to a machine to such an extent without at the same time damaging and partially paralyzing his intelligence. The strict regimentation of an army, with its concomitant of army politics, often crushes initiative and in the end makes it impossible for the underling to think of new things. Since a man can come to command only after long service in subordinate positions, conservatism is inherent in the army. Because an army, by and large, cannot bring out the best in a man, fails to use the best of a man's potentialities and in fact sometimes destroys that best, one may argue that an army always tends to be inefficient just because it is an army—a fault it shares with all bureaucracy.

An army always prepares for the last war, runs the popular remark, or for the last but one. In any case, the conservatism of peacetime armies is proverbial. Recent decades have witnessed many instances in which the military wisdom of such men as Mitchell and De Gaulle was smothered by tradition-bound brass hats. In peace, the Colonel Blimps hold undisputed sway in most armies, but war weeds them out. In the United States, the wartime influx of a great number of civilian-minded officers usually gives us a very effective army, after these men have learned their army jobs, which usually takes a couple of years.

Some Part of Every Soldier Fights the Army

Certainly the human animal is not perfectly adaptable to military life. He is quickly bored by it and rebels against it. There are so many things that the soldier, as a human being, wants to do but cannot do because he is a soldier that boredom is almost universal in war. The soldier must spend much of his time waiting; he must run to get to some place quickly and then wait all day for others to arrive; he must wait for the zero hour and for the big attack. In an army of specialists, the technician must spend a great amount of time waiting for the chance to do the particular job for which he has been trained. Soldiers therefore develop a whole series of techniques and attitudes that help to minimize boredom and to pass the time.

No matter how hard he tries to conform, no matter how well and cheerfully he does his duty, the soldier, with some small part of himself rebels against the army. This rebellion shows itself in the perennial grumbling that has apparently been characteristic of soldiers since wars began. The songs that common soldiers sing frequently express very adverse opinions concerning commissioned officers high and low, but wise officers realize the importance of such verbal outlets and pay no attention to the singing and hardly more to the grumbling unless its tone becomes ominous. Most of all, of course, the soldier rebels by "soldiering" on the job. (Note the folk-wisdom inherent in that phrase, "to soldier on a job.") The man who is army-wise learns how to avoid certain duties without incurring unpleasant consequences, and is perhaps the better soldier for it.

Such phenomena, characteristic of almost any military establishment at times, do not necessarily indicate that morale is low. Morale may be defined as an adjustment of the wishes and attitudes of individuals to the purpose of the group. The purpose of an army is fighting, and so long as soldiers will fight, their morale is good. An army is not a seminary for young ladies, and it can afford to limit its demands to the business of war; in fact, it cannot afford to make any demands irrelevant to war—like the law, it does not concern itself with trifles. *Esprit de corps,* which the military often confuse with morale, is not quite identical with it. It helps morale, but is not its primary element. The essence of morale is simply that adjustment in individuals, that set of attitudes which causes them, when the pressure is on, to do their duty.

An army is not a school of character but a machine for fighting. When the civilian-turned-soldier has adjusted his personality to the demands of the military machine, he has thereby lost some part of his ability to adjust to the demands of civilian society.

He has learned to get by in the army, to look out for himself as a soldier, he has learned to take orders and to act in concert with thousands of others, but he has not learned to get a civilian job and to hold it, he has not learned to rise in the morning with no bugle or top sergeant to remind him, he has not learned to live without the incessant proddings of the military machine, he has not learned how to treat his wife and children or what attitude to take toward the opinions of the neighbors. Accustomed to receiving and giving orders, he can no longer comprehend that vast and alien civilian world where everything depends upon consent, where one must persuade, not order or forbid. In a world where externals are everything, where outward conformity is the sum of one's duty and one's whole life is devoted to the husk of things, he has had no opportunity to cultivate familiarity with the still small voice of conscience, has had, in fact, no right to have a conscience because he had no right to regulate his behavior by his own inner standards. When the soldier returns to civilian life, he must learn once more to take up the burdens of personal and moral responsibility.

The Soldier Is Alienated from the World He Left Behind

ONCE in the army, the civilian-turned-soldier is shut off from the main currents of communication characteristic of civilian life. In our society, communication with others is normally intense and continuous. We read newspapers, magazines, books, advertising, letters, signs, billboards, cards, and every kind of thing that mankind has designed to bear a written message. We listen to the radio, attend plays and movies, go to church, speak or listen at meetings. With those about us, we chatter endlessly, even when our talk has no meaning except to show the momentary absence of ill will. Gossip and ridicule control our behavior and confine us to the ways of our herd. Opinion is formed in the discussions at the village store, on the bus or club-car, in the pool-room and saloon. Folk-wisdom reaches us through this communicative process; and just so do we get our common sense, which we call common not because the majority of people have it but because it is derived from the common life. Our very selves are derived from the welter of words and gestures in which we live.

When the young man joins the army, he is almost completely removed from this communicative interchange. No one tells him the gossip about the woman next door, or the interesting details of the newcomers down the street. There is no garage man to repeat the witticism that a mechanic can't make any money pumping gas in explanation of a botched repair job done at a filling station. There are no prudent neighbors to raise their eyebrows at his behavior. No one speaks to him of family pride, and no one listens to his stories about his job. He is in a different world now, a new country.

The soldier does not read much, the Armed Services Editions

notwithstanding. Although our army is doubtless better educated than any previous American army, less than half of the men have been through high school, while another one-fourth has finished high school but no more. Furthermore, the soldier has little time for or interest in books. Trained for action, he lacks the scholar's *Sitzfleisch;* immersed in the daily routines of the soldier, he cannot settle down to Plato. When he does read, his goal is not ordinarily self-improvement, and he prefers Super-Man and other comics to the Five-Foot Shelf. He is a doer now, not a talker or a thinker, and the intellectual climate in which he lives is unfavorable to the growth and development of complex ideas. The so-called "intellectual" is sometimes broadened a bit in his human sympathies; he learns at length that truck-drivers are people, but he is in a position to profit only because he begins by being, as regards concrete human relations, not, as he believes, the broadest, but the narrowest of men.

The Army World Is the Real World to the Soldier

The soldier becomes a part of a tightly organized social world so deeply engrossed in its own concerns that it has no interest in most of the things that concern civilians. The army is an intense world, compact, replete with meaning. While it is free and easy about many things important in civilian life, the army is pedantically precise and exacting in military details. Its problems are either crucial or utterly trivial, either of life or death or how to get a twenty-four hour pass. Its contexts and meanings are almost the complete antithesis of civilian society.

The new soldier is sometimes amazed to learn how important the head man of some little part of the organization can be in the army. The head man's characteristics are subjected to minute scrutiny, because he is the holder of immense, and, to the soldier, apparently arbitrary power over the lives and destinies of his men. Unlike the civilian's immediate superior, the head man in the army has controlling power twenty-four hours a day.

Far more than in a civilian community, rumors determine the public opinion of an army. They start nobody knows how and circulate through those unknowable channels that we call the grape-vine: The outfit is going overseas at once, or it is going back home; such and such a program or practice is being discontinued; there are going to be thirty-six hour passes for everybody; there is saltpetre in the food; the war is all over and the big shots are just holding back the news. Rumor plays such an important part in the army precisely because of the absence of the normal channels of news dissemination. When the newspapers are suppressed or the news is too heavily censored, rumor comes to occupy a similar position in civilian life.

The soldier is so busy, so engrossed in his own concerns, so tired, so far removed from such matters, so military-minded that he finds it impossible to care greatly whether Lawyer Sharp or the Honorable Do Much gets elected to Congress back home. The issues cannot come alive for him; he has no stake in them, and hardly any attitude except that he resents them. He wants to get the war over; and next to that, he craves a woman and a drink, in the language of the last war, a steam-heated flat and a blonde. The political struggles back home seem trivial compared with such driving necessities.

In a sense, there is not even as much war talk in the army as in civilian life. It is not just a joke when a man joins the army to get away from the war, or to get his mind off the war. The soldier has his war and does not need to think about it any more; he is free from the driving impulsion to discuss strategy (which in any case is no concern of his) that motivates the civilian at home. It is true that the soldier's single concern is war, but with this qualification: The civilian discusses the war, while the soldier discusses the army or a part of the war. The soldier trains in one particular company in a certain training camp; if he gets to the front he sees a small part of a great battle; perhaps he spends the war doing paper work in Iceland; whatever happens to him is his personal and particular war. It will be a matter of years before he learns about the rest of the war.

The Army Breeds a Culture of Its Own

The army has its own culture, and as the soldier becomes immersed in it, it becomes a part of him, and he grows away from his civilian personality. The army speaks a special language. Forms of speech are carefully prescribed and usually mirror conventionalized relationships. Military language contains many cherished archaisms, such as the "Aye, Aye, sir," of the Navy, as well as the uniform and the now abandoned mode of marking time by bells and watches; the function of such mannerisms of speech is to set a service apart and to isolate the members of that service from the remainder of the world. Army abbreviations alone are almost sufficient to make military speech incomprehensible to the civilian. A letter from one old army sergeant to another is likely to be such a collection of initials as to seem like a code to the uninitiated, but when translated it is direct and simple speech. On the other hand, military language is sometimes superior to ordinary speech in modernity and lack of ambiguity; an example of which is the present twenty-four hour nomenclature of the services. Not only is the soldier's way of telling time different from that of the civilian, but the attitude toward it is different, the meaning of time being almost wholly a function of social habits.

Service humor is also characteristic of the army world. It deals pre-eminently with service situations, expressing attitudes often incomprehensible to civilians. There is a frequent element of gallows humor in it. Caesar recounts some of the sour witticisms of his own soldiers, not too different from the military brand of today. But nothing can match the grim humor of the Johnny Reb who prayed:

> Now I lay me down to sleep,
> While gray-backs o'er my body creep;
> If I should die before I wake,
> I pray the Lord their jaws to break.[1]

The army love of humorous abbreviations gave birth to the famous SOL of World War I, and to the more ingenious snafu (variations, susfu, fubar, and tarfu) of the present war. A certain type of army humor, particularly the recruit jokes, seems to be intermediate between service and civilian humor. *Dere Mable* appealed to both soldiers and civilians, but *See Here, Private Hargrove* leans definitely to the civilian side. American Legion publications contain a good deal of this intermediate kind of humor, being in themselves intermediate in attitude.

[1] Quoted by R. D. Meadie, N. Y. Herald-Tribune Book Review, April 16, 1944, p. 7. The reader whose cultural opportunities have been limited will be interested to learn that the grayback is a louse.

Service men's songs follow along the same lines. Manufacturing his own folk music and embellishing old tunes with new words, the American soldier displays much ingenuity. The famous song of the 1918 A.E.F. was the "Mademoiselle from Armentières;" which, should the reader not be familiar with it, describes the lady's characteristics and behavior with frankness and detail. The 1943 "Dirty Gertie from Bizerte" was supposed to be another such ingenious creation until some doubt was cast on its authenticity. Soldier's songs may be, and often are, exceedingly sentimental. Many come direct from Tin Pan Alley. But though they are often difficult to interpret, they undoubtedly contain significant clues to the soldier state of mind.

The Soldier Becomes Estranged from His Loved Ones

One important phase of the soldier's isolation is his severance from family life. There are women in the army now, but they are not there as women, and the soldier is almost entirely devoid of the feminine influence. Nor can his parents or the elders of his community exert any further control over him. Relations with the family are kept up only through letters and very occasional visits. These letters are tremendously important to the soldier, greatly affecting his morale, but they can hardly take the place of family contact.

Sometimes even the most sophisticated soldier is shocked when he suddenly recognizes the gulf that has arisen between himself and his loved ones. The writer attended a dinner party in an eastern city, in honor of the furlough homecoming of the soldier of the household. The talk flowed rich and warm, between the soldier and the people at the table—his young wife, his mother, his older sister, in particular. Of course everybody wanted to know how the young soldier "liked army life," and he was more than willing to talk about the subject. In fact, he talked so fully (though not with particular enthusiasm) that he himself grew aware of it. "Here I am back home," he suddenly remarked, "home where I've been longing to come—where I had so many questions to ask—and all I talk about is the army! I've been thinking about nothing but all of you, but I keep talking about the rest of the army guys." A week after the soldier had returned to camp, his young wife received a letter that said, in part: "All the time I was with you, I had the most curious feeling that I was waiting to go back—to go 'home' to Camp X———. Now I realize why. I'm really home now, hard as it is to say this. But that's what happens, it seems, when you join the army. You don't feel that you belong anywhere else— you can't, when you're in a uniform. The army seemed strange when I first got into it, but now everything else *but* the army seems strange."

The soldier's relations with his loved ones at home probably continue to carry a heavy emotional charge. He lives for his girl's letters, and she for his, but strange misunderstandings somehow arise. It is not, however, hostility but mutual idealization that chiefly hinders communication between the soldier and those he loves. For the duration of the war, communication between loved ones may well continue on an apparently high level of understanding, but it is delusive and unreal, because each person has meanwhile built up idealized conceptions of the other. The clash, the proof of non-communication, comes later when the man shoulders again the burdens of daily living and finds himself chained by his previous commitments and perhaps by legal ties to one who is now an utter stranger.

For these and other reasons, the former civilian who has become a soldier finds himself drifting almost imperceptibly away from his former ways of thinking and his accustomed attitudes. He is now enmeshed in a different communicative world, and it has made another man of him. No matter how he tries, he can never quite recapture his former self; he cannot find the road back nor yet go home again. In particular, he loses the art of dealing with other people who have wills of their own,—and have a right to them. In his world there is no wooing, no persuading, no justifiable arguing and no winning of consent; one takes orders or gives them. The moment the soldier's grasp of the arts of consent becomes uncertain, he has become alienated from a great segment of the social world. Generals who have become politicians have often demonstrated this incapacity to win consent from those to whom they cannot issue orders.

The soldier is likely to find himself unintentionally acting with some hostility toward civilians, behaving on the unspoken and perhaps unrecognized premise that civilians are not quite human and do not matter very much. With the greatest of good will on both sides, the soldier is likely to discover that there is much in his life and his attitudes—whole systems of values—that he cannot share with civilians. And he may fall into the habit of saying, again and again, "Of course a civilian would hardly understand such a thing, but ——" Or perhaps just thinking it, and not speaking at all of these incommunicable matters.

The difficulties of communication between civilians and soldiers symbolize the gulf between their two worlds. Even the mere physical distances that cause the mail to take a long time are an obstacle. But a letter is a poor thing at best, merely a set of marks on a piece of paper, and when values and attitudes have changed subtly, communication is most difficult. When a man has been in the army for a while, words have altered their meaning; words have a changed emotional context because his emotions themselves have changed, for the soldier must adapt even his emotional life to the army routine.

He No Longer Speaks the Language of Civilians

Sometimes incidents occur that demonstrate very clearly that the words which mean so much to the civilian mean very little to the soldier. Even the greatest master of spoken language often fails to reach the man in uniform. The writer witnessed the utter failure of two great speakers of 1918, Theodore Roosevelt and Billy Sunday, each in his own way a master of eloquence. They extended themselves and tried all their tricks but all they received was a sullen and unfriendly hearing from their audience of service men.

Reporters of the current war tell us that abstract words mean little to the men in the front lines, and chaplains relate the same discovery. In a marvellously acute bit of introspective writing, Hemingway told this story some years ago:

> I did not say anything. I was always embarrassed by the words sacred, glorious, and sacrifice and the expression in vain. We had heard them, sometimes standing in the rain almost out of earshot, so that only the shouted words came through, and had read them, on proclamations that were slapped up by billposters over other proclamations, now for a long time, and I had seen nothing sacred, and the things that were glorious

had no glory and the sacrifices were like the stockyards at Chicago if nothing was done with the meat except to bury it. There were many words that you could not stand to hear and finally only the names of places had dignity. Certain numbers were the same way and certain dates and these with the names of the places were all you could say and have them mean anything. Abstract words such as glory, honor, courage, or hallow were obscene beside the concrete names of villages, the numbers of roads, the names of rivers, the numbers of regiments and the dates.[2]

After a time the soldier loses some of the ability to put his feelings into words. Ernie Pyle tells a moving story that illustrates this point:

In this war I have known a lot of officers who were loved and respected by the soldiers under them. But never have I crossed the trail of any man as beloved as Captain Henry T. Waskow, of Belton, Texas.

Captain Waskow was a company commander in the 36th Division. He had been in this company since long before he left the States. He was very young, only in his middle twenties, but he carried in him a sincerity and gentleness that made people want to be guided by him.

"After my own father, he comes next," a sergeant told me.

"He always looked after us," a soldier said. "He'd go to bat for us every time."

"I've never known him to do anything unkind," another one said.

I was at the foot of the mule trail the night they brought Captain Waskow down. The moon was nearly full and you could see far up the trail, and even part way across the valley. Soldiers made shadows as they walked.

Dead men had been coming down the mountain all evening, lashed onto the backs of mules. They came lying belly down across the wooden pack-saddle, their heads hanging down on the left side of the mule, their stiffened legs sticking awkwardly from the other side, bobbing up and down as the mule walked . . .

Then a soldier came into the cowshed and said there were some more bodies outside. We went out into the road. Four

[2]Ernest Hemingway, *A Farewell to Arms.* Scribner, 1929, p. 196.

mules stood there in the moonlight, in the road where the trail came down off the mountain. The soldiers who led them stood there waiting.

"This one is Captain Waskow," one of them said quickly.

Two men unlashed his body from the mule and lifted it off and laid it in the shadow beside the stone wall. Other men took the other bodies off. Finally, there were five lying end to end in a long row. You don't cover up dead men in the combat zones. They just lie there in the shadows until somebody else comes after them.

The uncertain mules moved off to their olive groves. The men in the road seemed reluctant to leave. They stood around, and gradually I could sense them moving, one by one, close to Captain Waskow's body. Not so much to look, I think, as to say something in finality to him and to themselves. I stood close by and I could hear.

One soldier came and looked down, and he said out loud, "God damn it!"

That's all he said, and then he walked away.

Another one came, and he said, "God damn it to hell anyway!" He looked down for a few last moments and then turned and left.

Another man came. I think he was an officer. It was hard to tell officers from men in the dim light, for everybody was grimy and dirty. The man looked down into the dead captain's face and then spoke directly to him, as though he were alive:

"I'm sorry, old man."

Then a soldier came and stood beside the officer and bent over, and he too spoke to his dead captain, not in a whisper but awfully tenderly, and he said,

"I sure am sorry, sir."

Then the first man squatted down, and he reached down and took the captain's hand, and he sat there for a full five minutes holding the dead hand in his own and looking intently into the dead face. And he never uttered a sound all the time he sat there.

Finally he put the hand down. He reached up and gently straightened the points of the captain's shirt collar, and then he sort of rearranged the tattered edges of his uniform around the wound, and then he got up and walked away down the road into the moonlight, all alone.[3]

[3] Ernie Pyle, "The Death of Captain Waskow." Scripps-Howard newspaper column, 1944, and Henry Holt, publishers.

Most people, probably, civilians as well as soldiers, find them-selves inarticulate when faced by a loss that strikes them deeply. Nevertheless these soldiers, in civilian life, would have found some form of words more appropriate and more expressive of their grief than "God damn it!" In any event, the civilian would have *tried* to find the "right" words—would have plucked the air for some-thing appropriate to say—because a varied and abundant range of words is the normal response of men in civilian life.

Spoken language is an automatic, natural expression of thoughts and feelings; and civilian life, being various, wide in range, and filled with shades of feeling, requires and consequently uses a vari-ous, wide-ranged, complex tongue. Not so, the military life. Because his world is rigidly confined and his activities dictated for him, the soldier has no need for a varied vocabulary. He can get along very well with a few words, and he tends to use these universally. That is why a certain four-letter word (tabooed from polite conversation but found wherever small boys can find room to scribble it) is used by American soldiers today to express practically everything and anything. It is the universal verb of our army, for ex-teamsters in uniform as well as ex-professors in uniform.

The soldier does not need an ample vocabulary. His fellows will understand what he means; they will realize that "God damn it!" spoken in the presence of a dead beloved comrade carries a vast meaning. Knowing the context, the soldiers understand, but the civilian will not. And the civilians can not because they, as civilians, are strangers to the soldier's world; just as the soldier is a stranger to the civilian's world. When he comes back to live in society again, the soldier will have to learn this estranged world of peacetime complexity. He will have to resume communication on a civilian level, which will come to him quickly enough once he becomes renaturalized into society.

He Learns the Deep Meaning of Comradeship

ARMY life, by its very nature, necessarily frustrates most of the basic needs of the human animal. One need, however, it certainly gratifies, as civilian life does not: the hunger for solidarity with one's fellows. This sense of solidarity embraces many things that we express imperfectly by different forms of words. It is a feeling for the common life; it means that one knows that something is shared or held in common with others. It means that men do not live to themselves alone, that they are members, severally, of one another, that they are all one flesh. Solidarity is the soul, and perhaps the whole, of religion. It is an imponderable, and outweighs everything else. In solidarity there is a kind of security; men will sacrifice all for it and count the world well lost. Solidarity— the need of it, the yearning for it—is a mainspring of social life. It is comradeship. It is approval by one's fellows. It is the sure sense of belonging. It is one of the few solid rewards of army life.

A man may be completely unaware of a desire for a child, but when the child appears and he calls it his own it becomes the joy of his life. A man may not be aware of his hunger to be one with his fellow man, but when the experience of solidarity comes, he gladly surrenders himself to it, his mind, his separate self, his reason, taste, and comfort. The sense of solidarity is most often found in a cause, a religion, or a community. A man can lose himself in a cause or a religion; that is how one loses his soul in order to find it. A cause, as experience has often shown, does not need to be good in order for men to regard it as holy. Whatever men in masses devote themselves to is sacred to them. Solidarity is the source of values and the great excuse—for irrational beliefs, for hatreds, atrocities, and behavior that contradicts all the principles of ethics and morality. "I am doing as the others do and therefore I am doing right" is a dangerous principle, to be sure, but the one most often followed; it is especially dangerous when applied by a group of men removed from the controls of family, church, and community. Other situations than war and army life give some opportunity for this flight from free individuality into a tight-knit social unity: football games, political rallies, drunken parties, and lynching mobs.

The Hunger for Solidarity Is Satisfied

In modern life, this profound need for saying "we" is often frustrated. Our self-feelings keep us apart from one another. Competition keeps our souls separate, makes us suspicious, causes us to cheat ourselves by striving to out-do another. In peacetime society, our lives are wrapped in small bundles, like families, and we know little and care less of the loosely tied large bundles such as nations. Canyons of race and religion, chasms of class, keep us from mingling with the herd. This frustration of the sense of solidarity, this separateness and selfness, has much to do with the anxiety and insecurity that underly our modern neuroses.

In war all this is changed. The nation is threatened. Its citizens spring to its defense in a fever of patriotic emotion. People discover their love for their country, lose their puny egos in devotion. Hatred for the enemy binds men together with strands of steel. In the release with full social approval of the usually tabooed emotion of hostility, people find one more thing in common, one more joy of fellowship. Barriers are down. People speak without introductions. Neighbors get together, act as one. Everyone shares somewhat in a slightly hysterical sense of well-being. Even the humblest task acquires new meaning from its place in the common effort; the taxi-driver and the garbage collector suddenly have their own dignity as men who do their part. In this early period, this honeymoon of war, the people ask for sacrifices—and solidarity. Their leaders, if they are wise, give them blood, sweat, and tears—and solidarity. Although this experience of solidarity usually lasts only a few months, it is an important ingredient of war. As the war proceeds, its sentimental assets are gradually expended. Some solidarity, however, must remain, or the war must stop. For when people lose the sense of solidarity, they also lose the will to fight.

The Soldier's Loyalty Is Stronger Than Death

The army as the instrument of the nation at war necessarily reflects the temper of that nation. But the army, with its masses of marching men, its discipline, its packed assemblages of human bodies, its landscapes of faces and uniforms, its songs and battles and death and comradeship, is far better adapted than civilian society to give the sense of belonging to an inclusive unity and of struggling for a common cause. "In war one is seldom alone." Barriers between persons are down in the army. Class, religion, social origin and even race are supposedly forgotten. Everybody is buddy, Jack, soldier, Joe. No soldier ever needs an introduction to another soldier. Food and luxuries are shared. Men risk their own lives to recover a wounded man, or even to pay respect to a corpse.

Many find something mysterious and rewarding in this comradeship of men at arms. Here all suffer from a common fate and struggle for a common cause. They recognize that kind of justice at least which arises when all alike have given up certain rights. They enjoy the lack of personal responsibility, and do not mind its cost. They discover that at least there is security in the army. The soldier knows that when the boss looks at him in a certain way, that does not mean he is going to get fired; he does not need to worry lest someone speak ill of him to the owner of the business. The soldier's status in the world is humble but secure. He walks in ranks, not thinking whether to go right or left, just doing what the others do. To this one may come when he is "sick of revolt, of thought, of carrying his individuality like a banner above the turmoil."[1] In the army there is an end of all the old sort of competition. "Work together," says the drill-sergeant to the recruits. "Cooperate, boys," say the instructors at the OCS. "There are commissions enough for all of you." There will be glory enough for all who are willing to pay its price. There is blood and death enough to go around. "Many enemies, much honor."

In particular, the front-line soldiers have their own sense of fraternity.

Look at that fellow over there. He's on leave too, straight from the trenches; I recognize the type. For all I know, he may

[1] John Dos Passos, *Three Soldiers*. Modern Library edition, p. 22.

be from Verdun. If we met somewhere at the front I should mean nothing to him and he would mean nothing to me. But here there is a bond between us. We've been through the same ordeals in the ritual sense of the word. There is a free-masonry of front-line fighters; they form a sort of order.[2]

Hitler has often appealed to this solidarity in his speeches by refer-ring to himself as a "front line fighter." *Forsan et haec olim memi-nisse iuvabit,* says Virgil, perchance we shall take pleasure in remembering even this. Perchance we shall but we shall not remember it because of the dirt and hunger and death, nor because of the glory, only because we were together. "Looking back," says one writer, "one forgets the horrors and hardships, and one sees only the convivial side of life, happy dug-out days—a strange phrase, except to those who, looking back to some cushy dug-out, remember happy half-hours, snatched, as it were from the very feet of death."[3]

Ernie Pyle, reporter of the human side of the present war, tells of "the ties that grow up between men who live savagely and die relentlessly together." "There is," he says, "a sense of fidelity to each other among little corps of men who have endured so long and whose hope in the end can be but so small." Pyle tells of Sergeant Buck Eversole, a battle-hardened Westerner who had been in the front lines for more than a year. As such non-coms sometimes do, he began to feel guilty about leading green men to slaughter; he began to think of himself as a sort of Judas sheep. On the eve of an attack, he was ordered back to the rest camp. He tried to get out of the assignment that would take him away from the battle, but he failed. Then he took a long time in saying good-bye, shook hands all around, wished his men good luck over and over again. As at last he walked away he said to Pyle, "I feel like a deserter."

Uriah the Hittite said it thirty-five hundred years ago: "And Uriah said unto David, The ark, and Israel, and Judah, abide in tents; and my lord Joab, and the servants of my lord, are encamped in the open fields; shall I then go into mine house, to eat and to drink, and to lie with my wife; as thou livest, and as thy soul livest, I will not do this thing."

Uriah the Hittite said it thirty-five hundred years ago and

[2] Jules Romains, *Men of Good Will;* Vol. VIII, *Verdun.* Knopf, 1940, p. 436.
[3] G. B. Manwaring, *If We Return: Letters of a Soldier of Kitchener's Army.* Lane, 1918, p. 161.

Sergeant Buck Eversole said it the day before yesterday. Such is "the powerful fraternalism in the ghastly brotherhood of war," always the same, since men went first to battle.

The Best Leadership Rests on Comradeship

The task of leadership is always to build this inclusive unity of fighting men. In "Portrait of a Soldier" Colonel Edward S. Johnstown has told how Major Rasmussen, a gifted officer of World War I, took over a dispirited and disorganized battalion and made it into a great fighting unit.[4] A principal part of Rasmussen's task was to instill the sense of solidarity. He believed, and he taught his men that the battalion came first, and that "in war nothing else mattered so much as the comradeship of fighting men," that "somehow privations were not so onerous when you bore them as one of a band of brothers." He encouraged platoon spirit also, but subordinated these units to the larger whole. He taught his men pride in their appearance, their toughness, and the morale of their outfit. He helped them to overcome their repugnance toward corpses, extending the solidarity of living men to include the bodies of their slain comrades. He checked competition within his group, pitting his men against external obstacles. He defended them and fought for them, for he had learned that first principle of leadership that in order to get loyalty one must give it. The result was a magnificent fighting unit, pervaded by "the confidence born of unity—the sense of being one no matter what betide." The battalion retained its spirit even after the death of the major.

Less orthodox methods, but also based upon the principle of building solidarity as the basis of morale, were followed by Evans Carlson, leader of the famous Raiders.[5] His *gung ho* system was really an institutionalization of solidarity, and it rested upon the mores of comradeship. In the military world, Carlson's destruction of the barriers between officers and men was audacious, something that could be done only under exceptional circumstances by a leader of great ability. We have had a few other such experiments, probably a little less daring, in the history of our armies. Roosevelt's

4 Colonel Edward S. Johnstown, "Portrait of a Soldier," in *Americans vs. Germans.* Penguin Book and The Infantry Journal, 1942, pp. 11-36.
5 Lucien Hubbard, "Colonel Carlson and His Gung Ho Raiders," *The Reader's Digest*, Dec. 1943.

Rough Riders must have had a splendid group feeling that derived from the character of their leadership. And when the men in the ranks shouted remarks and suggestions to Uncle Billy or Marse Robert or Old Jack, everyone knew that there was then no question of disrespect; and that was leadership.

Ordinary officers, perhaps, could hardly hope to copy the methods of such natural leaders as Rasmussen and Carlson. And yet many men who were not exactly geniuses of war have realized that a certain solidarity of officers and men is an essential of leadership. A story is told of a young Polish captain who was sent to the front in one of Poland's wars. He equipped himself with silk underwear and shirts, thinking in this manner to protect himself from lice. He reported to a wise old colonel, who scolded him violently for his forehandedness. If the men suffered from lice, the colonel said, then the officers must have lice too, else how could there be any brotherhood of men at arms? The colonel was also a noble and a count, and a man who in time of peace felt no such sense of kinship with the common people, but in time of war he knew that these common men were his brothers.

Relationships between officers and men in the German army are reported to be excellent, and largely because of the systematic cultivation of the sense of solidarity.[6] The officer, it is said, must be the teacher, the mentor, of his men rather than a mere institutional superior. He must keep in intimate touch with them. There must be daily inspections, personalized as much as possible; the officer should look each man in eye, and he should show interest in the attempts of the men to decorate their bare rooms. (Such attempts at decoration were encouraged because they were thought to promote individuality.) The officer must never expose the soldier to ridicule, or hold him responsible for the officer's mistakes. The officer is supposed to congratulate the man on his birthday, being careful to ascertain the date from the files and not from the man himself. The soldier dresses in his best to receive these congratulations, the officer in his best to give them. Afterwards, the officer sends congratulations to the soldier's family as well. Thus a principle of American salesmanship has been applied to the promotion of Nazi army morale.

6 See Ladislas Farago (ed.), *German Psychological Warfare*. Putnam, 1942, pp. 87 ff.

Veterans Yearn to Recapture Their Lost Comradeship

In the post-war period, the ex-soldier tries once more to recapture the experience of solidarity, a subject that many post-war novels treat with vivid realism. The ex-soldier's cynicism is in great part a reaction to the thing that he had once and misses now. When he was one of a group of comrades his life had purpose and meaning, and he resents the fact that such sacred things could end so badly. The ex-soldier's organizations, his reunions (which necessarily grow increasingly pathetic through the years), are means for reaching out for the things that he sought and found not in civilian society. When ex-soldiers get drunk at their conventions, when they whistle at women and dress in ridiculous costumes and throw furniture out of hotel windows, they are merely trying in a stupid way to recapture their youth and vanished comradeship.

For many veterans, the comradeship in war remains the high point of their lives. Men do not often have the experience of fighting for a cause in concert with their fellows. The war and the army becomes the Alma Mater of many a man who never goes to college.

Victory or defeat does not really affect this attitude. Whatever the outcome, the soldier remains a soldier still, and sighs for the old days, for the war that was really a war, and for all his vanished comrades. Such values remain meaningful to him, even though he rejects them. Perhaps, like Robert E. Lee, he will not permit any one to say in his presence that the struggle was bootless and his time in the army wasted. Perhaps, like Hemingway, he conceives a great distaste for the words "in vain," and believes the slaughter was as meaningless as that of the Chicago stockyards would be if nothing were done with the meat except to bury it. Such opposing attitudes are merely two different *responses* to the same essential conflict.

We have said that the event of victory or defeat does not matter in the subsequent evaluation of a cause. That is not quite right. The truth is that the advantage is probably on the side of defeat. For sentiment's sake, it is better to lose. The cause that was lost, like the suitor who was rejected, like the child who died in youth, remains forever enshrined in memory and never undergoes the tests of maturity or the blemishes of age. A cause that wins must later be rigidified into an institution of some sort and administered by mortal and probably venal men; it must be sullied by corruption and bickering and avarice. The Union had its carpetbaggers and its era of good stealing; the South had only the memory of its Glorious Lost Cause. The Allied nations won their war to make the world safe for democracy in 1919, but their cause lost its luster before six months had passed. The Germans retained their cause and kept its memory alive. So it was for a century or more, with the bonny prince over the water, and with dismembered Poland. In terms of human sentiment, there can be no cause like a lost cause.

But whether he belonged to an army that won or an army that lost, the soldier has been profoundly enriched by the experience in human solidarity. Having satisfied the hunger for "belonging to a group"—a hunger that can never be quite satisfied in our world of individual enterprise and "each man for himself"—the soldier will always cherish the memories of this comradeship. The exhilaration of working together, in a common bond for a common purpose and in a common world twenty-four hours each day, can never be matched by such gratifications of individual civilian achievement as the average soldier is likely to know.

But like most deeply gratifying experiences, the soldier's remembered sense of solidarity is a mixed blessing. Once he is returned to civilian life, he will feel the lack of the security of solidarity—there will be a great void in his life. He will remember the companionship; it will haunt him and he will seek to recapture it. No one can deprive him of the memory of this sense of unity, which is, from a practical point of view, an unfortunate thing. For if he could erase it from his mind, his adjustment to the "Root-hog-or-die" code of civilian living would be incomparably easier. Because of his life with his fellows and their consummate bond, the soldier-returned-to-civilian-life will never be quite the same.

He Learns to Be
Cruel and Merciful

THERE is in every human being a set of tendencies to hurt others, to strike, to wound, to thwart, to deflate, to ruin, to kill, or otherwise to do damage to the lives and personalities of other human beings. We shall hereafter designate these behavior patterns as sadistic-aggressive tendencies. Though we do not know to what extent they are ingrained in the native equipment of human beings, we do know that they are modified by a great deal of social conditioning. In war, these tendencies undergo strange transformations.

In civil life, the expression of sadistic-aggressive attitudes encounters many obstacles. Often there are strong components of hate in the complex attitudes which one has toward members of his family, but such hatreds can rarely be adequately expressed. Rebellion against one's father, rivalry toward a brother or sister, and other attitudes toward family members may become nodules of festering self-contradiction and eventually lead to neurosis. Women, especially when outside the family circle, are expected to keep a tighter rein upon aggressive tendencies than are men.

The expression of aggressions in civil life follows complex and little understood patterns. The principal mode of release is furnished by persons who deviate from the established "rules" of society; the violation of these mores by one person gives others an opportunity to vent their pent-up hatreds upon him. Righteous indignation is the most socially acceptable way of releasing one's accumulated hostility. For this reason, the criminal makes a contribution to society—law-abiding citizens can hate him with impunity and with an easy conscience.

In our civilian society, superiors are able to express anger toward subordinates, the boss toward his employees, the white man toward the Negro. Children formerly furnished a very satisfactory outlet for the aggressive tendencies of adults. Adults were encouraged to be harsh by the venerable maxim "Spare the rod and spoil the child," but the newer theories of child-care have largely removed this innocent pleasure from our lives. Subordinated social groups, such as women and Negroes, are forced to express their aggressions indirectly or upon members of their own group. None of these outlets for hatred is altogether satisfactory. When war comes to a nation, many civilians find it exhilarating because it gives them a satisfactory hate experience. We can hate satisfactorily only when we are permitted to hate, which means, for most of us, that we do not hate enough, not hard enough or often enough for the demands of our own mental hygiene. Therefore we welcome the plenary indulgence of war for cruel thoughts and words.

The Soldier Takes Hatred and Cruelty for Granted

In the army, all this is changed. The soldier has an entirely legitimate outlet for his hatred; in fact, he has several more or less legitimate outlets, which is fortunate, because his life situation is such as to give him a great deal of hatred to express. Without any official encouragement, the soldier often hates his non-coms with passion, usually enjoying in this hatred the concurrence and approval of other enlisted men. Formally and officially, the soldier is encouraged to hate the enemy with all his heart and soul. But his hatred of the enemy, like any other attitude around which life is organized, tends to recede from the forefront of consciousness into the realm of the taken-for-granted. The soldier is also isolated from the civilian communication-system, which is another reason why he hates the enemy in a manner different from that of the civilian.

In any event, the army does not rely solely upon hatred to make men fight, or indeed upon the consent of the soldier to anything that the army commands him to do. It is worth remembering that the army is far more successful in controlling the soldier's habit systems than in forming his opinions or summoning his emotions; it conditions him, trains him, controls him by organization, but it does not depend too much upon winning his consent. Soldiers fight because they are in the army; an army is a machine for fighting, and the soldiers in it have to fight. The soldier's business, of course, is killing, and the army does a good job of conditioning him for it. The soldier learns to kill in a cold-blooded, professional way, with weapons if possible, with bare hands if need be. The frustrations of army life—the denial of sex, the want of comfort, the exactions of non-commissioned officers—these and other similar army facts that make a soldier annoyed, irritable, and angry add to his aggressiveness with steady accumulations.

For most men, war becomes a perfect excuse for killing, so that war experiences are completely dissociated from ordinary life. They may have little remembrance of them in later years. A German veteran of 1914-1918 once remarked to the writer, "Oh, I could never kill a man. Such a thing would be impossible for me." A few minutes later he remarked, having recalled the matter with some surprise. "Of course, I have killed many men. I used to run a trench mortar. I know I killed them because I used to see their bodies flung out of the trenches when the shells exploded." Thus with a certain gentle professor of philosophy who had devoted his life to the development of a not very intelligible system of philosophical thought; he was a kindly man who would not harm a fly, but he used to be a machine-gunner who mowed men down by hundreds, always trying to shoot them in the belly; he never thought of that any more. He had managed to exclude it from his consciousness as veterans always strive to do, once they are civilians again and weaned away from the thought of war.

On occasion, however, the sadistic-aggressive tendencies of men in uniform get out of control. Soldiers may kill their officers, as they often threaten to do but actually do very rarely. Soldiers may fight among themselves, being, in Shakespeare's phrase, "sudden and quick in quarrels." The greatest perversion of these tendencies, however, occurs where soldiers tire of fighting the enemy and begin to compromise, to trade or otherwise to fraternize with him. This is a perennial problem of the leaders of armies. Charles Horton Cooley called this curious phenomenon "the sympathy of percussion."

War-Weary Soldiers Fraternize with Their Enemies

The aberration of the fighting spirit by virtue of which soldiers fraternize with the enemy is not necessarily inconsistent with valor in battle, but officers rightly regard it as dangerous to the morale of troops. Apparently it arises because the soldier comes to see that the enemy is a soldier like himself and like himself a human being caught in the deadly maelstrom of war. Respect for the other man's soldierly qualities is often involved in this sympathy. The ferocious civilian speaks of the enemy as the dirty Boche or dirty Jap or the Hun or Nazi, but the soldier knows that the enemy is a brave man and an able soldier, and he can speak of him almost affectionately as Jerry; nowadays the Germans are "the Krauts" to American soldiers. The contrast between the unrelenting civilian and the soldier is often illustrated when the time comes for making peace. Grant's terms to Lee were generous and fair, but they did not please some of those who had remained safely at home. Petain vainly relied on this mechanism when he asked Hitler for a peace, speaking as one soldier to another.

Our own Civil War furnished many examples of the sympathy of percussion. Indeed, the tendency toward fraternization seems to have been strong throughout the war. A trade in tobacco, coffee, newspapers, and jackknives flourished between the lines. On occasion the fraternization reached dangerous proportions, and one Illinois regiment had to be disarmed and put under guard. Such an instance, however, was rare, and fraternization was not usually inconsistent with high morale. Sandburg describes the intercourse between the two armies as follows:

> On the picket lines flung out at night after the day's fighting were laughter and good will across enemy fronts, Meade's staff man Lyman writing, "These men are incomprehensible—now standing from daylight to dark killing and wounding each other by thousands and now making jokes and exchanging newspapers, despite orders to the contrary. You see them lying side by side in the hospitals, talking together in that prosaic way that characterizes Americans. The great staples of conversation are the size and quality of rations, the marches they have made, and the regiments they have fought against. All sense of personal spite is sunk in the immensity of the contest."[1]

General Meade himself wrote, "I believe that these two armies would fraternize and make peace in an hour, if the matter rested with them; not on terms to suit politicians on either side, but such as the world at large would acknowledge as honorable, and which would be satisfactory to the mass of people on both sides."[2] Lin-

---

[1] Carl Sandburg, *Abraham Lincoln, The War Years.* Harcourt Brace, 1939, Vol. III, p. 64.

[2] *Ibid.,* p. 64. Note the slighting reference to politicians.

coln himself welcomed evidences of "a fraternal feeling growing up between our men and the rank and file of the rebel soldiers.

The literature of World War I contains frequent references to this same phenomenon. One of the best of these is the following passage from Robert C. Sherriff's *Journey's End:*

> RALEIGH: The Germans are really quite decent, aren't they?
> I mean, outside the newspapers.
> OSBORNE: Yes. [*pause*] I remember up at Wipers we had a man shot when he was out on patrol. Just at dawn. We couldn't get him in that night. He lay out there groaning all day. Next night three of our men crawled out to get him in. It was so near the German trenches that they could have shot our fellows one by one. But, when our men began dragging the wounded man back over the rough ground, a big German officer stood up in the trenches and called out, "Carry him!"—and our fellows stood up and carried the man back, and the German officer fired some lights for them to see by.[3]

In that war there were occasional Christmas truces, and Alan Seeger noted that in 1915 fighting was becoming rarer and rarer along the front.[4] Other instances follow:

> It was so bad in parts of the line during November storms that whole sections of trench collapsed into a chaos of slime and ooze. It was the frost as well as the rain which caused this ruin, making the earthworks sink under their weight of sand-bag. German and English soldiers were exposed to one another like ants upturned from their nests by a minor landslide. They ignored one another. They pretended that the other fellows were not there. They had not been properly introduced. In another place, reckless because of their discomfort, the Germans crawled upon their slimy parapets and sat on top to dry their legs, and shouted, "Don't shoot! Don't shoot!"[5]

It is perhaps too soon to expect full-fledged examples of the sympathy of percussion to be reported from the present war, but there are signs that the attitudes from which this sympathy arises are developing. War Correspondent Leland Stowe recently reported as follows:

> My friend, War Correspondent H. R. Knickerbocker, has just sent me some highly pertinent testimony about our Italian

3 Reprinted by permission of Coward-McCann, Inc., from *Journey's End*, by R. C. Sherriff, copyright 1929.

4 Alan Seeger, *Letters and Diary*. Scribner, 1917, pp. 100-101.

5 Philip Gibbs, *Now It Can Be Told*. Harper, 1920, pp. 208-209.

campaign. He says: "I heard the boys of the famous Iowa Division, who had been in the Cassino battle thirty-five days and had lost a pitiful number of their comrades, say, 'We ain't mad at anybody.' " [6]

Compare this statement with that of Corporal John F. O'Neill, of Maplewood, Missouri, who was recently repatriated after a stay in German hospitals and prison camps. He said, "German front-line soldiers are always gentlemen. The experiences of all our wounded have proven that." [7]

From many wars one may gather indications of this strange bond of sympathy between sworn enemies. The same soldier who at the beginning of a war strained with fury to "rip the guts" of the enemy can, when he has seen men die and had his fill of killing, look the other way when the enemy offers a convenient target for a bullet. His own personal hatred of the enemy has been lost in the immensity of the conflict, in the vast impersonality of war. He has come to realize that the enemy soldier is a fellow sufferer, a man like himself and like himself helpless against the human storm, nearer to him in spirit and in destiny than the civilians at home. He has learned that the enemy is a fellow craftsman even though he works for a different boss. The army is wise not to depend too much upon hatred, or upon any other emotion, to make the soldier fight. Hatred is for civilians, killing for soldiers, killing and forbidden acts of mercy.

The ominous fact concerning the sympathy of percussion is that in terms of experience, training, temperament, and generalized attitudes the soldier may begin to feel that he has more in common with the enemy soldier than with the people back home. The dangers latent in such a feeling need no elaboration. When the soldier returns, his adjustment problems are vastly aggravated if he comes to hate civilians more than he ever hated his enemies. The pent-up sadistic-aggressive tendencies will not have been completely spent in war, for the things that feed them continue long after the last shot has been fired. It is society's urgent concern to remove from the path of the returning soldier any conditions that might impel him to vent his accumulated, unspent fury on society itself.

[6] From a broadcast by Leland Stowe, April 21, 1944, Blue Network. By permission of Leland Stowe. Later in the same broadcast Stowe quoted the following from the Soviet reporter, Ilya Ehrenburg: "War without hatred is as shameful as cohabitation without love."
[7] New York Herald Tribune, June 8, 1944.

He Learns to Live with Fear, Horror, and Guilt

THE control of fear is one of the soldier's—and the army's—principal problems. There is an extensive literature on the subject as well as a considerable body of practical knowledge. John Dollard, however, on the basis of a study of 300 veterans of the Abraham Lincoln Brigade, in the Spanish Civil War of 1936-1939, has given us our most exact information about the matter.[1] For the most part, Dollard's findings accord very well with the military tradition that has been built up through experience. Most soldiers know fear. Three-quarters of Dollard's veterans reported feeling afraid when they went into their first action, but most of them found that fear diminished in subsequent engagements. Military writers sometimes speak of this first action, the moment when a man suddenly realizes that those others are really shooting at *him*, the moment when troops become "blooded."

According to Dollard's study, the bodily symptoms of fear in battle are the same as in civilian life: pounding heart and rapid pulse in 69 per cent of the cases, muscular tenseness in 45 per cent, a "sinking feeling in the stomach" in 44 per cent, dry mouth in 33 per cent, and clammy hands in 22 per cent. Soldiers were most afraid of wounds in the abdomen, eyes, brain, and genitals, in that order. Green soldiers were more afraid of showing cowardice than of being crippled or disfigured, but battle-tried veterans had a greater fear of being crippled. Dollard's group felt that regimental pride, belief in war aims, leadership, training, and materiel were very important in controlling fear. They also believed that fear should be frankly admitted and discussed before battle.

Fear is a reasonably clear-cut, recognizable emotional state. Some-

1 Dollard, John, privately published by The Institute of Human Relations, to be republished by The Infantry Journal.

times it is mingled with horror, and often horror predominates. War is full of horrors. Many soldiers carry with them into life after the war the memory of these jumbled emotions of fear and horror. For some, at least, these emotions are complicated by feelings of guilt. For most soldiers at most times, war is a situation outside their personal codes of behavior, and only occasionally does it become personal and human. Not only is battle impersonal, but it carries with it its own anaesthesia, in the form of stupefying noise, confusion, movement, and emotional turmoil, so that memories are less sharp and clear than they might otherwise be. But some small fragment of experience is apt to be singled out and preserved as a symbol of the whole chamber of horrors, and it is likely to seem extremely personal.

An Episode Sometimes Condenses the Whole of Horror

A former ambulance driver of World War I, holder of one of the highest awards for heroism, will say little about the war except that many times he put three live ones in his ambulance and removed three dead ones. Another tells of a time in the trenches when the shells kept digging up the dead, who had to be buried over and over again after each progressively nauseous exhumation. A shell-shocked veteran traces the origin of his difficulties to a relatively slight incident in which he pulled a man's body out of a wrecked plane and found it without a head. Another soldier's horror was centered in the recollection of the body of an unknown in the middle of a road, mashed as flat as wall-paper by passing traffic. A veteran of Singapore tells of a bomb that hit a sick-bay, and of pieces of human flesh embedded in the steel walls of a ship, a situation reminiscent of one described by Hemingway, when the members of his outfit had to pick small pieces of female flesh off the strands of barbed wire after an explosion in a munitions plant. A young aviator in the recent novel, *Shore Leave*, by Frederic Wakeman, reports with grim humor an incident in which he was shelled and the man in the next bunk killed; he was unable to wash for a few days and began to stink, and when he finally took off his clothes to wash he found a few pounds of human flesh in them. Our war with the Japanese is replete with horrors, from which the ingredient of cruelty is not absent. Some soldiers knock the teeth out of the mouths of dead Japanese and keep them for souvenirs or use them as articles of commerce, gold teeth being especially prized for this purpose. Or, one may cut off the upper portion of a Japanese skull, throw it to the rats and the ants, and when these humble servitors have obligingly cleaned it, use it as a very superior kind of ash-tray. A German soldier is said to have accumulated a considerable fortune by assiduously collecting gold teeth and gold fillings from Russian corpses.

A stock situation of the war novelists is that in which a soldier is brought face to face with a man he has mortally wounded, and he must then watch that man slowly die and as the man dies he becomes no longer a hated enemy but just a man and a son and a husband and a father who wanted to go home to his family and had no wish to fight or kill or to meet death in a shell-hole. Of course, this sort of thing probably occurs rarely in modern war, because most killing is done at long range. A less hackneyed guilt situation is that described with excellent psychological insight in *The Red Badge of Courage,* where the young Union soldier leaves a crazed and wounded comrade to die, and knows that he will carry the memory of that heartless act to the grave.

Guilt Feelings Arise from One's Own Conflicting Motives

Often only a narrow margin separates the horrible from the pleasurable. Sometimes it seems that feelings of guilt arise not so much from the cruel things one must do in war as from the pleasure one inadvertently finds in them. The good warrior must exult in battle, but the good Christian can take no pleasure in killing. Even the gentle Lee—a tender nurse of sick women—could feel the joy of battle, and he was afraid of it. When the victory of his army was being forged at Fredericksburg, he turned to Longstreet and "revealed the whole man in a single brief sentence: 'It is well that war is so terrible—we should grow too fond of it.' " An utterance, as a British correspondent who stood by believed, of "antique heroism."[2]

That is the kind of memory that men bring out of battle, of a confusion of action and movement and a mingling of fear and horror and guilt. The extreme reaction of the psychoneurotic

2 Douglas Southall Freeman, *R. E. Lee.* Scribner, Vol. II, p. 462.

soldiers to such incidents certainly has its basis in the previous experience of a poorly balanced organism. In many cases the shocking situation is so mild in nature that it is difficult to understand the extreme reaction to it. But there is every evidence that normal men react in the same way to a lesser degree. We may suppose that every soldier who has seen front-line service is at least mildly shell-shocked, as well as a great many who got nowhere near the front. This is an important clue to the understanding of the personality of the veteran.

The mental state which we have called the sense of solidarity is the greatest antidote to fear and probably also to horror and guilt. Dollard's findings and the best military tradition agree on the importance of solidarity. All but 3 per cent of Dollard's cases thought that pride in one's outfit would have some effect on them, while 77 per cent put belief in war aims highest in the list of factors combatting fear. Dollard's cases would probably be inclined to over-emphasize ideology. They were unusual soldiers, all volunteers, all politically minded and idealistic to such a degree that they were willing to go abroad to fight for a country not their own, and they were not very well-trained as soldiers.

While we should not on that account disregard the opinions of these men, many lessons of experience warn us against an over-emphasis of belief in a political cause as a basis of good military performance. Some of the best soldiers have been mercenaries, including some excellent troops serving in the present war. Franco's Moors, opposing the Abraham Lincoln Brigade, were mercenaries who certainly had no cause to fight for, but they fought well none the less. The truth seems to be that it is solidarity that most opposes fear, and there are various ways in which to get this sense of solidarity in a military organization. Solidarity may come from belief in a cause, but that is the hardest kind of solidarity to obtain and the least dependable. The quickest, easiest, and surest way to get solidarity is through good organization and good leadership, through such methods as are described in an earlier chapter. Leadership and organization can do more to help the average man to overcome his fear than any amount of attempted indoctrination with a cause.

But this same sense of solidarity that enables the soldier to conquer feelings of fear and guilt may also, in an indirect manner, be the cause of them. Two army psychiatrists recently reported some astonishing findings bearing on this point.[3] The psychiatrists first describe the manner in which group solidarity develops in a unit of the army, and then analyze the feelings of guilt with which individuals torture themselves because of real or fancied violations of this solidarity.

"One of the most amazing revelations derived by our uncovering technique," say Grinker and Spiegel, "has been the universality of guilt reactions, not only in men who have been removed from combat because of anxiety states but also in those who have successfully and honorably completed their tour of duty. These guilt reactions are related to the most varied, irrational and illogical experiences. A comrade was killed on a mission which he took instead of the patient. Hundreds of little acts which the patient did or did not do are the bases of self-accusations and we often hear the guilty cry, 'I should have got it instead of him!' The intensity of these guilt feelings is proportional to the severity of the inner conflicts."

It is well known that flyers often become mentally disorganized as they approach the end of a tour of duty. They become anxious because they are soon to leave their squadron and thus to violate their deepest loyalty. As Grinker and Spiegel put it, the flyer "becomes intensively anxious on his last, or next to last, mission, feeling that he will never reach his goal. This is the initial displaced manifestation of guilt over the anticipated desertion of his squadron."

Flyers on leave often develop queer psychological quirks as a result of this same basic conflict. They may become chronic alcoholics, or develop severe digestive disturbances at this point, in this manner inflicting upon themselves the penalties of desertion. The flyer who returns to his home and is lionized for heroic exploits may still torture himself with the feeling of unworthiness and guilt. Drs. Grinker and Spiegel add an ominous note concerning a report from one of the overseas air forces in which "it was clearly brought out that men who had successfully finished a tour of duty showed

3 Lieutenant-Colonel Roy R. Grinker and Major John P. Spiegel of the Army Air Forces Medical Corps. Their discoveries were made in the process of "narco-synthesis," a sort of "talking cure," administered with the aid of drugs. A digest of their paper was published in the New York Times, May 17, 1944.

a quantity of aggressive behavior so great that they have been likened to delinquent adolescents, or 'dead-end kids.' "[4]

It is certainly obvious that these highly disturbing emotional experiences will handicap many of the soldiers when they return to civilian life. Many may be expected to break for reasons of psychoneurosis, years after the end of the war, when the difficulties of civilian life put some unusual strain upon a weakened segment of their emotional structure. This is in accord with our experience of World War I.

The problem of helping these psychologically battered veterans to regain their balance is very great and most urgent, but not insoluble. If we are to solve it, we must begin now to train thousands of technicians to deal with such cases. We discuss some of these matters at greater length in Part IV of this book.

---

[4] Without displaying any psychiatric insight into the matter, Frederic Wakeman describes such behavior in his novel, *Shore Leave,* which we have elsewhere discussed.

He Learns a New
Code of Morals:
Courage Is All

ANY features of army life contribute to a certain moral irresponsibility on the part of the soldier. The soldier is isolated from the family that nourished him and kept him in tutelage until he entered military service. He is more or less out of contact with the young women of his own age who would ordinarily be his eligible mates; ordinarily he cannot marry and if he does marry he cannot live with his wife in the normal manner. The church with which he was formerly associated can reach him no more; in its place stands the army chaplain who, hardworking as he probably is, can hardly hope to control his flock of young men. The local community with its thousands of Mr. and Mrs. Grundys and its small groups of people whose opinion matters cannot any longer keep watch on the boy now in uniform and regulate his behavior by gossip. In a word, the soldier is emancipated from most, if not all, the controls of civilian life.

Economically, the soldier does not need to strive. Financial incentive is, for all practical purposes, non-existent. Food, shelter, clothing, and medical care are free goods, all made available to him without his asking. No planning or management on his part is likely to enable the soldier to obtain more than these elementary necessities plus a few equally elementary luxuries. He must do his military duty, and the army will take care of his needs.

Money does not and cannot mean to the soldier what it means to the civilian. It does not stand between him and starvation, guarantee his future, or purchase social position. It may therefore be spent recklessly or gambled with, and gambling is in fact a sort of fighting play that grows out of sadistic-aggressive tendencies cultivated by the army. While money has no real value for the soldier, simple luxuries are often extremely rare under war conditions; if he wants them badly enough he will not hesitate to pay fantastic prices—and, in fact, he has paid as much as three dollars for a lemon, five dollars for a bottle of 3.2 beer, fifty dollars for a bottle of whiskey. From the civilian's point of view, this is irrational behavior. In the soldier's world, it makes sense, because money has little value. In the case of the officer, long trips and sudden changes of residence make it expedient for him to keep large sums of cash in his pocket, which similarly produces an attitude toward money utterly alien to the civilian.

Because the soldier's life is not under his own control, he is freed from the sense of personal responsibility. He cannot plan, because he has no control over his future. His task is to play the part that the military machine assigns to him and to await the decisions of an inscrutable destiny. Even his time is not his to budget and to organize; it is all but useless for him to keep a date book or a schedule of engagements. Time is not money to the soldier and not a dimension of self-initiated designs. It is merely something that belongs to the army and that passes. Death is always possible, and it may be just around the corner. Any day, any hour may be the last. Small wonder that the soldier snatches eagerly whatever satisfactions his life affords without weighing the implications of his behavior with too great a degree of moral nicety.

The solidarity of soldier society gives plenary indulgence to those sins that soldiers are most likely to commit. Everyone else commits them, or so it seems, and therefore one's own behavior has social justification. The army attitude toward sex behavior traditionally permits a certain license. The rest of the world expects the soldier to behave with some freedom in such matters. Similarly, prescriptions and taboos concerning property change their nature when one goes from a civilian life to the army. Property may not only be appropriated and used by persons other than its legal owner, but it may also be put to many uses for which it was never intended, and it may be wantonly destroyed. Where masses of men are concerned, it does not seem to matter very much whether they are a group of chaplains or recruits for the regular army; both groups are highly destructive except when military discipline brings this tendency under control. However, the soldier's morality combined with his feelings of brotherhood in war demands the sharing of property to a degree unknown in civilian life. It is reported that

Marines on Tarawa shared their last cigarettes, carefully fluffing up the package to hide the fact that it was the last. Such incidents have been reported many times in the annals of war. This is morality, and a high morality, although it is opposed to the customary practices of our society.

And it may come about that the soldier's morality demands the sacrifice of life itself. The current newspapers are full of tales of such heroism as that of Lieutenant Robert Craig, who, on July 11, 1943, at Favoratta, Sicily, charged a group of a hundred Germans in order to draw their fire away from his men—a feat from which there was no possibility of personal survival. Lieutenant Craig received the Congressional Medal of Honor posthumously. Such instances are recorded in the annals of almost every nation. Apparently such things have always been, and men have always admired them.

He "Takes the Cash and Lets the Credit Go"

Almost inevitably, the soldier falls into a short-term hedonism. In the place of the accepted morality of civilian society, the soldier regulates his life by individualistic, hedonistic adjustments on a short-term basis. Morality is a matter of the long pull; it involves long-term rewards and punishments. The college boy studies now, content in the belief that he will collect his greatest rewards thirty years from now. He is continent, because he intends one day to marry; honest, not only because he has been taught to be honest but because, in the long run, it is much the best policy. But if the soldier has no future, as all too often he has not, morality cannot have much appeal. The soldier "takes the cash and lets the credit go," hoping to "live a little while before he dies forever." Giving up hope of the first-rate and despairing of the worth-while, he grasps eagerly at the cheap and quick and tawdry. When he returns to civilian life, it is difficult for him to adjust his life to long-term planning once again. It is harder for him to work for the distant future than it can ever be for the man who has never known war and the luxury of living entirely for the present.

The recent novel Shore Leave tells of the reckless hedonism of the front-line fighters of the present war.[1] The novel, recounting

1 Frederic Wakeman, Shore Leave. Farrar and Rinehart, 1944.

certain episodes in the life of four young naval aviators, centers around one Crewson, a fabulous character who has a hectic love affair with a gorgeous creature named Gwynneth. These young men pride themselves on having seen the worst of war and braved its deadliest perils; only fighters count in their universe. They prefer their gold-braid tarnished and their uniforms almost in tatters, preferences that cause much grief to the shore-bound admirals and the special police. Civilians—male civilians—are vague creatures who mean little in the combat pilot's world. The chatter of civilians is so much hog-wash. Men of battle and of the sky need not even trouble to tell the truth to civilians; it is useless to try to communicate anything to them anyhow, and better to spin out some fantastic yarn. When a civilian explains that he would like to do his part, but what can he do with a wife, three children, and a mortgage, the young aviators become slightly nauseated. They joke, as did the soldiers of World War I, about what they are doing to maintain the morale of civilians. War aims are not for such men. They are for civilians; they are big sloppy words and combinations of words such as civilians like. The Four Freedoms? Big, sloppy words. Why do these men fight? Says Crewson, "You fight to win, period." One forgets so easily the end of war when he is actively engaged in the war process.

Like many other men who have a rendezvous with death, these young aviators have the morals of alley-cats. "All I ever see of a town any more are the bars, the hotels, and the women," as Crewson puts it. Crewson has a wife, but she is far away, and he may never have another shore leave, and the others have wives also, but such things do not matter in war. Crewson's wife is no more to him than a nasty reminder to call Operator Six at Great Neck. No property rights mean anything any more; money does not mean anything; nothing counts but liquor, women, and fighting. Like Hemingway's characters, the young men of Wakeman's novels philosophize sometimes and strike off crisp cynicisms when they are not too drunk. At least from the surface of their minds they exclude the thought of the morrow.

Courage and Valor Are the Highest Virtues

That the soldier develops compensatory virtues should go with-

out saying. His job is to fight, to die if need be with antique
courage. The pages of history are full of the names of brave soldiers
who did their duty unto death, and literature abounds in eloquent
tributes to such men. One of the best of such eulogies is Carlyle's
little oration concerning the Swiss Guards at the Tuileries. It
illustrates our point well.

> Oh ye stanch Swiss, ye gallant gentlemen in black, for what
> a cause are ye to spend and be spent! Look out from the
> western windows, ye may see King Louis placidly hold on his
> way; the poor little prince royal "sportfully kicking the fallen
> leaves" . . . And ye? Left standing there, amid the yawning
> abysses, and earthquake of insurrection; without course, with-
> out command; if ye perish, it must be as more than martyrs,
> as martyrs who are now without a cause! The black courtiers
> disappear mostly; through such issues as they can. The poor
> Swiss know not how to act; one duty only is clear to them,
> that of standing by their post; and they will perform that . . .
> Surely few things in the history of carnage are painfuler.
> What ineffaceable red streak, flickering so sad in the memory,
> is that, of this poor column of red Swiss, "breaking itself in
> the confusion of opinions"; dispersing, into blackness and
> death. Honor to you, brave men; honorable pity, through long
> times. Not martyrs were ye; and yet almost more. He was no
> king of yours, this Louis; and he forsook you like a king of
> shreds and patches; ye were but sold to him for some poor
> sixpence a day; yet would ye work for your wages, keep your
> plighted word. The work now was to die, and ye did it. Honor
> to you, Oh Kinsmen; and may the old Deutsch *Beiderkeit* and
> *Tapferkeit,* and valor which is *worth* and *truth,* be they Swiss,
> be they Saxon, fail in no age! Not bastards; trueborn were
> these men; sons of the men of Semback, of Murten, who knelt
> but not to thee, Oh Burgundy! Let the traveler, as he passes
> through Lucerne, turn aside to look a little at their monu-
> mental lion; not for Thorwaldsen's sake alone. Hewn out of
> living rock, the figure rests there, by the still lake waters, in
> lullaby of distant-tinkling *ranz des vaches,* the granite moun-
> tains dumbly keeping watch all round; and though inanimate,
> speaks.[2]

All sorts and conditions of men have contributed to these armies,
great and small, that died for duty and for honor—white, black, red,

[2] Thomas Carlyle, *The French Revolution,* Vol. II, Chap. VII.

and yellow men, slaves and freeborn, criminals and law-abiders, infidels and God-fearers, all have been martyrs with or without causes. Often they were mercenaries who died so; sometimes they were poor "pressed men" forced all unwilling into service. They may have been evil men whose only goal was booty; possibly they were patriots enamored of a cause. It does not seem to have mattered very much: they were soldiers. Men will die just as readily—and as heroically—in a bad cause as in a good one. Housman tells of the army of mercenaries who "took their wages and are dead;" they "saved the sum of things for pay," but they might just as well have "died in defence of a chicken-brained harlot." They could equally well have been patriots who offered up their lives in a glorious cause. Their valor was their justification whether they died in good causes or bad. That is the implicit creed of the soldier. Valor is the great virtue—courage, steadfastness in duty, bravery.

So urgent is this virtue in the mind of the soldier that Christian civilian society accepts it unquestioningly, even though the implications are strongly pagan. The very Christian Robert E. Lee remarked after the Battle of Gettysburg: "The conduct of the troops was all that I could desire or expect, and they deserved success in so far as it can be deserved by heroic valor and fortitude."[3] The major premise is clearly that success is deserved by courage and not by the merits of one's cause. How far is this from the "might is right" slogan that America uttered with such scorn when Kaiser Wilhelm proclaimed it in the 1914-1918 years? Not only is Lee's premise amoral in terms of Christian civilization; it is also the soldier's philosophy implicit.

Lincoln subscribed to the same credo in speaking of the same battle. In his Gettysburg Address he expressed sentiments utterly non-Christian in nature but marked by a high religious tone. "But in a larger sense, we cannot dedicate, we cannot consecrate, we cannot hallow this ground. The brave men, living and dead, who struggled here have consecrated it far above our poor power to add or detract." Religious, certainly; but certainly non-Christian; for Christianity, custodian of absolute truth, cannot grant that two opposed ideals can both be true—can both be virtuous. The conse-

[3] Douglas Southall Freeman, *R. E. Lee*. Scribner, 1934, Vol. III, p. 155.

cration, therefore, that Lincoln pays tribute to, is one that arises from courage—great, valorous courage of men dedicated to *an* ideal. By implication the ideal itself—content of the cause—cannot matter because any army dedicated to an ideal and valorous in behalf of an ideal must be virtuous and capable of consecrating the battlefield. The content of the ideal (the end) is secondary; the valorous act of striving (the means) is primary.

It is interesting in this connection to examine our word "virtue." Its Latin root *virtus* is best translated as "valor." The roots of the pagan cult of bravery are in fact very deep in our culture. We cannot believe that any man who is brave can be wholly bad. The most abandoned criminal, the cruelest outlaw, if he dies bravely, wins a portion of our admiration and so softens somewhat our condemnation of his acts. For his courage has "consecrated the act" in our eyes—our still somewhat pagan eyes!

This central virtue of the soldier—like the other new virtues that constitute his new morality—is far from useful in peacetime society. A man does not have much chance to be brave in civilian life. In fact, physical bravery does not matter greatly either by its presence or absence once the war is over. If a man is a coward, that rarely interferes with his business or profession; if he is brave, he rarely receives any credit for it. So with the other virtues of the soldier; they are often irrelevant to competitive peacetime living. If a man is loyal to his friends, very good, provided he does not carry the matter to extremes, but if he is too loyal, so that he sacrifices himself for others, then the more fool he.

By and large, virtue in the soldier inheres in just one kind of thing for which there are many names—adherence to duty, loyalty, steadfastness, bravery, call it what you will—and this one intensive and solidary virtue matters to the civilian hardly at all.

He Revalues
"Civilized Attitudes"
and Religion

I F A PERSON has a tack in his shoe and keeps on wearing the shoe
and does not remove the tack, after a time he develops a callus.
The callus is a sore spot, but it covers the tack and is the best
protection that Nature could improvise. So if one has a gnawing
anxiety in his mind or a yearning and a hungering in his soul, these
things also give rise to callusses—mental growths, protective devices
which, however unsuitable they may be ordinarily, nevertheless help
to deal with an abnormal situation.

The soldier suffers many hardships, hungers, anxieties, and irri-
tations. From within himself he calls forth a bitter strength, and a
kind of humor that enables him to bear the burdens of his existence. He suffers physical deprivation and hardship; in order to
bear such things he becomes physically hardened. He yearns for
love but cannot have it; he degrades it by obscenity and coarseness
so that it will seem not worth having. He fears death; therefore
he makes light of death. To buttress all these attitudes, he develops
little snatches of philosophy, which like other philosophies befog
unpleasant certainties and befool the mind with illogical logic. He
develops belief systems, and like anyone else is emotionally attached
to those beliefs in proportion to the degree of his suspicion that
they are false. In short, the soldier develops a mental system, complete with attitudes, behavior patterns, forms of logic, beliefs and
philosophy, custom-tailored to the needs of his life.

The soldier's life is bitter hard, and because it must be bitter
hard there arises a kind of cult of hardness and fitness to give men
the qualities to stand it. The soldier must call upon his body for
incredible exertions, long marches with heavy packs, and days without sleep or food. He must sleep on the ground, live in a foxhole,
endure dirt and flies and the assorted insects served on the menu

of each locality. To meet these trials, he develops physical fitness, and not only fitness but also the belief that fitness is a great virtue. Proud of his endurance, he soon comes to look down on the soft civilian. Perhaps he resolves never to let himself get soft when he returns to civilian life, happily oblivious to the stubborn fact that few men in civilian pursuits are ever able to exercise all day; unaware that diligence, in most civilian pursuits, consists precisely in applying the seat of one's pants to a chair for long periods of time. But while the soldier is in the army, physical fitness serves him well.

To meet the other hardnesses of army life, there arise other kinds of fitness. The necessity of preparing to be a killer engenders in the soldier an almost prideful attitude toward murder and its instruments. When soldier and civilian meet, the soldier sometimes says and more often thinks, "I could kill you. One smash of a gun butt would splatter your brains all over the sidewalk. And I know several sure-fire ways of killing you with my bare hands." And he may add, "Perhaps you have more money than I have. You don't deserve it. I could take it away from you if I wanted to." But in the back of his mind the soldier, reared to be a peaceful and not a murderous citizen, still revolts at brutality; he is uneasy about it and it hurts his conscience sometimes. From such conflicts, humor provides a mode of escape, and brutality comes to be regarded as screamingly funny.

> It was astonishing how loudly one laughed at tales of grue-some things, of war's brutality—I with the rest of them. I think at the bottom of it was a sense of the ironical contrast between the normal ways of civilian life and this harkback to the cave-man code. It made all our old philosophy of life monstrously ridiculous.[1]

The soldier has an unfulfilled and unfulfillable yearning for love, and because this yearning cannot be satisfied he degrades love by cultivating obscenity. This obscenity is apparently characteristic of all armies; the speech of soldiers is always coarse and doubtless there were many dirty remarks among Joshua's warriors when they stormed Jericho and, in faithful execution of their orders, spared no one but Rahab the harlot who was also a fifth columnist. The

---

[1] Philip Gibbs, *Now It Can Be Told*. Harper, 1920, p. 130.

psychology of obscenity is simple. One longs for love, not mere carnal gratification, one cannot have love, and therefore one degrades it by referring to it constantly in the crudest, coarsest, and most undignified terms that language provides. Thus one attempts to persuade one's self that this thing which one cannot have is not worth having anyhow.

Like other love-starved men and women, soldiers take great delight in pets. Sometimes this need for something to love causes them to cherish strange creatures, such as lice and fleas and other fauna rarely cultivated by civilians. More often they turn to animals more in keeping with the ordinary tastes of mankind, the most popular pets of soldiers, as of civilians, being dogs and little children. The affinity of dogs and soldiers is proverbial, a love match lasting since men were men and dogs were dogs. A soldier in a training camp writes as follows concerning the rôle of the dog in army life:

> There is no question that the dog is man's best friend but in the army man is the dog's best friend. When I first arrived at camp I was immediately struck by the number of dogs of all descriptions running loose. There wasn't a single company that didn't have at least several dogs to attend all formations and follow each group as it marched to details.
>
> A position we moved into had a Great Dane who'd been the pet of the first sergeant of the preceding unit. He slept in a bed of his own in the sergeant's barracks and was carried on the ration list as a private first class. Whenever a jeep went out of the area he rode proudly in back. The men of our group took to him at once and he soon had his court of admirers and caretakers. He was joined at intervals by various house pets who had strayed from nearby homes to the easy food and exciting life of an army dog. Rarely were there less than three mutts on hand.
>
> The Great Dane really came into his own as an idol of the enlisted men when he wandered away to the regimental headquarters one day and reared up onto the colonel's shoulders, knocking the latter to the ground. A traffic accident brought the Great Dane to an ignoble end. He was buried with full military honors near the flagpole. The battery commander read a posthumous good conduct medal citation which was placed in the coffin. The bugle played Taps and his special friends lowered the body into the grave.

A gargantuan Saint Bernard was brought in to fill the void left by the untimely end of the Great Dane, but could not gain the universal favor of his predecessor. Having been brought up as a watchdog by a private family, he couldn't seem to get used to large groups but became the special care of one great hulk of a fellow. This man was of somewhat dull normal mentality. His wife had had a child shortly after his induction and he'd seen the child only a few times. Many an evening I've seen the great brute sleeping on the floor of the recreation room with his huge human friend rocking in a chair beside him and beaming proudly as everyone else made cautious detours of the neighborhood. The Saint Bernard was found to be too unsociable, and, after tearing a number of jackets and trousers, was returned to his former owner. His friend still carries his photo and will discourse at great length, upon the slightest provocation.

Soldiers also adopt children, children of all races, children of enemy countries about as readily as any others. Ernie Pyle writes as follows of the pets of American soldiers in Italy:

I've told you time and again about the dogs our soldiers have taken as pets and mascots. Running second to dogs, I believe, are Italian kids. There's no way of estimating how many Italian boys have been adopted by our troops, but there must be hundreds.

An outfit will pick up some kid, usually one who has been orphaned by bombing and has no home and no place to go. The children come along of their free will, of course, and they begin having the time of their lives.

The soldiers cut down extra uniforms and clothe them in straight GI. The youngsters pick up English so fast it makes your head swim. They eat better than they have eaten in years. The whole thing is exciting and adventuresome to them. The units keep them in areas as safe as can be found when they go into action . . .

I do know of Sicilian adoptees who were brought along on the invasion of Italy, just like the animal pets. And I've heard of two other adoptees, already written up by some of the other correspondents, who stowed away and went on the Anzio beachhead landings.[2]

The possibility of death and the fear of death are central prob-

2 Ernie Pyle, Scripps-Howard newspaper column, 1944, and Henry Holt, publishers.

lems of the soldier's life. The most direct answer to these problems is the cult of courage to which we have already referred. As to fear, the front-line soldier accepts it and is not ashamed; perhaps he even slightly overdoes the pose of being always horribly afraid. Dollard's Spanish Civil War veterans showed a considerable degree of tolerance for the soldier who cracks up under fear-producing situations, and the same tolerance was shown by soldiers of World War I. Civilians are probably less tolerant in this respect.

He Takes on New Attitudes to Make Life Bearable

Many systems of attitudes and beliefs are devised by the human mind to make the risk of death easier to bear. Death in war is glorious; *dulce et decorum est pro patria mori*—it is sweet and fitting to die for one's country. Death for the cause is glorious, for by that death we shall gain a better world. Death is bad, but better than defeat; better to die than to be ruled by Fascists. Better a dead lion than a live hyena. Such things people say in war, and everyone nods his head and says, "True, true! How true!" but relatively few persons are really convinced by such sayings. We whistle words to keep our courage up.

Fatalistic creeds flourish in war; they become the common speech of the day. Death will come to you only from the bullet that has your name on it, and that bullet has not been manufactured yet; death will come for others, of course, but not for you. Death will take you when your time comes, but not before; nothing can change the date of your fated rendezvous with death, your appointment in Samara. Perhaps one pins his faith to some charm or amulet, a pocket testament, or a rabbit's foot. As Gibbs remarks, "They became fatalists after a few fights, and believed in their luck, or their mascots—teddy-bears, a bullet that had missed them, china dolls, a girl's lock of hair, a silver ring. Yet at the back of their brains, most of them, I fancy, knew that it was only a question of time before they 'went west.' "[3]

The fear of death gives rise to curiously amusing intellectual contrivances. One is either at the front, or not; if not, there is nothing to worry about. If at the front, the enemy is shelling or he is not; and if not, there is nothing to worry about. If he is

3 Philip Gibbs, *op. cit.,* p. 389.

shelling, one gets hit or not, and if not, there is nothing to worry about. If one gets hit, he is killed or not; if killed he need not worry. If one is wounded, the wound is serious or not—and so on to the end. A similar formulation proves with fairly valid logic that when a man is killed in war it is an accident.

Other philosophies belittle or make fun of the Grim Reaper himself. "Death," says A. H. Gibbs, "we faced daily, hourly, with a laugh."[4] As Philip Gibbs puts it, "Death, their own, or other people's does not mean very much to some who, in the trenches, sat within a few yards of stinking corpses, knowing that the next shell might make such of them. Life was cheap in war. Is it not cheap in peace?"[5] Death, perhaps is not so hard to take, when one has toughened himself to war, but the waiting for death is never easy.

"Death is nothing," said one young officer just down from the Somme fields for a week's rest cure for jangled nerves. "I don't care a damn for death; but it's the waiting for it, the devilishness of its uncertainty, the sight of one's pals blown to bits about one, and the animal fear under shell-fire that break one's pluck. . . . My nerves are like fiddle-strings."[6]

He Is Reported Overwhelmingly Indifferent to Religion

There are many honest and sincere people who believe that the answers to the soldier's problems are to be found in conventional religion. These people have seized upon the saying, "There are no atheists in fox-holes," and upon a few dramatic incidents as proof that there is a great revival of religion among the armed forces. While there is some difference of opinion, the facts do not seem to support this belief. In the early months of 1944, *Time* magazine presented convincing statements from Dr. Daniel A. Poling, Dr. Bernard Iddings Bell, and an unnamed Catholic chaplain. Certainly none of these men has a bias against religion; not one of them but would welcome a religious revival if he saw evidences of it.

Dr. Poling, just returned from a tour of many battlefronts, re-

[4] A. H. Gibbs, *Gun Fodder, The Diary of Four Years of War.* Little Brown, 1919, p. 205.
[5] Philip Gibbs, *op. cit.,* p. 553.
[6] *Ibid.,* p. 333.

ported in his forthright way that "two things more than all others have troubled me, two things that are not good for America. First: positive bitterness against organized labor (perhaps I should write: against leaders of organized labor). Second, overwhelming indifference to organized religion."[7] Dr. Bernard Iddings Bell, High Church Episcopalian, was reported as in complete agreement. As to the no-atheists-in-foxholes dogma, Dr. Bell concurred with the opinion of a chaplain that if this is true it is because there are few atheists anywhere.[8] A Jesuit chaplain who remained anonymous corroborated these reports to the full. Even franker than his Protestant colleagues, he stated, "If you read the Catholic press nowadays you get the impression that there is a great religious revival going on in the armed forces. Personally I think that is a lot of tripe. So do the few Catholic chaplains I have talked with."

This Catholic chaplain, according to his letter reprinted in *Time,* considered that an attendance of 300 at his Sunday Mass was an excellent showing—even though his flock numbered 900. The Protestant ministers apparently envied the size of his audience.

Like other thoughtful religionists, this chaplain expressed deep concern about the effect of the hatreds released in the course of combat experience. Like others, he considered that the Church would find it extremely hard to reach the ears of men conditioned by a war of extermination. He deplored the failure of the churches to keep in touch with the men who were in the front lines, risking their lives. He added:

"They don't care very much about words, least of all about abstract words. Campaign ribbons are going to count an awful lot with them after the war, and the man or the priest who has 'been there' with them is going to have their ears."[9] Perhaps the ideal chaplain's attitude is that of the chaplain of a famous ship and veteran of many battles who expressed the matter in this way, "I am very much attached to the human race, having lost all hope for it."

Members of the clerical profession aware that army life has rendered a tenth of our population "overwhelmingly indifferent to religion," nevertheless are prone to regard the Church as uniquely qualified to assist the veteran in his readjustment to

[7] *Time*, January 3, 1944. [8] *Time*, January 31, 1944. [9] *Time*, Feb. 21, 1944.

peacetime living. Rev. Dr. John Sutherland Bonnell, pastor of New York's Fifth Avenue Presbyterian Church, put forth this point of view in a sermon, when he remarked that the demobilization of 10,000,000 service men will "present a tremendous challenge to the Christian church."

> The therapeutic values of Christian worship and preaching should be developed. . . . The emphasis on educational and vocational rehabilitation must not be allowed to overshadow the profound need that will exist for spiritual orientation. Inevitably there will exist, to a considerable degree, psychological maladjustments manifested in disillusionment, resentment toward civilians, depression, and a sense of guilt. Spiritual therapy available in the resources of the Christian faith can accomplish most in overcoming these problems."[10]

Dr. Bonnell's faith in the powers of religion is fairly representative of one clerical point of view, hopeful of channeling the "aggressive instincts developed in service men," as he puts it, "into a noble crusade against intolerance, ignorance, poverty, and hate."

One's attitudes are the function of one's life situation. The soldier revaluates the civilian attitudes of his former self, because his new life situation as a warrior forces him to revaluate them. It will not be possible to lead the returning soldier into a church and expect him to follow the exhortations of the sermon. The fact is that he will not understand these exhortations because they are the values of the civilian world which he does not understand any more, and to which he must be re-introduced by gradual and persistent stages.

The values that the soldier has learned to respect in war are the values of war and not the values of peace. The hardness, obscenity, fatalism, and apathy to religion cannot suddenly be dispelled by an inspiring sermon, regardless of the speaker's sincerity and eloquence. These "soldier values" can be dispelled only by the successful experience of civilian living; for the veteran will have to be "shown" that the civilian values he discarded under military necessity are really worthy of his allegiance.

[10] Reported in the N. Y. Times, May 22, 1944.

He Is Bored and
Rebels, Rebels and
Is Bored

A<small>T THE END</small> of a hard march after several days of hard marches a Confederate general was standing by the road while his weary troops struggled grimly through the mud. Seeing a battle-toughened old veteran in the ranks, he called out,

"Well, how are you getting along, John?"

John looked up, paused briefly, and replied, "Oh, I'm all right, General. I'm all right, I guess. I'm doing fine, thank you. But God damn my soul if I ever love another country!"

When a man, under the gentle compulsions of his draft board, gives himself over to the army, he gives his consent to the things the army does to him, he surrenders and swears away many of his rights as a human being. He determines to be a good soldier, to do whatever is required of him. But the man hardly lives who can fulfill such a promise, who can do all that an army requires of him without some inward rebellion.

The army shoves a man around, the American army figuratively, others literally. It forces him to perform unpleasant, menial tasks, and imposes an endless number of discomforts on him. It takes him from his wife and children, or prevents him from having wife or children. It takes away the years in which he had planned to progress in his career and forces him to spend those years on work that benefits him but little.

The army denies a man the right to answer back, to argue, to question orders, to ask the reason of things; the army permits no discussion, demands unhesitating and unquestioning conformity. The free-born American was not born to this, nor was he ever taught to accept it. He resents being ordered about, hates and rebels against the Frederick-the-Great, cannon-fodder type of discipline. When an American is forced to submit to army regimentation, he is likely to feel that he has been cheated of his birthright.

Perhaps the worst ordeal of all is the boredom. Boredom is almost universal in war. War has often been characterized as long periods of boredom punctuated by acute periods of fear. Long periods of waiting for something to happen, lonely vigils in inaccessible places, isolation from one's ordinary circles of association and channels of communication, the drudgery of routine tasks, the want of incentive, the absence of stimulating companions, the lack of recreation —all conspire to inflict exquisite boredom upon the soldier. There is no way in which to break the circle of tiresome thoughts. As A. H. Gibbs once put it, "One's mind was tied to war, like a horse on a picketing rope, and could only go round and round in a narrow circle."[1]

For such reasons the soldier always rebels against the army and the wise commander of men permits some rebellion. A good officer pays little attention to grumbling, and he does not appear to hear some of the unfavorable comments made *sotto voce* about himself. General Meade apparently did nothing when he heard one of his men characterize him as a "goggle-eyed old snapping turtle." Nor did Lee object when his men, toiling to erect earthworks around Richmond, referred to him as the King of Spades. As long as the officer can pretend not to have heard such mutterings, he can afford to overlook them. The intelligent officer is careful not to take in a personal way the common soldier's songs, jokes, with their lewd references to officers and astonishingly vivid descriptions of the behavior of the officers behind the lines. Nor does the officer interfere with the amusements of the men—gambling, drinking, women, or cock-roach races—unless circumstances compel him to do so.

For many soldiers, however, these forms of release are insufficient. Such men fulfill to a minimal degree the demands made upon them, rendering unto Caesar just enough to keep out of the guardhouse and not one whit more. They salute in a sloppy manner, spend a great deal of time in the latrine, neglect their clothing and equipment, and frequently go on sick call. They "soldier" on the job; they gold-brick and occasionally malinger. The goldbricker is in fact a well-recognized social type among soldiers. His job is wriggling out of work and he is good at it. Sometimes he is

[1] A. H. Gibbs, *Gun Fodder, The Diary of Four Years of War.* Little, Brown, 1919, p. 210.

a competent soldier and a good man in combat. Gold-bricking under combat conditions may take the form of deliberately incurring a minor wound or even a self-inflicted one.

Modern armies have a great deal of trouble with such things. Minor points of rebellion center about the uniform. Where dress is prescribed in its minutest details, a man who can vary it a little bit is able thus to save some small part of his individuality from the crushing weight of regimentation. A soldier who can wear a uniform a little better than the Government Issue and not quite in accord with regulations, or a sailor who can wear a dress cap that looks unusually salty has won a mighty victory in his mind. Such deviations from regulations are relatively harmless, and may, because of their effect upon morale, be militarily useful. Generals, of course, dress pretty much as they please.

Other soldiers, without going in for overt rebellion, put up a desperate struggle to save some part of themselves from the army. As they put it, they want to be able to call their souls their own, and therefore they fight the army unceasingly. Intellectuals particularly tend to engage in this kind of spiritual sabotage, for which reason they are usually not good soldiers. These rebels for their souls' sake are actually very poor psychologists. A man can save more of himself by giving way completely to the military machine and thus winning concessions for good behavior than by forever fighting against it. Over-conformity is easier than under-conformity and may serve exactly the same purpose.[2]

Boredom Comes from Frustration

The boredom of war is one of the things men rebel against, one of the chief complaints against a military experience. Boredom is something to rebel against, but it is more than that: boredom *is* rebellion. Boredom is an unsuppressible, un-put-down-able mutiny, the most damaging form of resistance to authority. Boredom is the great social force before which all compulsion fails. Strangely, bore-

---

[2] A veteran who has seen hard service once explained how he had avoided any feeling of conflict between himself and the army. He said, "I just did what I was supposed to do before anybody could order me to do it. I knew the bugle would blow at six o'clock and wake me and I would have to get up and I would resent it. So I just got up five minutes early and everything was fine." In this way he not only avoided conflict, but preserved the illusion of spontaneous behavior.

dom, or ennui, has received little attention from the sociologists and psychologists, and there is, apparently, not even a familiar essay on the subject comparable to Stevenson's *On Falling In Love*. Ennui is the rebellion of the human soul against regimentation. It sets the limits beyond which the individual cannot go in conforming to external compulsion. It is the curse of institutions, flourishing always in armies, prisons, schools, and churches. It afflicts many marriages. Hans Gross, the great criminal psychologist, even regarded it as one cause of crime.

Boredom is an automatic, uncontrollable reaction to frustration. The mental state of boredom is characterized by an apathy toward the stimuli of the current situation, by mild repugnance to the situation and by a psychic withdrawal from it. There is involved in it a desire to be somewhere else and to do something different, to escape from the boring stimuli; often it produces a restless turning from one boring situation to another. Boredom is a recognizable mental state, but though every one knows what it is many people cannot easily distinguish it from mild anger or disgust, and in fact mild anger or disgust, if there is no means of escape from them, may be an element in ennui. In ordinary life, the boring person is the one who overwhelms us with his undisguised vanity, the egotist, who has sometimes been defined as the person who talks about himself when you want to talk about yourself.

Two kinds of boredom may be distinguished, introverted and extraverted. The introvert is bored when the external world imposes itself upon his mind in a manner alien to his own inner desires. The extravert is bored when he has nothing outside himself to occupy his mind. The extravert is bored when he is alone, the introvert, more often, when he is in company. Persons who experience protracted periods of boredom unfailingly reveal some deep-lying frustration. They want to get married, and cannot; or they want to get a divorce or go to college or quit their jobs, and cannot. Boredom, with its consequent apathy and inability to conform to the demands of the external world, is subject to only a slight degree of control on the part of the person who suffers it; only within narrow limits can the individual help being bored. It is subject to much external control by other individuals; to bore others acceptably, as in school or church, or not to bore them, may be made the basis of a career.

He Devises Ways of Escaping from Boredom

Prison officials are familiar with a state of mind in which, as a result of extreme ennui, a man reacts in a habitized, stylized fashion to his accustomed environment, but actually dwells continually in his phantasies. He goes through all the outward motions of prison life but his mind is not in it; he is barely conscious of the external world. Rebelling no more in his overt behavior, he lives in his beautiful dreams. Such a man is said to be "prisonized," to have "prison-stupor," to be "stir-crazy." Probably few prisoners avoid a touch of this disease. Similar reactions appear in the army, and soldiers with their customary taxonomic ingenuity have invented many descriptive terms. A man may become "barrack-wacky;" on the North African desert he is "lurgy-lurgy" or "sand-happy;" in Iceland or Greenland he is "glacier-happy." The mechanism is the same in all cases: Reality has become intolerable and the individual has taken refuge in phantasy.

The attempt to find relief from boredom motivates much of our behavior in civilian as well as military life. To escape boredom civilians go to the theatre, play cards or chess, take trips, read books, get drunk, change wives, or do any of a thousand wise or foolish things. Soldiers have not so many resources, but they do the best they can with what they have. They gamble, for that is the "proper use" of money, and the winner goes on a spree. They fight among themselves. They spread rumors, make up slang, compose and sing dirty songs. They amuse themselves with mental games, tell tall tales. They talk about what they did on their last leave and what they are going to do on the next. They write letters, read and reread the letters they receive. They have cock-roach, louse, and bed-bug races, and make special pets of the worthy performers. In every way that circumstances permit, they strive to combat boredom.

Minor creature comforts such as Coca-Cola, chewing gum, and candy-bars help to prevent boredom and to relieve nervous tension. But the soldier's most important resource when he is nervous or bored is tobacco. In fact, tobacco plays such an important part in modern war that one wonders how wars were fought before its use was discovered. It wakes the soldier in the morning and puts him to sleep at night, whiles away the time in the endless waiting of war, dulls discomfort, substitutes for food, checks the fears of men about to die and calms their executioners, and helps the grave-diggers to overcome their repulsions. Tobacco may not do any of these things, but men use it for such purposes and a thousand others. Little is known about the physiological effects of tobacco and no more about the psychological. We do know that its use among soldiers is almost universal and that soldiers prescribe it for themselves in such situations as those described. In some strange way it helps to overcome the frustrations of the military way of life and substitutes for the comforts of home. Without tobacco man's experience of war would be very different.

Probably more than any other soldiers, prisoners of war suffer from ennui. Soldiers, as Paul Cohen-Portheim puts it, lead a danger-ous and a terrible life, prisoners a helpless and a useless one.[3] A prisoner realizes that his sufferings are useless and futile; there is no point in them at all. There have been plenty of horrors in the prison camps of the past, and there are plenty today; there is brutality, thieving, murder, starvation. Boredom remains one of the greatest horrors, and imprisoned men fight it as best they can. When they fail, as they must often do, they develop the *maladie du fil de fer barbèle*, the barbed-wire sickness, which is prison stupor by another name.

[3] Paul Cohen-Portheim, *Time Stood Still, 1914-1918*. Dutton, 1932, p. 83.

When Peace Breaks Out, The Army Collapses

WHEN peace or armistice comes, the military machine falls apart. If, as the saying goes, "war raises hell with an army," then peace is all but indescribable. A modern army is assembled for a specific purpose, and the instant that purpose is accomplished the soldiers want to go home.

A story now current illustrates a widespread attitude. Two soldiers, a sergeant and a private, were being tried for gross insubordination. It seemed that at an inspection the two of them had kicked a general. The sergeant gave his explanation first:

"It was just a bit of reflex action, and no offence was intended. I have a very sensitive toe, and when someone steps on it my leg automatically kicks out and I can't help it. Just as the general was passing me, somebody stepped on my toe, and my foot went out and hit the general. I didn't intend any disrespect."

The judge turned to the private, "And what is your explanation?"

"Well, sir," said the private, "My action was due to a mistake. I just happened to look up and see the sergeant kicking the general, and I thought the war was over!"

The Soldier Thinks the Army's Job Is Done

Peace always seems to come suddenly. As the soldier sees it, the terrible enemy disappears all at once, and with him disappears the army's reason for existence. The soldier does not realize that it is necessary to keep an army in being in order to win the respect of one's allies, he does not understand by what a devious route diplomacy must travel from a state of war to a state of peace; he cannot comprehend why the routines of demobilization are so long-drawn out and tedious. He gives his consent to the submerging of his personality in the military machine no longer.

Morale—in an army, a football team, a gang, a nation at war, a school, a prison—is merely an adjustment of the wishes of the individual to the purposes of the group. The purpose of the army is to fight a war. The soldier submits to the army regime because he concurs in that purpose. He identifies himself with the army and its cause, hates the enemy, and loses himself in the mystic solidarity of his fellows; he gives his assent to being regimented and the army does the rest. When war ends, there is no point in being a soldier any longer. Hence, he ceases to give the basic assent upon which the army maintains its system of compulsions.

A World War I sergeant has supplied the following account of what happened at Camp Gordon (Atlanta, Georgia) when peace broke out in November, 1918:

> The first noticeable relaxation of morale occurred with the false armistice. It seemed obvious to the men that the officers had been ordered to bear down on discipline. The men were apathetic in drill, and in barracks they varied between being very talkative about peace and extremely dull and moody.
>
> At the news of the real armistice there was wild confusion. Everybody cheered and said, in effect, "to hell with duty." There were two or three days of celebration and of marching in town. Then an attempt was made to return the camp to the former discipline.
>
> The enlisted men didn't change noticeably for about two or three weeks; and then orders began to come from headquarters to the effect that morale officers had been appointed. This gave rise to the first great change. These officers were looked upon as a sort of boy-scout organization. The men made ribald jokes about the morale officers and there was frequent talk of "going over the hill."
>
> The next step occurred when the men were ordered to turn in their rifles and side-arms. The men didn't mind this at all. They were given wooden guns to drill with in some cases, and in other cases they were taken out to close-order drill. At each rest period on the field, more and more men disappeared—they went back to the barracks to sleep or they went to the canteen to eat ice cream or drink pop. As time went on, it became the habit for most of a company to disappear after the first rest period. Drill was more or less given up.

There was a great deal of growling about staying in camp though the war was over. Some entertainments were arranged for the men, but these things didn't change the general attitude of "to hell with it, let's go home!"

Shortly, orders were given to disband regiments and transfer them to the depot brigade. Most of the men transferred reported for rations and quarters, but they were told that the area was jammed and to go and find a place in an empty barracks. Empty officers' quarters were taken first, and then the overflow went to empty barracks. Instead of going to the depot brigade for rations, men circulated from kitchen to kitchen where there were accumulated mess funds, and they ate in these kitchens whenever possible. When not possible, they went to the depot brigade.

A desultory period followed when headquarters selected men to duty in the discharge of casual troops [unassigned]. Men were discharged quickly to make room for these casuals, most of whom were colored work battalions from places like Bordeau and Brest. Heavily infected with venereal diseases, these men were reported to the general hospitals for treatment before discharge. They were very impatient and didn't respond to the argument that this hospitalization was being ordered for their own good.

More and more confusion and aimlessness followed because the troops that had been in the camp did not have fixed routines or quarters. Passes were handed out freely and morale officers weren't heard of anymore.

This confusion and dissatisfaction continued until we were all discharged. I was discharged three months after November 11.

The writer of the account adds, significantly: "Note that once the arms were taken away, it was hopeless to try to maintain morale. A soldier deprived of his arms feels that he has been returned to the status of a rookie."

At the end of the war, the sense of struggling for a cause disappears; in all probability the meaning of the struggle is destroyed in the post-war bickerings of allies. Such things damage the solidarity of the army, if they do not destroy it altogether. Discipline decays. The men grow careless in appearance and make a point of not saluting. Military offences multiply. The soldiers rarely get what has been promised to them; people have not been careful, during the war years, to be literally exact in their promises to soldiers. Soldiers suspect the motives of those who desire to keep them in the army; each one who remains under arms resents the fact that others are being released and are grabbing the few available jobs. Parents and friends join the soldiers in this resentment and build up political pressure to get the boys out of the army.

Soldiers have told in many ways of this debacle of the military spirit. As one veteran of the A.E.F. of 1918 put it, "When the peace came the soldiers at the front felt as though we were let down, like a man feels when he's lost everything. Before it came, I always pictured that the joy and happiness would be so very great that it would be beyond human power to live through it. And then when it came we felt almost sad." This sort of reaction has not been at all unusual with American armies. Our saddest army at war's end was probably the Revolutionary army, which was in such a serious mental state that the news of the end of the war was almost suppressed. Unpaid for months and years, underfed and ill-clothed during the entire war, cheated and wronged at every turn, the soldiers who won the Revolution had a right to be discontented if ever men had.

Victory celebrations do not help the malady. The greatest celebrations are for civilians; civilians are able to delight in the joys of the victory which they did little to gain, and then immediately turn their minds to the things of peace. But the soldiers are still in the army, still dirty, lousy and uncomfortable. And with every step on the "tortuous, narrow path to home" the soldier grows more and more impatient.

Entr'acte:
Society Changes
While the Soldier
Is at War

THE boy who comes back from the wars is not the same boy who went away, and the society to which he returns is not the one he left behind. The most important changes in the soldier are those of personality that have taken place in his own *mind*. The soldier-turned-veteran is such a man as army living has made him. And while he has been living in the peculiar world of the army, while he has been cut off from his accustomed world, while he has been isolated, great currents of social change have swept through the home-land. The fact that the soldier has lost touch with the rest of the nation at a time of rapid change contributes heavily to the problem of reassimilating him into his former world.

While the nature of wartime changes in society is well-known, it is perhaps worth while to pass them before our eyes in rapid rehearsal, paying particular attention to those changes that affect the soldier's prospect of readjustment.

The effects of war upon the economic system are devastating. In modern wars, certainly one-half and possibly two-thirds of the national income may be devoted to the purposes of combat. When one reflects that in time of peace the national income is only just sufficient to furnish the barest living to large sections of the population, it becomes clear that widespread poverty is an inevitable concomitant of the wastes of war, in spite of any increases in national income during war. There soon arises a shortage of goods and of labor. The labor shortage draws large numbers of women into industry, and opens many doors to Negroes and other under-privileged groups. Money in the hands of many new war workers helps to unsettle price schedules. Some degree of inflation there necessarily is, with its inevitable effects upon fixed incomes, savings,

and the relations of borrowers and lenders. Rising prices produce
labor troubles; there are strikes and work stoppages. Consumption,
instead of being encouraged, is controlled by various rationing
schemes. The strain of war also produces deterioration of capital
goods, through manpower shortages, material shortages or sheer
neglect—forcing the railroads to allow their roadbeds and rolling
stock to fall into disrepair and the farmer to neglect his fences.

War Takes Over the Economic System

In the economic changes of war, it is probable that the service
man and his family have fared badly. The soldier's wages are low,
and allowances for his dependents are meager in the extreme. On
his return home, the soldier finds that his economic status is inferior
to that of persons who did not go to war. The problem of reemployment of millions of soldiers, of which economists speak in general
terms, is a very personal problem for the soldier. Whether the
soldier will get any job is a serious question, but the problem of
what kind of job he will get is also important. Though his skills
probably do not fit him for a high economic status, his expecta-
tions are bound to lead in that direction. The officer, and especially
the airforce officer, has often attained a degree of "glamor" as well
as a rate of pay, which he can hardly expect to equal when he
comes home.

In wartime, the State expands its power in order to control the
economic system and otherwise to regiment the life of the people.
The returning soldier finds a great number of new agencies controlling production and consumption, allocating materials and
labor, awarding contracts, regulating labor relations, commending
some business firms and condemning others. The State expands its
power in other ways, finally assuming wide control over the lives
of its citizens. In this expansion of State power, the executive has
gained at the expense of the legislative and judicial branches. Such
things, as we know, are inevitable in war. Nevertheless, the soldier
is likely to be shocked by the damage that has been done to the
free and easy, democratic world with which he was familiar in the
years before the war.

In time of peace the family is the most important social institution. In time of war the State dominates the entire social scene,

and necessarily does great damage to the pattern of family life. The family must give up members to the army, to war work; it loses its hold upon the minds of the young. The family must adjust its budgets to taxes, and inflation, its consumption to shortages and rationing systems, its sentiments and attitudes to the demands of official propaganda. War forces a change in the entire peace-time system of family living.

War Plays Havoc with Family Relationships

War separates family members. When a man is away from his home for a period of years in military service, he tends to grow away from his family and the other members of the family tend to grow away from him. While he is away from home, either he or his wife may form other attachments, and either or both may get used to living alone. Tender attachments—engagements and understandings—between unmarried persons are even more vulnerable to the accidents of war. While the soldier is at war, his girl—or wife, for that matter—is open to the advances of other men, and either may respond. Other separations are produced by war work. Many women leave the home in time of war, not infrequently, as social workers know, deserting a brood of young children. And a great many persons, men and women, get more money in time of war than they are accustomed to handle, and in the process of spending this money they form habits and attitudes inconsistent with their previous pattern of family life. As every social worker knows, a sudden increase in income can disrupt a family as effectively as a sudden decrease.

Soldiers and civilians alike participate in the relaxation of sexual morality in time of war. Wherever men and women meet, they may join in illicit unions. This condition is so widespread in the present war that a British bishop has recently suggested that all such offences be condoned, that at the end of the war the separated pairs forgive all wartime lapses of morality, go through another marriage ceremony, and start all over again. We may be sure that the bishop would not make such a radical suggestion unless conditions warranted it.

In time of war, women leave the home, take up new work, enter new fields of achievement. They gain freedom, attain economic and social equality, but lose something of their status as women; war gives them jobs, temporarily at least, and denies them husbands, often forever. After a war, women do not easily give up their new-found freedom, and since men are scarce and morality in general relaxed, the post-war period tends to be a time of experimentation with new family customs and forms.

Children are neglected in time of war. Parents are busy elsewhere, and schools deteriorate rapidly. The teen-age group, too young to go to war, too old to be kept in ignorance of it, is particularly affected. Teen-age boys produce an unusual percentage of thugs and hoodlums, teen-age girls, of sexual delinquents. Statistics of many wars in many countries have shown this phenomenon clearly. Post-war youth is a disorganized generation. With the returning veterans and the disillusioned civilians, these children who have come to maturity in time of war give to the post-war period its characteristic tone by devoting themselves to a peculiar kind of gaiety from which the element of happiness is entirely absent.

Juvenile Delinquency, Education, Boom Towns

By these changes in the family, the soldier is profoundly affected. His is the age-group in which these things take place, and his the economic level on which they have the greatest effect. The impact of war upon the family cannot be adequately pictured by rows of cold statistics showing numbers of divorces, delinquencies, and cases of venereal disease. We must think instead of millions of blasted lives, of millions of human beings confused and in trouble. Many returning soldiers will be in this group of persons for whom the effects of war on the family are no mere academic or theoretical proposition.

The educational system is one of the most pathetic and neglected casualties of war. From the first, the teaching profession is literally and figuratively emasculated, literally, because the men leave, and figuratively because the best of the men and the best of the women leave. Teachers quit their profession by the hundreds of thousands. In the year 1943-44, there was a shortage of at least 150,000 trained teachers in a teaching population of about 900,000, and the exodus of trained persons still continues, while the teacher-training schools can supply only a fraction of their former number of recruits. We have been forced to turn over the work of teaching to thousands of ignorant, untrained youngsters who are barely more than children; small wonder that there is a general decay in discipline and a decline in the effectiveness of the schools. The soldier is not likely to become directly aware of the war damage to the schools, but he readily perceives its effects in the form of the youth problem of the post-war world.

Communities likewise become disorganized in time of war, and in such ways as the returned soldier cannot fail to observe. Populations move about in great droves, war workers by the hundreds of thousands migrating to areas where the tools of war are produced. Housing shortages become fantastic; hundreds of thousands must live in trailers, and trailer camps in some cities stretch out for miles; people must bear and bring up children in such trailer-camp communities. The sex ratio of these boom-town communities is thrown out of balance, with thousands of surplus males in one area and corresponding surpluses of females in another.

Only with the greatest of difficulty can the ordinary community services be made available to these dislocated populations. The children of newly arrived war-workers strain school facilities to the utmost, and there may be a tax problem as well, because it is difficult to collect taxes from those who have only just arrived in a community. Churches likewise have difficulty in reaching war-workers. In fact, it is often difficult to supply even the most rudimentary sanitary facilities to these newcomers.

But these war-workers have money to spend, sometimes fantastic sums, and if they cannot rent suitable houses, they can buy automobiles and they feel themselves entitled to C cards which give them an ample supply of gas for joy-riding. Partly because of bad living conditions, they turn to drinking and to hectic gaiety, suffering from hang-overs on the morning after and producing a serious problem of absenteeism in the war-plants. When the soldiers learn of these things, their anger rises.

While the community faces these pressing problems, it loses those leaders who might be able to meet them. It must give up many of its leading citizens to the army and the bureaucracy; others become so involved in the conduct of their own business that they have no time for community affairs. The decay of the school system reduces the ability of the community to deal with its youth problem. Since the community must often give up a large proportion of its doctors (the nation as a whole has given up about a third), there is a slow deterioration of health conditions, with the ever-present danger of one or more of those serious epidemics that usually harass populations at war, killing more, as a general thing, than die of battle wounds.

Race Riots and Other Explosions

In the United States, the race problem nearly always becomes worse in time of war. There were frightful riots in various cities during and after World War I, and outbreaks have been numerous, some of them serious, in World War II. "Thirty-four Americans died and more than one thousand others were wounded in the streets of Detroit—in the heart of the 'Arsenal of Democracy'— during Negro-white clashes the week of June 20, 1943," and more than 1,000,000 man-hours were lost to American war production.[1] Instances of anti-Semitism and other nativist aggressions, sometimes taking the form of physical assaults, defacing of buildings, and desecration of cemeteries, are part of the annals of the home front. Strained race relations are carried over into the post-war period, when very likely, they reach their terrible fruition with the re-injection into the population of one more dynamic element, the veterans returned from war. Explosions in the racial field are closely connected with other forms of social disorganization, such as juvenile delinquency, which as already noted, flourishes in war. It is noteworthy that, in World War II, numbers of teen-age boys have been involved in the race riots that have taken place thus far.

The soldier-turned-veteran cannot overlook these symptoms of community disorganization. They stare him in the face. It is in such communities that he must try to find the road back to the life of peace.

Changes in the class system of the nation are most interesting to the soldier,—so interesting that he has followed them from afar and has already formed violent opinions concerning some of them. Our American society is never unified, never a whole, but rather a collection or heap or mound of conflicting and competing groups that somehow manage to live together. The white man and the

[1] A. M. Lee and N. D. Humphrey, *Race Riot,* Dryden Press, 1943, p. 2.

Negro contrive to inhabit the same society by means of a system of social arrangements fully as complex as the caste system of India, and very like that system in many ways. Capital and labor, Catholic and Protestant, gentile and Jew, farmer and urban worker—these pairs, too, have worked out patterns of relationship, but each member of such pairs is distrustful of the other, and each such relationship is dynamic in the extreme. It is the business of politics to effect alignments in such a society and to keep the various members of this band of potential murderers from flying at one another's throats.

The soldier leaving for war is well aware of his own position in this complex pyramid of conflicting and competing groups. When he goes to war, he assumes that nothing will be done to change the fundamental pattern of social arrangements. The theory is that when the nation is threatened, most of its citizens shelve their private feuds, and face outward to meet the common enemy. The unspoken truce of war becomes explicit in such arrangements as Germany's *Burgfrieden* of World War I, or the Union Sacrée of the French, or a coalition government. Actually, many groups in the nation do not, perhaps cannot, recognize this unspoken truce. Capital tries to make large profits. Labor tries to make gains. So do the farmer and the Negro. When the soldier returns, if not before, he becomes very much exercised about the situation, feeling that others have taken advantage of his absence in war to change the character of the nation that he has helped to defend. He left a society at "peace," he returns to find it openly at war within itself.

A similar situation prevails with regard to other social reforms. In general, social reform is brought to a stand-still by war. President Roosevelt has recognized this fact by rather belatedly announcing the demise of the New Deal. Some reforms can still be carried over by hitching them up to the war effort—as, for example, Prohibition in World War I. The returning soldiers were bitter about this, feeling that it was a violation of the unspoken truce, and that the reformers had changed the American social order while they were away. Soldiers are at present alert for similar moves and resent them hotly. For example, a recent ban on *Esquire* brought indignant protests from men in uniform, who feared the blue-noses were at large again.

Civilians Are the First to Weary of War

During a war, the morale of the civilian population usually suffers a slow decline. The war begins with a sort of honeymoon stage, an exalted phase in which solidarity is high. People cheer a lot and comedians tell cheap, unfunny jokes about how easily we shall dispose of the Japanese Navy. Nobody as yet knows anything about war or realizes that such jests may later be regarded as almost sacrilegious. The second state is one of grim struggle and high morale; people hang on, struggle, take privations in their stride, develop the cult of austerity, try not to hope for too much in order that they will not be disappointed. This was the phase in which, long ago, we used to read, "Paris refrains from rejoicing." Then a stage of war weariness sets in. The germs of defeatism take hold and flourish. France is said to be bled white. There is a great deal of ill-humor in this stage and the one preceding. The process ends in victory or defeat, and the saying becomes current that the victory goes to the nation that manages to hold out fifteen minutes longer than its opponent. The discordant and conflicting elements of the population have much to do with the ultimate decline of morale. As Negro-white, capital-labor conflicts develop, they undermine the solidarity of the nation at war. The management of such cleavages, therefore, is a fundamental problem in maintaining morale.

An army does not go through these stages, at least not in the same way. An army can maintain and sustain morale better than a civilian population. When morale in an army declines, this results not merely from military defeat but from defeatism in the civilian population. Thus Chambers remarks that it was the experience of all defeated nations of World War I that the morale of the army declined more slowly than that of the civilian population.[2] It is this situation that gives Hitler's "stab in the back" myth its plausibility, enabling him to say that Germany was never really defeated but was betrayed by certain elements in its own civilian population.

[2] Frank P. Chambers, *The War Behind the War, 1914-1918.* Harcourt Brace, 1939, p. 118.

The Chasm between the Army and Society Deepens

As war proceeds, the alienation of the army from the people goes on apace. Inevitably the chasm widens, for reasons which we have attempted to make clear. Attitudes and opinions of the army develop in one direction, in accordance with their own inner imperatives and the laws of their being. Attitudes of the civilian population pursue a different course of development in accordance with the laws of their being. As war continues, the divergence becomes sharper. In early 1943, the Germans of Konstanz, Germany, were concerned about the attitudes of soldiers. Their newspaper, the *Rundschau*, remarked that the men on leave "seem like foreigners . . . Many of them don't speak a word, spend the whole three weeks alone, avoiding everyone."[3]

In previous American wars, the alienation of soldiers and civilians has sometimes reached extremities. In a recent speech, Secretary Stimson commented on the process as it has occurred in this country in the present war:

> Suddenly what happened? To our troops looking over their shoulders from the battlefields of the Mediterranean and the steaming jungles of the South Seas, the American front at home suddenly seemed to be on the point of going sour. A host of what seemed to our soldiers petty controversies in industry and labor, each one of which threatened to put a check in the production of priceless weapons, arose throughout our land. The three vital industries of the home front, upon which basically all our production of weapons and transportation depend, were threatened with, or actually experienced, nation-wide strikes—coal, steel, and the railroads.
>
> It does not require great imagination to realize the effect of these occurrences upon our troops fighting on those battlefields which have marked our steady progress toward victory. It is my duty to visit and inspect the units of the Army, to visit the wounded in the hospitals and talk to them, and countless letters come to the War Department from them and their families bearing upon this situation.
>
> I can tell you that today that situation, the industrial unrest and lack of sense of patriotic responsibility which it seems to evidence in large numbers of our population, has aroused a

[3] *Time*, Jan. 31, 1944.

strong feeling of resentment and injustice among the men of the armed forces. I believe it is hazardous to belittle the effect which such a situation will have upon the ultimate welfare of our democracy.

If it continues, it will surely affect the morale of the Army. It is likely to prolong the war and endanger our ultimate success; and when those troops come back to us again at the close of the war and we are faced with the acute problem of demobilization it may have an effect upon the future unity of our nation which is disturbing to contemplate.

The men in the Army see this country divided into two entirely distinct classes. On the one hand are the men who are in the armed forces. Their enlistment has been carried out with the aid of the selective service law, a process of selection applied to them by their nation under the sanction of compulsion. They have been told not only that they must serve, but the time, the place and the method of their service has been chosen for them in the light of their respective aptitudes to fit the requirements of the nation.

They are facing a duty which they cannot escape and which involves the possibility of death or mutilation.

On the other side they see that the government imposes no corresponding duty upon the remaining men of the nation and even permits them to leave the most important war jobs without regard to the needs of their country.

Our democracy has been founded upon a basis of equality and justice. I tell you that today the men in the armed forces are beginning to believe that they are being discriminated against in a matter which is one of fundamental justice as between man and man."[4]

4 From a statement by Henry L. Stimson, Secretary of War, to the Senate Military Affairs Committee on January 19, 1944.

The Soldier-Turned-Veteran
Comes Back to an Alien
Homeland

The Veteran
Is Bitter —
And With Reason

WHILE the war is on, the soldier works hard at the job of learning to kill his enemy and to live to fight another day. There are techniques of survival—they are the skills of war and the soldier learns them well. By facing death and enduring discomfort and risking mutilation and disease—and by being in the army—the soldier gains the attitudes of war.

Military Skills Are Useless for Peacetime Living

The skills and attitudes of war are of little value in civilian life. Some soldiers, the older ones, can return to their former status, their wives and children, the jobs they once held. It is worse for the younger ones, who have learned no trade but war. Of a group of such men Remarque wrote:

> The smoke of pipes and cigars fills the room. Desires, thoughts, ambitions in seething confusion. God only knows what will come of them. A hundred young soldiers, eighteen lieutenants, thirty warrant officers and noncoms, all sitting here, wanting to start to live. Any man of them could take a company under fire across "No Man's Land" with hardly a casualty. There is not one who would hesitate for an instant to do the right thing when the cry "They are coming" was yelled down into his dugout. Every man has been tempered through countless, pitiless days; every man is a complete soldier, no more and no less.
>
> But for peace? Are we suitable? Are we fit now for anything but soldiering? [1]

So it was with the vanquished, but the victors, the conquerors of Germany, fared little if any better.

[1] Erich Maria Remarque, *The Road Back*. Little Brown, 1921, p. 130.

Who cared for the men who had risked their lives and bore on their bodies the scars of war? The pensions doled out to blinded soldiers would not keep them alive. The consumptives, the gassed, the paralyzed were forgotten in institutions where they lay hidden from the public eye. Before the war had been over six months "our heroes," "our brave boys in the trenches," were without preference in the struggle for existence . . .

What knowledge had they of use in civil life? None. They scanned advertisements, answered likely invitations, were turned down by elderly men who said, "I've had two hundred applications. And none of you young gentlemen from the army are fit to be my office-boy." They were the same elderly men who had said, "We'll fight to the last ditch. If I had six sons I would sacrifice them all in the cause of liberty and justice." [2]

When they return to civil life, victors and vanquished are very much alike. Their skills are equally useless. They are equally unready for "the savage wars of peace."

When the soldier returns to the home of which he has dreamed through the years of war, he finds it smaller, dingier, more sordid than he had ever imagined it to be, and his life within it is flavorless. Something has gone out of him that once gave zest to the old life, and there is nothing to take its place. The parents whom he has idealized seem strange to him; he cannot find words to talk with them, he cannot tolerate their well-meant ministrations. He is unwilling to accept his place in the economic world, not yet ready to tie himself to the drudgery of detail, not prepared at all to take up the sort of status for which his experience qualifies him.

Perhaps the soldier realizes that the lack is in himself. "The difficulty," says a young veteran recently discharged, "The difficulty, I find, is to regain those lost emotions which enable a man to take his place in civilian life . . . I can understand now why members of the so-called 'lost' generation of the 1920s went to such extremes in their search for animation. It may sound like exaggeration, but I actually feel like a stranger in my own home, because everyday living in America requires emotional responses which I am incapable of giving." [3]

[2] Philip Gibbs, *Now It Can Be Told.* Harper, 1920, p. 549.
[3] Edgar L. Jones, "The Soldier Returns," in *The Atlantic Monthly,* Jan. 1944.

The literature of World War I contains many similar bits of introspection. A character of Romains phrased it well:

> I sometimes find myself wondering, in a sudden panic, whether I'm not in the way of developing great numb patches in my sensibility of which I shall never be cured—even if I do come through this war. Delicacy of feeling. What a wonderful expression! Shall I ever again know what delicacy of feeling is? I may be nervous, irritable, exasperated by trifles, but shall I ever recover that sensitiveness which is the mark of the civilized man? I sometimes see myself in the future transformed into a sort of invalid who has suffered an amputation of all his delicate sentiments, like a man who has lost all his fingers and can only feel things with a couple of stumps. And there will be millions of us like that.[4]

One of Remarque's characters becomes a schoolteacher and has a moment of vivid awareness of his maladjustment in society, created by the disparity between what he knows and what he is supposed to teach.

> Morning comes. I go to my class. There sit the little ones with folded arms. In their eyes is still all the shy astonishment of the childish years. They look up at me so trustingly . . .
> What should I teach you then you little creatures, who alone have remained unspotted by the terrible years? What am I able to teach you then? Should I tell you how to pull the string of a hand-grenade, how best to throw it at a human being? Should I show you how to stab a man with a bayonet, how to fell him with a club, how to slaughter him with a spade? Should I demonstrate how best to aim a rifle at such an incomprehensible miracle as a breathing breast, a living heart? Should I explain to you what tetanus is, what a broken spine is, and what a shattered skull? Should I describe to you how brains look when they scatter about? What crushed bones are like—and intestines when they pour out? Should I mimic how a man with a stomach wound will groan, how one with a lung wound gurgles and one with a head wound whistles? More I do not know. More I have not learned.
> Should I take you to the brown and green map there, move my finger across it and tell you that here love was murdered? . . .
> About your brows still blows the breath of innocence. How

4 Jules Romains, *Men of Good Will*; Vol. VIII, *Verdun*. Knopf, 1940, p. 430.

then should I presume to teach you? Behind me, still pursuing, are the bloody years . . . How then can I venture among you. Must I not first become a man again myself? [5]

The Soldier Comes Home Angry

The soldier is glad to come home, but he comes home angry.

In the early months of 1919, the writer talked with a great many other demobilized soldiers on Chicago streets. Although he had felt something of the service-man's rebellion, he was as astonished as any civilian at the intensity of their fury. They were angry about something; it was not clear just what. The writer questioned many of them, but found not one who could put his grievances into understandable form. But there was never any mistaking their temper. They hated somebody for something. There were angry men on West Madison Street in 1919, and, as one learned later, there was rancor on Market Street in St. Louis and at Eighth and Race in Philadelphia, and in all the little angry knots where soldiers gathered were bitterness and disillusion and discontent.

These men, these veterans-on-the-street, the reader remarks, were hardly typical veterans. That is true; they were a sort of residue of men whom industry had not employed and family and community life had not yet reabsorbed. They were not average veterans. But we can best understand the average by studying the reactions of extreme cases; the statistically unusual man may be representative; he may stand for something, express something that is in us all; and so it seems to be with veterans.

The attitude of these men was puzzling, even to one who participated in a milder way in their feelings. Not one of them was able to explain why he felt as he did. For years the writer has been trying to puzzle it out and to understand what these inarticulate men wanted to say. In order to make sense of what they said it has been necessary to find words for them, to supply logic for their grievances, to sort out and throw away minor grievances in the attempt to penetrate to the great feelings of injustice from which these smaller complaints arose. When, some years after 1919, the war novels and autobiographies began to appear, they were help-

[5] Remarque, *op. cit.*, pp. 252 ff.

ful, especially for the verbalization of attitudes, but for the most part they merely expressed and recorded attitudes and stated the reasons for them only by inference. Still it is a contribution to express a complex state of mind clearly, and novels are very valuable in this respect, even though they have little utility as proof. Autobiographies, of course, have greater value as evidence.

Perhaps the reader, in his struggle to understand the soldier's bitterness, should start with what the returned soldiers said on West Madison in 1919. They said, specifically, "God damn the obscenity obscenity obscenity! Of all the obscenity obscenity raw deals! The obscenity obscenity obscenities!" They said, "The next war, if they want me, they'll have to burn the woods and sift the ashes." They said, with a knowing wink, "The next war, they'll be two guys don't go, me and the guy they send after me." They said, "Brother, I've had a belly full!" For twenty-five years the writer has been trying to decipher the meaning of their inarticulate rage.

Whom does the soldier hate? Jules Romains has an excellent answer, so far as it goes.

If you were to ask me who it is we despise and hate the most, whom it would give us the greatest pleasure to punish, my answer would be: First of all, the war profiteers, business men of all kinds, and, with them, the professional patriots, the humbugs, the literary gents who dine each day in pajamas and red leather slippers, off a dish of Boche . . . Next in order come the soldiers who have worked themselves into nice safe jobs, officers for the most part. They form a very special category—fellows who are lucky enough to have been posted to some back-area town, twenty or thirty miles behind the line, where they are in no greater danger than you are in your boot store, but play the brave soldier and say, "We in the trenches." Those are the men who put in a claim for decorations, and who get them—before we do. They'd be perfectly happy if the war went on for ten years. Never in their lives have they touched so many perquisites as now. And don't they love one another! Their time is as much taken up with intrigues, backbiting and plots as the most squalid of peace-time garrisons! The worst offenders are the regulars, the men who deliberately chose the army as a calling in the days before the war, but who now when we civilians are asked to spill our blood, just take to cover. Their fellow soldiers hate them as bitterly as we do. Whom else shall I mention? Certain ambitious generals, with hearts of stone, to whom the lives of thousands or tens of thousands mean nothing if, by sacrificing them they can assure their own advancement, or, moved by slightly less selfish motives, carry through pet schemes of their own . . . Oh, but I was forgetting perhaps the most symbolic of all these back-area figures, the well-set gentleman of a certain age, in a nice warm suit, freshly bathed and pomaded who sips his chocolate and reads the communiques and says: "Damn slow progress. Trouble is the Staff's too timid. The important thing is to know when to make sacrifices." [6]

Some of these hatreds are readily understandable. Others might require further elucidation. But they are all real. American soldiers felt the same way in 1919.

Why is the soldier angry? Because he was the one singled out to fight and die and suffer and see horrors. He feels akin to everyone who has suffered as he has, even the enemy; he hates everyone who has not. There is a famous speech to this effect in *What Price Glory?*

Oh God, Dave, but they got you. God, but they got you a beauty, the dirty swine. God damn them for keeping us up in this hellish town! Why can't they send in some of the million men they've got back there and give us a chance? Men in my platoons are so hysterical every time I get a message from Flagg, they want to know if they're being relieved. What can I tell them? They look at me like whipped dogs—as if I had just beaten them—and I've had enough of them this time. I've got to get them out, I tell you. They've had enough. Every night the same way. And since six o'clock there's been a wounded sniper in the tree by that orchard angle crying "Kamerad! Kamerad!" Just like a big crippled whip-poor-will. What price glory now? Why in God's name can't we all go home? Who gives a damn for this lousy, stinking little town but the poor French bastards who live here? God damn it! You talk about courage, and all night long you hear a man who's bleeding to death on a tree calling you "Kamerad" and asking you to save him. God damn every son of a bitch in the world who isn't here! [7]

[6] Romains, *op. cit.*, pp. 440-442.
[7] Laurence Stallings and Maxwell Anderson, *What Price Glory?* Harcourt Brace.

In the same play is another speech, almost as eloquent, by Flagg.

> Show him, Kiper. Damn headquarters! It's some more of that world-safe-for-democracy slush! Every time they come around here I've got to ask myself is this an army or is it a stinking theosophical society for ethical culture and the Bible-backing uplift! I don't want that brand of Gideons from headquarters. Now you watch that door. Watch it! In ten minutes we're going to have another of these round-headed gentlemen of the old school here giving us a prepared lecture on what we're fighting the war for and how we're to do it—one of these bill-poster chocolate soldiers with decorations running clear around to his backbone and a thrilling speech on army morale and the last drop of fighting blood that puts your drive over to glorious victory! . . . The side-whiskered butter-eaters! I'd like to rub their noses in a few of the latrines I've slept in keeping up army morale and losing men because some screaming fool back in the New Jersey sector thinks he's playing with paper dolls.

It is easy to understand why the soldier hates the young man of his own age who manages somehow to escape military service. The draft board in its wisdom decides that Tom Jones must go to war, and off goes Tom to be a soldier. But Henry Smith, who lives next door, has had the foresight to get entrenched in a necessary industry; he stays at home, works for high wages, wins a promotion, gets married, and buys a little home in the suburbs. When Tom returns, Henry is still a necessary man in industry, still entrenched; he keeps his job and Tom goes on relief. The soldier's animosity toward such people is deep and powerful. After World War I they were known as slackers. When it was discovered that Jack Dempsey had suffered through World War I as a shipyard worker, he became so unpopular that he was jeered at on the city streets. (The fight promoters were able to turn this unpopularity to good use by arranging a match with Carpentier, who was a glamorous veteran but did not belong in the same ring with Dempsey.)

Not only the soldier, but all his relatives and friends take up the burden of such feelings of hostility. There is no resentment deeper than that of the mother whose son has been taken when some other mother's son has been left behind. And if her son dies, she carries that hatred to her grave. There is no way of avoiding such injustices except by taking every member of an age group, say from 18 to 25, exempting only those with such obvious physical defects as a missing leg or arm, and allowing no one to stay home because he is a medical or engineering student or a ship-yard worker or the sole support of eleven children. We are apparently moving toward such an arrangement, and after a few more wars we may attain it. Our current draft arrangements are infinitely fairer than those of the Civil War. During that conflict, the reader will remember, a conscripted man could hire a substitute to fight for him, or he could buy himself off for only $300. (This was a survival of the medieval custom of scutage.) The Civil War was truly a rich man's war and a poor man's fight. These arrangements provoked deadly riots, probably the worst in American history, in that great European city on the banks of the Hudson—never a center of martial spirit except in time of peace. Troops were rushed to the city, their ears still roaring from the Battle of Gettysburg, to quell the riots. Apparently the riots were successful: the draft thereafter received only nominal enforcement in New York.[8] We have had nothing of quite that sort in subsequent wars.

Scarcely less violent is the soldier's hatred for that other soldier who manages to wangle for himself a safe position behind the lines. The soldiers particularly resent officers in this category, those swivel chair heroes who distinguish themselves in the Battle of Washington, which, we are to understand, is a fierce and sanguinary engagement. There are young men who have secured commissions in the Navy although "the only ship they have ever seen is a junior partnership," who have never missed a meal or a night of sleeping with their wives, who yet have become very nautical, even salty, in their language and are accustomed to welcome their guests of the evening by saying, "I'm very glad you are on board tonight." In World War I there were other dashing and intrepid gentlemen who wore spurs the better to control their plunging swivel-chairs, or side-arms to protect themselves against the hazards of Washington streets. For such men, determined never to risk their necks during the war and equally determined to play the hero afterwards, the soldier has an abiding contempt. But there is nothing he can

---

[8] Carl Sandburg, *Abraham Lincoln, The War Years*. Harcourt Brace, 1939, Vol. II, p. 377, Vol. III, p. 284. The trick, a very shady one, was to count naval enlistments at New York City in the New York quota. Thus when a boy from the Middle West joined the Navy in New York, he was counted toward the New York City quota.

do about it; the swivel-chair heroes will be heroes just the same. These *embusqués* will always win; they will have their safety and their glory too.

The soldier is angry because he knows the war is bitter hard for him, and at the same time realizes that for many of the people back home it is a distinctly pleasant experience. While soldiers die, speculators and profiteers get rich, and politicians make capital of campaigns that cost the lives of many men. Workers at home draw fabulous wages and still go on strike, as many of the soldiers believe, for frivolous reasons. The soldier resents the striker more than he does the profiteer, because what the striker does is readily visible, and besides, the striker is a man from his own world, a man with whom he can compare himself, while the profiteer remains a rather shadowy figure. The soldier resents the dancing and the gaiety of the people at home, and remarks bitterly that he can hold out, he can stand anything, but he does hope that the civilians at home manage to keep up their morale.

Miners were striking for more wages, factory hands were downing tools for fewer hours at higher pay, the government was paying any price for any labor—while Tommy Atkins drew his one-and-twopence and made a little go a long way in a wayside estaminet before jogging up the Menin road to have his head blown off . . .

In all classes of people there was an epidemic of dancing, jazzing, card-playing, theatre-going. They were keeping their spirits up wonderfully. Too well for men slouching about the streets of London on leave, and wondering at all this gaiety, and thinking back to the things they had seen and forward to the things they would have to do. People at home, it seemed, were not much interested in the life of the trenches; anyhow, they could not understand . . .

The British soldier was gay and careless of death—always. Shell-fire meant nothing to him. If he were killed—well, after all, what else could he expect? Wasn't that what he was out for? The twice-married girl knew a charming boy in the air force. He had made love to her even before Charlie was "done in." These dear boys were so greedy for love. She could not refuse them, poor darlings! Of course they had all got to die for liberty, and that sort of thing. It was very sad. A terrible thing —war . . . Perhaps she had better give up dancing for a week, until Charlie had been put into the casualty lists.[9]

9 Gibbs, *op. cit.*, pp. 535 ff.

My mental attitude towards the war had changed. Whatever romance and glamour there may have been had worn off. It was just one long, bitter waste of time,—our youth killed like flies by "dugouts" at the front so that old men and sick might carry on the race, while profiteers drew bloated profits and politicians exuded noxious gas in the House . . .

How *dared* they have valets while we were lousy and unshaved, with rotting corpses round our gun wheels? How *dared* they have wives while we "unmarried and without ties" were either driven in our weakness to licensed women, or clung to our chastity because of the one woman with us every hour in our hearts whom we meant to marry if ever we came whole out of that hell? [10]

The soldier is bitter because civilians see the glamor of war and gloss over its ugliness by beautiful speeches. Remarque's ex-soldiers make reply to the principal of their school in the following passages:

The Old Man's voice sinks to a minor. It puts on mourning, it drips unction. A sudden tremor passes over the black flock of masters. Their faces show self-control, solemnity.——"But especially we would remember those fallen sons of our foundation who hastened joyfully to the defence of their homeland and who have remained upon the field of honor. Twenty-one comrades are with us no more—twenty-one warriors have met the glorious death of arms; twenty-one heroes have found rest from the clamor of battle under foreign soil and sleep the long sleep beneath the green grasses——"

There is a sudden, booming laughter. The principal stops short in pained perplexity. The laughter comes from Willy, standing there, big and gaunt, like an immense wardrobe. His face is red as a turkey's, he is so furious.

"Green grasses—Green grasses!"—He stutters. "Long sleep? In the mud of shell holes they are lying, knocked rotten, ripped in pieces, gone down into the bog—Green grasses! This is not a singing lesson!" His arms are whirling like a windmill in a gale. "Hero's death! And what sort of thing do you suppose that was, I wonder? Would you like to know how young Hoyer died? All day long he lay out in the wire screaming, and his guts hanging out of his belly like macaroni. Then a bit of shell took off his fingers and a couple of hours later

[10] A. H. Gibbs, *Gun Fodder, The Diary of Four Years of War.* Little Brown, 1919, pp. 141-144.

another chunk off his leg, and still he lived; and with his other hand he would keep trying to pack back his intestines, and when night fell at last he was done. And when it was dark we went out to get him and he was full of holes as a nutmeg grater.—Now you go and tell his mother how he died—if you have so much courage . . .

"Mr. Principal," says Ludwig in a clear voice, "you have seen the war after your fashion—with flying banners, martial music, and with glamour. But you saw it only to the railway station from which we set off.—We do not mean to blame you. We, too, thought as you did. But we have seen the other side since then, and against that the heroics of 1914 soon wilted to nothing. Yet we went through with it—we went through with it because there was something deeper that held us together, something that only showed up out there, a responsibility perhaps, but at any rate something of which you know nothing and about which there can be no speeches."

Ludwig paused a moment, gazing vacantly ahead. He passes his hand over his forehead and continues, "We have not come to ask a reckoning—that would be foolish; nobody knew then what was coming.—But we do require that you shall not again try to prescribe what we shall think of these things. We went out full of enthusiasm—the name of the 'Fatherland' on our lips—and we have returned in silence, but with the thing, the Fatherland, in our hearts. And now we ask you to be silent too. Have done with fine phrases. They are not fitting. Nor are they fitting to our dead comrades.—We saw them die. And the memory of it is still too near for us to abide to hear them talked of as you are talking. They died for more than that." [11]

How the soldier hates the men of talk, especially those who prattle of ideals and honor and fighting for the right! An inexplicable attitude? Not at all. Because the soldier has come to believe, and with considerable reason, that those who talk about ideals do not fight for them, and that those who fight for them do not talk about them. The soldier knows that when the nation fights for freedom and for justice in far-flung areas of the world, he must lose his freedom, his comfort, even his identity for the duration of the conflict. The ideals for which he is fighting can have little meaning for any soldier so long as the war lasts, while for those

[11] Remarque, *op. cit.*, pp. 123 ff.

who die and for many of the wounded they can never have any meaning at all. He knows that those who speak so glibly of ideals have no conception of what the process of enforcing those ideals means in terms of pain and starvation and death and horror; perhaps he comes to realize that for many civilian orators, fighting for ideals, being "alert to the danger" was a very good business and a short road to promotion and pay. Perhaps the soldier returning from this war will be told that few of the really vocal Hitler-haters ever managed to get near the front line, that none of them ever missed a meal, and all of them will die in bed after they are heavy with years. Possibly he will hear once more the bitter jest that a patriot is a man who is always willing to lay down his life for his country, while an orator is willing to lay down your life for his country.

When the British had won the great victory at El Alamein, the civilian populace rejoiced, but the sound of their rejoicing as it came in over the radio did not make the soldiers happy. It seemed a little premature to the soldiers, because they were still in the desert, they were still suffering from flies and dirt and heat and cold and hunger, and they were still getting killed by Stukas. For the soldiers victory or defeat meant just another battle with an enemy who was still full of fight.[12]

When the soldier comes home, he hears his victories extolled by an unctuous radio-announcer who has taken good care of himself during the conflict, and he thinks that the announcer is just a "cheap chiseller" who is trying to "muscle in" on the soldier's prestige, and it is a little sickening to hear him "make cracks" about what we are doing, have done, or are going to do to the little yellow devils in the Pacific and talk between whiles of bath salts and a superduper cereal which will help the war production.

Perhaps the soldier returns to college, and learns about America's predestined role as the savior of the world from an amiable gentleman who takes all his opinions from the liberal press—the very best opinions, mind you—who can never be quite sure what he thinks of anything until he has read the latest copy of *The New Republic*, having devoted his best thought for twenty years to just one subject, and that being the best method of cleaning a pipe, a subject upon which he expended all the ingenuity of his fertile

[12] Jones, *op. cit.*

brain when the war produced a shortage of implements designed for that purpose.   Or perhaps the soldier goes to his philosophy class and learns that human beings must always be treated as ends, and must never, never, never be treated as means; yet he knows very well that while he was a soldier he was only a means and not an end at all, and as for those who died in the war, well, that was an end of their being either an end or a means.

The returned soldier of any mental level is less enthusiastic than he might be about a program to furnish a quart of milk for every Hottentot child when he himself has been living on indescribably vile powdered eggs and an execrable brand of canned meat. If he is intelligent, he may begin to question the whole species of humanitarianism which leads A and B to decide to send C to fight D for the sake of very problematic benefits to E, while A and B, if they really wish to further human welfare, have only to cease and desist from persecuting F and G.

And the veteran knows that these men of words, who irritate him so much and are so often in his way, could not have lasted very long or amounted to much in the world in which he has been living. As one young soldier recently remarked, and as many said in 1919, "A smash of a gun butt over the head would soon dispose of ——, of him and all his thoughts and clever tricks. Such and such, an illiterate truck driver, is a better man than he is."

One day the soldier will be subject once again to men of talk—perhaps he never escapes them at all—but they will be men who express to him his own prejudices, men who talk against talk, politicians who denounce politics, and such men are exceedingly dangerous. In his disdain of men of words, men who make their living through the little shams, poses, and hypocrisies of the world, the soldier is more than half right. But he does not realize that our society could not exist without such men and that the men of talk whom the soldier chooses as his very own are likely to be ten times worse than the others. Here, as elsewhere, the soldier's anger is reasonable, at least nine-tenths justified, but its expression is often unreasonable.

In the end, the soldier is almost certain to feel that his sacrifices have not been fully appreciated. There is a brief period of glory in which those who have done least and come home first play the greater part. The soldier receives the grateful thanks of the nation, and that is all. He finds himself left behind and permanently disadvantaged in competition.

How Far Is This Bitterness Justified?

In considerable part the soldier's bitterness is justified. He has been the victim of the worst injustice that any modern civilized society visits upon its members. He has given everything and received very little in return, nothing in fact except a highly perishable kind of glory. At no point does the conflict between the individual and society become more intense than with regard to military service. A notice of induction is for most young men a sentence to hard labor, and for some a sentence of death; for others it is a sentence to lose a limb or an eye—disfigurements that no civilized society can now impose as a punishment for crime—at least it is distinguished from these things only by the fact that it is associated not with disgrace but with honor. The concepts of honor and duty have been invented to make such sacrifices acceptable. What, then, if the honor that is the soldier's due in the bargain be withheld? What if the Purple Heart or the Croix de Guerre become equivalent in a few years to the little bronze medal that the eight-year-old child receives for attending Sunday School on twenty-six successive Sundays? What if the veteran, in his need, must pawn his medal for heroism in order to buy food for himself and his children? The windows of America's pawnshops were full of medals for heroism in the nineteen-twenties.

"It is true," says Lorenz von Stein, "that victory brings to the sum total of the State, to the people, the highest profits, whereas at the same time it remains forever unable to restore to the individual what it has taken from him." [13] At the very least, the state has taken from the soldier some years of his youth, and it can never give them back.

The essential injustice to the soldier inheres in the fact that a competitive society decides to fight a war. Less injustice is involved when a socialistic society fights a war. In a hypothetical communist state which would take from each according to his abilities and give to each according to his needs, there would be no injustice at all in taking a man for a soldier. There is, as Quincy

[13] Quoted by Alfred Vagts, *A History of Militarism.* Norton, 1937, pp. 18-19.

Wright has noted, a natural affinity between socialism and war:
"States at war have tended to become socialistic; and socialistic
states have tended to be at war." [14] Wright comments further that
socialistic economies have produced the most warlike states of history, citing, among other examples, the socialistic empires of Assy-
ria and Peru as well as socialistic Sparta. [15] Along the same line is
Powell's conclusion that autocracies have seemed to suffer less from
veterans' problems than free societies.[16]

The social arrangements of modern America are such as to guarantee that we cannot wage war without inflicting the maximum
of injustice upon the soldier. Ours is a competitive society. Every
man is supposed to take care of himself.[17] It is the part of virtue,
and almost the whole of virtue, for a man to try to get ahead in
the world. The essential American idea is that it is possible for a
man to rise to high position through industriousness, that the
status which a man attains in society adequately reflects his ability
and conscientiousness. All we ask of the young man is that he work
and make the most of his own abilities. He is brought up to believe that that is his full social duty. In ordinary times, military
service is no part of what one owes to the world. In periods of
peace, we are inclined to hold the soldier in disrepute. We turn
much of the work of education over to pacifists, thus conditioning
our young men against military service. What is even more fatal
is that the soul of our society is civilianism, which, rather than
pacifism, is the true antithesis of militarism.[18]

When war comes, we take these young men trained for peace
and send them off to fight. Having conditioned our young men to
compete and to look to their own interests, we compel them to
sacrifice their personal good and their personal lives to the collective good. They could hardly have been worse prepared for the
experience of war. We remove them from the competitive society
for which they have been trained, and demand of them services
and sacrifices that can really be justified only in a communal society in which each person lives for others. Then, with a pat on the

---

14 Quincy Wright, *A Study of War*. U. of Chicago Press, 1942, Vol. II, p. 1172.
15 *Ibid.*
16 Talcott Powell, *Tattered Banners*. Harcourt Brace, 1933, p. 5.
17 Our society is really a competitive, familistic society, the family being the
competing unit, a unit in which competition is not supposed to take place; but
that does not matter for the present argument.
18 Cf. Vagts, *op. cit.*, p. 15, for the contrast between militarism and civilianism.

back and some hypocritical words of praise, we return them to competitive society, where, for a time at least, they compete at a considerable disadvantage.

If we took all the young men of a generation, that would seem less unfair to the soldier. And though he would still be disadvantaged in comparison with other age groups, his own generation would start even. However, we do not take all the members of an age group by any means. We grant full exemption from military service to many men who have minor physical defects. We reject many others for minor psychoneurotic disorders. We exempt others because they have special skills of use in war production—or are thought to have such special skills—and we excuse many others, less defensibly, because of the essential jobs they hold in war industries, even though their skills are admittedly not particularly great. We grant exemptions to some in special cases because of family obligations. When so many can escape, the one who is ordered to serve has some reason to feel abused. All this, of course, is part of the fundamental injustice of the situation. No one is personally responsible. No one planned it that way. Draft boards and others have done their best to administer our intrinsically inequitable laws in a just manner.

While the man selected for military service is giving his time to the collective effort, others forge ahead in the competitive race of civilian life. Imagine a foot-race in which a hundred performers start even, all with high hopes of winning. When the race has just begun, we take a few of the runners out of the race and demand that they fix the track. We keep adding to our labor force in the same way until we have removed about half the contestants. When the work is over and the laborers are fatigued, we release them in the same haphazard way, give them our hearty thanks, and tell them to resume the race. That is the way the system works.

While we were away, as Vera Brittain put it, "others stayed behind and just got on—got on the better since we were away." The absence of the soldiers and the demands of war industries have created the best labor market of a generation. What a labor market! According to information received from confidential sources, the average IQ of persons hired by a large defense plant in late 1943 was in the middle eighties (84)—the average IQ. The average weekly pay of these intellectual giants, who were also, of course, completely untrained, was about $41, at the start, with more to come later, naturally.

What the soldier believes is not, of course, wholly and unqualifiedly true. It is easy to understand why the soldier resents the high wages of war workers, and yet the advantage is not always on the civilian side in financial matters. Many civilians with fixed incomes, notably white collar workers, have been severely pinched by rising prices and taxes. Even the war workers do not fare so well as the gross earnings indicate; there are deductions to be considered: union dues, the social security tax, the withholding tax, and the bond purchases, which are obligatory in most war industries. While the soldier's apparent income is low, allowances for his family are considerable and are free of taxes. Furthermore, soldiers in certain types of service are paid at rates which compare favorably with war industry and some young officers, especially in the air corps, undoubtedly touch more perquisites than they are likely to attain in civilian life for many years. When we consider these things, the comparative position of the soldier is less unfavorable than the uncorrected figures would indicate, although the *net advantage is still on the side of the civilian in the majority of cases.* Furthermore, it is unlikely that the veteran will be interested in refined calculations of comparative advantage. He will be convinced that he has received a raw deal, and there will be evidence enough to support his case.

While stating the soldier's grievances, we should note that it is not necessarily the common soldier who is most set back in the struggle of life. Sometimes the officer is badly used. Doctors who have been taken into the service have often received very unjust treatment. A young doctor, aged thirty-three, was taken from a small city in up-state New York. He had educated himself at his own expense and had struggled for several years to build up a practice. He was, therefore, a business man with a considerable investment. Before the war, his practice was worth about $7000 a year, clear profit. The army made him a first lieutenant at $3300 a year. In order not to break up his family, he is consuming his savings, while his wife and children lead a most unsatisfactory existence in various training camp communities. If he had remained a civilian, his practice would be worth $15,000 a year. When the war is over, he must start again to build it up. Many thousands of other doctors will also be returning to practice, and will compete with him. This young doctor has lost nearly everything, gained nothing, not even, as he believes, any experience of value. If he should be killed in the service, his wife and children would be very poorly provided for.

When the soldier returns to civilian society, he is at a disadvantage for some time. His skills and attitudes are not applicable to civilian life. Undoubtedly the great majority of soldiers manage to overcome their initial handicap, and perhaps, because of the various preferences given to the veteran, some of them do a little better in competition than they might otherwise have done. A great many soldiers, however, do worse in competition because of their military service. The disabled have been really handicapped; and we recognize this and try to compensate them for it. Others have been injured in more subtle ways, and it is difficult to assess and evaluate their damages.

In every competition, however, some must fail. Some veterans fail because of what war has done to them. Others would fail anyhow. But all have a perfect excuse for failure, more than an excuse—an unsettled claim upon society. Because they once wore the uniform of their country, they feel that their country must take care of them. The problem of justice is to separate those who have a valid claim from those who have not.

How Long Does This Bitterness Last?

As in any other group of people, there is a wide range of variation in the attitudes of veterans. There is a core of anger in the soul of almost every veteran, and we are justified in calling it bitterness, but the bitterness of one man is not the same thing as the bitterness of another. In one man it becomes a consuming flame that sears his soul and burns his body. In another it is barely traceable. It leads one man to outbursts of temper, another to social radicalism, a third to excesses of conservatism. Much depends upon the veteran's temperament, upon where and under what circumstances he served, and upon his experiences after he is released from service.

The veteran is bitter because he has reason to be. After a time he becomes adjusted to civilian society once more, and his resentment disappears because it is no longer appropriate. Psychologists would speak of "extinction," and would refer to Pavlov's experiments with conditioned reflexes. If we ring a bell when we feed a dog, after a time the dog comes to salivate whenever the bell rings. This is a conditioned reflex. If the food is omitted when the bell rings, the sound gradually ceases to cause the dog to secrete saliva; the conditioned reflex has been disposed of through extinction. So with the veteran's anger. When its causes are removed, it gradually fades in intensity.

The veteran who suffers little inconvenience in readjusting to the world of civilian society usually recovers rapidly. If he returns to his former job, and is contented there, that helps, although he may still be angry because others have received promotions while he was away. If his family is undamaged by war, and his community and friends receive him graciously and take care of him, those things help too. If he was originally a stable personality, it is less likely that he has developed an outlook that will seriously interfere with readjustment. If after the war he becomes a success in life, there is little likelihood that he will be permanently embittered.

Even in the most favorable cases, however, it seems probable that the veteran's anger does not disappear altogether. Instead, the residues of resentment are redirected into different channels, usually into channels of class, race, and religious antagonism. Whomever a man would naturally hate he hates a little more because he has been a soldier. After the war, the soldier's sympathy with the enemy, born of the heat of conflict, apparently weakens for a time and is replaced by hatred, although the veteran's hatred of the enemy is often less keen than his hostility toward his former allies.

When the veteran must return to a degraded and oppressed status at home, he may become very dangerous to the established order. The Negro veteran is certain to be a storm center of trouble when he returns to his home community. He will resent discrimination and the doctrine of "The Negro in his place" as he has never resented such things before. All present indications are that Negro soldiers are in no very docile frame of mind. Some have gone from the South to the North and have had a taste of "equality," which, false though it is, unfits them for life in southern towns. Others have gone from northern cities to southern camps, and have learned what Jim Crowism means. All have been taught to kill, and to kill white men. Negroes have acquitted themselves like men in this war, as in all our wars, whenever they have had the chance; they have offered their bodies and their lives freely and have asked no odds of any man, whatever the color of his skin. Negro soldiers and civilians earnestly believe that they will never again submit to injustice as before, and even the gentlest and the mildest among them are beginning to believe that the time has come to fight.

There will be fierce and terrible men among the Negroes who come back from the war. Veterans make good revolutionaries. They have learned to hate and to kill. They have been shot over. They have lost their reverence for many of the word symbols that formerly controlled their behavior. On the other hand, the southern whites, earnestly convinced of the white man's right to rule, are among our best soldiers. Less than any others of our citizens did they require the gentle persuasions of the draft board to induce them to join the army. They have fought in every "Bloody Angle" of the present war; many have won distinction; many are officers. Veterans—and particularly veterans of that sort—make good counter-revolutionaries, if they believe there is need of a counter-revolution. And the Negroes are outnumbered ten to one, in the nation, though not in the South. The stage is set for conflict between the races.

If the veteran does not adjust to society, his bitterness persists through the years. Some veterans are unable to adjust because of disability, and it is understandable that they should cherish a lasting resentment because of this fact. Other veterans merely fail in competition and in life for reasons which have nothing to do with military service; they are the improvident, the unstable, the foolish, the stupid and the wrongheaded, the luckless ones who would have failed anyhow, the men who never would have been able to hold their jobs, their friends, their wives, or their self-respect. Now if these men had never been in an army they would have no socially acceptable excuse for failure. Since they have been in the army, they can hang all their feelings of guilt and resentment upon that peg, blame the war for everything that has gone wrong with their lives, the jobs they lost, the wives who betrayed them, the employers who bullied them, the friends who drifted away. The veterans who made up the Bonus Expeditionary Force of 1932 were just such pitiful maladjusts who had found a good excuse for failure. Failure to help the veteran in the post-war years leaves him with an unsettled claim upon society and thus facilitates this sort of rationalization.

The normal veteran who adjusts well to civilian life usually finds himself thinking rather pleasantly of his war in a few years. He never forgets the comradeship of men at arms and never ceases to think of it with a certain warmth. And, in time, he learns that there are a few real rewards in being a veteran. As a veteran, he has a place in society; some honor comes to him because he once served his country in time of war.

Many Things
Interfere With
The Veteran's Adjustment

A MONG the mistakes made by society in the past must be reckoned its failure to recognize that every soldier, and not merely the wounded, is in need of rehabilitation. As Robert Graves has pointed out, every soldier who returns to civilian life is still mentally and nervously organized for war—a condition that requires something more active than the passage of time for its cure. The soldier must give up his old attitudes toward civilian life and form new ones relevant to his changed situation, and the sooner he does this, the easier his adjustment will be. But we cannot intelligently expect him to achieve this unaided. Society must meet him more than halfway—for its own good, if for no more selfless reason.

The Civilian World Is Changed, Confused

The soldier's difficulties of adjustment inhere in the fact that his problem is a double one. Not only is the soldier changed from the man he once was, but the society to which he returns is a different society. We have seen the profound alterations of personality imposed upon the soldier by his army experience. Let us spend a few moments in examining the war-changed social order to which he returns, and into which he must now be "naturalized."

The soldier returns to a chaotic world in which values are confused and social structures are crumbling. There are widespread economic disturbances and disruptions involved in the process of returning industry to a peacetime basis. There may be further inflation in the post-war period, either of the boom type or of the runaway type; economists may argue as to whether or not inflation is really necessary, but political factors render it highly probable. Where there is inflation, there is usually an ultimate deflation.

There is a changed morality in the society to which the soldier returns, a very confused morality. Moral standards have partially adjusted to the changed situation but they remain unclear and confused on many points. Those who came to maturity in the pre-war period are subject to severe conflicts in this regard. A generation of post-war youth grows up with the wartime morality and escapes the conflict by flaunting many features of conventional morality. The crime rate is usually high in the post-war period.

The struggle between social classes, as well as between racial and religious groups, is bitter and intense. Wartime gains in many fields, such as labor and the status of minorities, are often largely lost in post-war reaction. Chaotic economic conditions make either revolution or reaction possible. Frequently, liberals are thoroughly discredited by the end of the war, and the backbone of liberalism is broken.

Curtailed civil liberties usually remain as a reminder of wartime solidarity.[1] Individuals voluntarily give up many of their liberties in time of war; at least they make no objection when the rights of free speech and free assemblage and the freedom of the press are abolished and such safeguards as the writ of *habeas corpus* suspended. *Silent leges inter arma*—the laws are silent in the midst of war. In the confused period following a war, it seems impossible to restore these rights at once. It is a matter of years before courts and legislators return to their usual procedures.

The chaos of a post-war period is almost indescribable. In 1920 James Westfall Thompson felt that the age might justly be compared with the period following the Black Death. He wrote as follows: "It is surprising to see how similar are the complaints then and now: economic chaos, social unrest, high prices, profiteering, deprivation of morals, lack of production, industrial indolence, frenetic gaiety, wild expenditure, luxury, debauchery, social and religious hysteria, greed, avarice, maladministration, decay of manners."[2] It would not be easy to find a better summary of the social and cultural aftermath of war.

---

[1] While civil liberties have fared somewhat better in this war than in most wars, there has been some abridgment, the most notable instance being the denial of their rights as citizens to American-born Japanese.

[2] James Westfall Thompson, "The Aftermath of the Black Death and the Aftermath of the Great War," in *The American Journal of Sociology*, March, 1920.

Every Veteran Is at least Mildly Shell-Shocked

Writers of the present day object to the use of the word "shell-shock," but the new terms proposed are equally misleading—perhaps intentionally so. There is nothing wrong with the old term provided that we realize that the state of mind to which it refers is not exactly shock and has nothing to do with shells. The soldier has been numbed somewhat by his experience, the frontline soldier more than others, but every soldier to some extent. He has his apathies and his intensities which seem equally incongruous to the civilian. "Sudden and quick in quarrels," as Shakespeare described him, he explodes and blows his top at unexpected moments, but often fails to react at all when he is expected to do so. He procrastinates concerning things that he ought to do at once and is in a tearing rush about things that necessarily take time. He is well aware that he is not emotionally in tune with his environment. The best and quickest way to describe his condition is to say that he is mildly shell-shocked, and the safest rule is to expect all soldiers to display these aberrations in some degree.

I was still mentally and nervously organized for war; shells used to come bursting on my bed at mid-night even when Nancy was sharing it with me; strangers in day-time would assume the faces of friends who had been killed. When I was strong enough to climb the hill behind Harlech and revisit my favorite country I found that I could only see it as a prospective battle-field. I would find myself working out tactical problems, planning how I would hold the Northern Artro valley against an attack from the sea . . . I still had the army habit of commandeering anything of uncertain ownership that I found lying about; also a difficulty in telling the truth—it was always easier for me now when overtaken in any fault to lie my way out . . . And other loose habits of war-time survived, such as stopping passing motorists for a lift, talking without embarrassment to my fellow-travelers in railway carriages, and unbuttoning by the roadside without shame, whoever was about. And I retained the technique of endurance, a brutal persistence in seeing things through.[3]

We had pictured it all otherwise. We thought that with one accord a rich, intense existence must now set in, one full of the

[3] Robert Graves, *Goodbye to All That.* London, Jonathan Cape, 1929, p. 352.

joy of life regained—and so we had meant to begin. But the days and the weeks fly away under our hands, we squander them on inconsiderable and vain things, and when we look around nothing is done. We were accustomed to think swiftly, to act on the instant—another minute and all might be out forever. So life is now too slow for us; we jump at it, shake it, and before it can speak or resound we have already let go again. We had Death too long for companion; he was a swift player and every second the stakes touched the limit. It is this that has made us so fickle, so impatient, so bent upon the things of the moment; this that now leaves us so empty, because here it has no place. And this emptiness makes us restless; we feel that people do not understand us, that mere love cannot help us. For there is an unbridged gulf fixed between soldiers and non-soldiers. We must fend for ourselves.[4]

I returned to Canada in February, 1919, on a troopship carrying six thousand men among whom were a few thousand minor casualties. We disembarked at Quebec, in a subzero temperature. Immediately upon stepping ashore, we were drawn up in parade formation on the landing quays because the Duke of Devonshire who was Governor General of Canada that year had made a special journey down from Ottawa to welcome us home. After letting us wait for two hours in a fierce cold, His Excellency and his aides finally drew up in a string of gleaming limousines. The officials were dressed in gorgeous blue uniforms with black fur collars. With this gala dress went astrakhan bonnets, polished riding boots and swords. We were called to "attention," and as the party of dignitaries slowly advanced toward us, their group presented such an unreal picture of Ruritanian movie splendor that the troops were struck speechless by the spectacle. The spell lasted but a moment. The next minute it exploded with a bang when someone in the rear ranks called out in a loud voice, "Look, boys, the soldiers are coming." Then there was no controlling the laughter; our officers stormed up and down the lines fuming, raging, swearing, and finally pleading for silence in the ranks, all to no avail. The Duke, a florid-cheeked man with puffy eye-lids, pretended not to notice the hilarity that his arrival had provoked and quietly mounted a small wooden platform of the kind Caesar used in the school book pictures to harangue his legions, and started to make a speech. The

4 Erich Maria Remarque, *The Road Back*. Little Brown, 1931, p. 165.

ranks grew silent at once. He began by telling us all about the war, the glory of it, the nobility of the services we had "so cheerfully rendered," and the reward that was not in store for us. That is about as far as he got, "Your King and country," he said, "thank you. And I say to you, from the bottom of my heart, henceforth nothing is going to be too good for you." At this point in the Duke's address, a crippled veteran whose stump was freezing exclaimed in a stentorian voice: "B . ." The Duke looked abashed for a moment as a new roar of laughter greeted the veteran's exclamation, shrugged his shoulders, and stepped down from the platform. We were then each presented with a walking stick and a white envelope which contained a mimeographed letter of gratitude from the Empire, with King George's and Queen Mary's signature rubber stamped at the bottom.

In the course of our short stay in the city of Quebec, the troops grew restless and began rioting. They had previously sacked the French base camp of Etaples, bombing their way past the British guard detachments posted at the bridges leading across a railway culvert from the camp into the town of Etaples, of which the taverns and brothels were "out of bounds" to all troops, which meant that they were reserved for officers only. The taverns were wrecked, the brothels invaded *en masse,* and the naked whores tossed high on the blankets found in the bedrooms. Thereafter they had raised a new rumpus in the camp of Rhyl, which was a concentration point for embarkation in Wales. In Rhyl, as in Etaples, many persons had been killed. It now looked as if Quebec in turn was about to have a taste of the *furor canadensis.* Dismissed from parade after the Duke's hasty departure, thousands of men marched into the city, tearing down street signs in the French language on the way. Streetcars were commandeered; local citizens found driving in their sleighs were stopped, pushed out, and forced to surrender their conveyances to the veterans. The walking sticks, donated by the patriotic citizens of Quebec, were used to batter in their own shop windows. . .

At military headquarters, where one returned every day along with thousands of others as if drawn by some ineluctable urge, officials were assuring the men that they would be properly looked after. There was going to be a gratuity, a bonus; land was going to be made available for settlement; convalescent camps were to be established; even broken-up homes were going to be mended by marital relations boards. All that sounded fine, but I had a feeling, nevertheless, that I had been the victim of an enormous nonsense. And not only I, but thousands of young men who had been deprived of everything that makes for human dignity by their submission to an arbitrary fate; men who had thrown their lives into the scales on the supposition that they were helping to preserve something precious in this world. All they had done was to clear the road for the same bourgeois democracy which had unleashed the storm just stilled, to start all over again. While we were stepping on the troopship's gangplank in Liverpool, the statesmen had started in Paris and London to lay out the tinder for the next conflagration. On the other hand, I was happy to have escaped with only a minor bodily injury. I was going to forget the nightmare, burn my uniform as soon as I would be finally discharged, throw my badges and tokens into Lake Ontario, and efface every trace of my shame and humiliation.[5]

After the trouble of demobilization came peace pageants and celebrations and flag-wavings. But all was not right with the spirit of the men who came back. Something was wrong. They put on civilian clothes again, looked to their mothers and wives very much like the young men who had gone to business in the peaceful days before the August of '14. But they had not come back the same men. Something had altered in them. They were subject to queer moods, queer tempers, fits of profound depression alternating with a restless desire for pleasure. Many of them were easily moved to passion when they lost control of themselves. Many were bitter in their speech, violent in opinion, frightening. For some time while they drew their unemployment pensions, they did not make any effort to get work for the future. They said, "That can wait. I've done my bit. The country can keep me for a while. I helped to save it . . . Let's go to the movies." They were listless when not excited by some "show." Something seemed to have snapped in them; their will-power. A quiet day at home did not appeal to them . . .

Young soldiers who had been very skilled with machine-guns, trench-mortars, hand-grenades, found that they were classed with the ranks of unskilled labor in civil life.[6]

5 Pierre Van Paassen, *Days of Our Years*. Hillman-Curl, 1939, pp. 88 ff.
6 Philip Gibbs, *Now It Can Be Told*. Harper, 1920, pp. 547-548.

The Veteran Is Somewhat Like a "Motherless Chile"

The proper term for what has happened to every soldier, and not just to the psychoneurotic, is perhaps not shell-shock but institutionalization. The regimentation of the lives of millions of men involves, as we have seen, some damage to their sense of self and to their power to think for themselves; it involves a redirection of their emotional life into channels acceptable to the military system. The soldier must form a soldier's habits, learn to be proud as a soldier is proud, learn to live—eat, sleep, dress, bathe—as a soldier, adjust his sex life to the soldier's necessities. Necessarily, he loses the sense of self-direction. A personality formed by such a milieu is thereby to some extent unfitted for civilian life.

Children who have spent a long time in institutions—orphans' asylums, schools for delinquents, homes for the deaf and blind, even, sometimes, expensive private schools—develop certain characteristic patterns of personality. Likewise, men who have been long in prison adjust their personalities so well to prison life that they are unfitted for life outside the institution. Like the orphan and the prisoner, the soldier has been institutionalized and thereby to some extent incapacitated for any life but the soldier's.

All such institutions rob the individual of his sense of self-direction and ultimately damage the capacity for it. Virtue in such institutions consists in having no preference about many things; in eating without complaint whatever is put on the table, in wearing what one is told to wear, in going to bed and rising again according to instructions, in making the best of things. The good institution member does not make choices or decisions. He submits and permits himself to be carried along, as it were, in a "moral automobile." When he returns to civilian life, his suddenly uncorseted soul seems flabby and incapable of standing alone.

Similarly all such institutions are alike in failing to furnish to the individual the feeling that somebody loves him. The institution cannot permit such a sense of individuality as life in the family normally engenders. It cannot and will not single out one child to tempt his appetite with tasty delicacies or feed his dinner to him by spoonsful as his mother might. (Spoon-feeding is a bad word in all such institutions.) The natural reaction to this denial of love makes the soldier, the prisoner, and the institution child destructive and demanding, makes them wasteful of whatever is given to them and forever unsatisfied in their demands for more. In all such groups obscenity appears to degrade the unattainable values of love into nothingness; obscenity becomes not merely a way of speech but a way of thinking and living.

Family living, because of the presence of mutual affection in a great many families, is usually a matter of living in some part for others. Institution living is living for one's self, living without love. The institution child never learns, and the soldier must forget, those little devices by which one demonstrates affection or calls out such demonstrations from another. Life in the institution renders the individual outwardly hard, cold, and expressionless, however much he might desire to be otherwise. The soldier undoubtedly suffers less from these things than the inhabitants of most other institutions, because his personality has been formed in the normal family, and also because comradeship with others who are likewise denied serves as a partial substitute for affection.

Reaction to the denial of love fuses with the general rebellion against the sacrifice of personality values in the Procrustean bed of institutional life. For the soldier, as we have seen, always rebels with some part of himself against the army and its demands. The soldier carries over into civilian life this incompatible mixture of dependence upon authority and rebellion against it. He cannot direct himself. Neither can he accept guidance gracefully. He is bitter over the denial of love, but does not know how to express love, or to elicit it in others. Lust, of course, he understands thoroughly, having explored its uttermost boundaries. He is so conditioned that he will sacrifice for others his life and his immortal soul, but he will not work.

As in all cases where a person must give up deep-rooted habit patterns, the returned soldier is restless. This restlessness, as Professor Burgess has noted, expresses itself in random movement with frequent changes of goal, in frequent projects eagerly conceived and abandoned before they can possibly be completed. As Remarque put it, "So life is now too slow for us; we jump at it, shake it, and before it can speak or resound we have already let go again." In addition, the soldier cannot at once get into effective communication with those who have stayed at home, his own attitudes being a principal barrier to such communication. The soldier is in very truth an immigrant in his native land.

And So, Is Often Dependent

Economically, the ex-soldier is often unable to fend for himself. He has lost, or never acquired, the skills of peace. He cannot accept the disciplines of peace. He is used to depending upon others for his daily bread. He does not know how to go about finding a job. His difficulty is enhanced by the fact that job-competition is usually severe in the post-war period.

But this man, who does not know how to work, knows how to kill. He knows very well what can be accomplished by force. He is not easily frightened; he is not much afraid of a burly policeman, and anyhow he has learned to accept the risks of death.

Modifying a little an old saw, we might say that every war leaves four armies: an army of heroes, an army of cripples, an army of thieves, and an army of panhandlers. Throughout history there have been thieves enough among the old soldiers, and a few cutthroats, but more beggars. A great many of us have a latent tendency toward dependency. Military service strengthens this tendency and gives it an excuse for expression.

Let us take a brief glance at the veteran of some three hundred years ago.

What became of discharged and destitute soldiers? In Elizabethan times, and indeed much later, a disbandment invariably meant an increase in the number of highwaymen, footpads, and thieves in general, and new dangers for all who traveled the King's highway. Something of the same sort happened after the close of the Civil War. Whitelocke notes in his *Memorials,* under 4th May, 1647, letters from the sheriff of Oxfordshire certifying "that many troopers, Irish and others, who had been in arms against the Parliament, robbed all passengers, and that he had raised the *posse comitatus* and apprehended about one hundred of them." James Hind, the most famous highwayman of the time of the Commonwealth, "the great robber of England" as his biographer calls him, had fought for Charles the Second at Worcester. In July, 1654, two years after Hind's execution, Hussey and Peck, two gentlemen who had once been officers in the King's army, were hanged at Oxford, "to the great reluctancy of the generous Royalists then living in Oxon." "They were out of commission and employ," apologizes Anthony Wood, "and had no money to maintain

them, which made them rob on the highway." Probably some
of the disbanded soldiers of the Cromwellian army took to
similar courses, but they were less conspicuous in the criminal
records of the time.

A more common figure still in the literature of the seven-
teenth century is the soldier turned beggar. Take for instance
the ballad called "The Maunding Soldier, or the Fruit of War
is Beggary."

> Good your worship, cast your eyes
> Upon a souldier's miseries;
> Let not my leane cheeks, I pray,
> Your bounty from a souldier stay,
> > But like a noble friend
> > Some silver lend
> And Jove will pay you in the end.

He then recites his services and perils:—

> Twice through the bulke have I been shot,
> My brains have boylèd like a pot:
> I have at least these dozen times
> Been blowne up by those roguish mines.

And concludes:—

> I pray your worship, think on me,
> That am what I do seem to be,
> No rooking rascall, nor no cheat,
> But a souldier every way compleat:
> > I have wounds to show
> > That prove it so,
> Then courteous good sir, ease my woe,
> > And I for you will pray,
> > Both night and day
> That your substance never may decay.

In another ballad called "The Cunning Northern Beggar"
an impostor describes how he personates an old soldier:—

> Now like a wandring souldier
> (That hath i'th warres been maymed
> > With the shot of a gunne)
> > To gallants I runne
> And begg, "Sir, helpe the lamed!
> I am a poore old souldier,
> And better times once viewed,

> Though bare now I goe
> Yet many a foe,
> By me hath bin subdued."
> And therefore I cry "Good your worship, good Sir,
> Bestow one poor denier, Sir,"
> Which when I've got,
> At the Pipe and Pot
> I soon will it casheere, Sir.

... On the other hand, a soldier willing and able to work found great difficulty in obtaining it. Hardly any pursuit but agriculture was open to him. . . . Cromwell . . . deserves the credit of being the first English ruler who attempted to find employment for old soldiers, for the adoption of this plan was due to his initiative. Thanks largely to it, the successive reductions of the army which took place during the Protectorate caused no disturbances, and it was also one of the reasons which made the peaceful disbandment of Monck's army so easy in 1660.[7]

The methods of the fraudulent wounded of Elizabeth's armies were direct, but effective. Some poulticed their arms with a mixture of rust, soap, and unslacked lime. When a blister appeared, they applied a linen cloth, waiting until it stuck, and then plucked it off. The result was a sore giving all the appearance of a gunshot wound. It was noted that right-handed beggars usually disfigured their left arms between elbow and wrist, where the sore would cause the least inconvenience. Another method was to use arsenic in the blister, which frequently poisoned the vagabond and did him serious injury. These spurious wounds were so much in evidence that they found a place in Elizabethan slang, and were called, "a soldier's maund."[8]

The United States has raised and disbanded some mighty armies but has suffered less than might have been expected from the mendicancy or criminality of its veterans. The panhandler who capitalizes on his military service is, of course, not unknown to us. He was a conspicuous feature of our street life in the years following World War I. There were some soldiers who periodically pre-

[7] C. H. Firth, *Cromwell's Army, A History of the English Soldier during the Civil Wars, the Commonwealth, and the Protectorate*. London, Methuen, 1912, pp. 272-276.
[8] Talcott Powell, *Tattered Banners*. Harcourt Brace, 1933, p. 39.

sented themselves to the Red Cross for rehabilitation in those years—and some who still do. Almost every American Legion post probably has a few hangers-on, demoralized veterans who receive help from the members in one way or another. The so-called Bonus Army, though composed of real veterans, contained at least a certain number who were accustomed to live by charity. However, panhandling and begging on the streets are not the favorite methods of the American veteran. His method is political action, culminating in the pension drive, which at least has the merit of giving to the deserving as well as to the undeserving.

And Sometimes Criminal

Sometimes the veteran has been so completely alienated from the attitudes and controls of civilian life that he becomes a criminal. Why this should be so is almost too obvious to need statement. The soldier must kill, must make a study of the art of killing, and overcome all his inbred repugnance to the taking of life. Perhaps he comes to enjoy killing. Military experience also weakens the taboos which protect property and hedge about sexual indulgence. Many soldiers suffer mental shocks which leave them with a form of psychoneurosis characterized by an inclination toward explosions of aggressive behavior; others are mentally disoriented in different ways. Many younger soldiers have learned no trade but war, do not know how to go about making a living; nearly all veterans have suffered some loss of the mental disciplines which go with civilian industry. Many veterans are discharged with disabilities which interfere with holding jobs. In addition, veterans are frequently restless and highly mobile, and thus they tend to drift away from the local communities which would either hold them in line or make allowances for their behavior.

For these reasons, many veterans become criminals, just how many we do not know, since the subject has never been studied as thoroughly as it deserves to be. There is a good deal of European evidence to the effect that crime rates go up during the postwar years. However, as Professor Sutherland remarks, it is not clear how much this is chargeable to war itself and how much to the inflation and general economic distress that war produces.[9]

9 E. H. Sutherland, *Principles of Criminology*. Lippincott, 1939, p. 32.

There is some evidence concerning the criminality of veterans in the United States.

After the Revolutionary War, ex-soldiers played a prominent part in the ruthless political struggles of the day, and doubtless committed many political crimes. The record does not show whether or not veterans were responsible for any great number of other crimes. There seems to have been an epidemic of horse stealing in that period.

At the end of the Civil War we demobilized two mighty armies which had had a long and arduous period of military service. Abbott and Rosenbaum have presented some evidence concerning the criminality of veterans in the post-Civil War period.[10] Rosenbaum quotes Wines as saying in 1870: "Immediately after the establishment of peace, however, there was a great increase in crime and disorder not only in the South, where conditions were abnormal, but throughout the North as well. And a very large proportion of the new offenders in the northern states were men who had 'worn the blue.'" At the Eastern Penitentiary in Pennsylvania there was an influx of soldiers in the last three months of 1865, and in 1866 an unprecedented flood of such cases. Many of these men, as Abbott remarks, were more fit for a hospital than a prison, and other writers have commented on the poor physical condition of the men discharged from the army. Criminality among the veterans was apparently general. "It was estimated that in 1866 two-thirds of all commitments to state prisons in loyal states were men who had seen service in the army or navy. In 1867 the figure was put at nearly half of the existing prison population."[11] One estimate put the number of veterans in prison at 5,000. In 1867 sympathy for the imprisoned ex-service men gave rise to a movement for prison reform.

Ultimately we absorbed our veterans into the population somewhat more easily, apparently, than Europeans had supposed we should. In length of service and in relative numbers of men mobilized, the Civil War probably furnishes a better parallel to the present situation than our experiences of World War I, although, for various reasons, it may prove harder to assimilate our

[10] Edith Abbott, "Crime and the War," in the *Journal of the American Institute of Criminal Law and Criminology*, May, 1918, and Betty B. Rosenbaum, "The Relationship between War and Crime in the United States," in the same publication in the January, 1940 issue.

[11] Rosenbaum, *op. cit.*

veterans at the end of this war than it was in the 1860s. At the close of the Civil War we were still predominantly rural, and our soldiers returned to farming without suffering much difficulty of readjustment, while their cross-roads communities were glad to listen to their tales and to bask in their reflected glory. Furthermore, we had a rapidly expanding economy at that time, with opportunity for all. The population was growing rapidly both by excess of births over deaths and by immigration. New immigrants were pushing the old settlers up the social ladder; new industries were being born daily and civilization was rapidly spreading across the continent. A soldier who wanted to get ahead in the world had every chance to do so in those days. And, for the really restless spirits who could never get war and killing out of their minds, we had a frontier where a man could indulge a taste for violence—fight Indians, hunt outlaws or be one, establish himself as "The Law West of the Pecos." After the present war, our soldiers must return to urban civilization and to the restricted opportunities of a matured and perhaps rigid economy. Possibly there will be a depression soon after the war, when the post-war boom has spent itself. And the soldiers will return to a nation facing embittered social and political struggles.

It is estimated that about one half of one per cent of the veterans of World War I, or about 20,000, served time in prison within four years of the end of the war. Criminologists regard this rate as high for such an age group, although not necessarily high for a group of veterans. In evaluating this percentage, which may seem small to the lay reader, we should bear in mind two facts: (1) That many serious crimes of ex-soldiers go unpunished because of sympathy for the accused, and (2) that even where there is no question of military service, only a small percentage of felony charges result in convictions. We must therefore suppose that veterans in prison constitute a small fraction of the veterans who commit serious crimes.

In 1922 ex-service men constituted 18.12 per cent of the population of a sample of twelve state reformatories and nineteen prisons. A Wisconsin investigation corroborates the estimated crime rate of one half of one per cent, and furnishes further details concerning a group of ex-soldiers studied in Wisconsin prisons.[12] Of this

12 W. F. Lorenz, "Delinquency and the Ex-Soldier," in *Mental Hygiene*, Vol. 7, 1923, pp. 472-484.

group of three hundred prisoners, twenty-five per cent had physical disabilities of service origin; just as in 1866, many of them were more fit for hospitals than for prisons. Fifty-four per cent of the Wisconsin group were mentally abnormal. Twenty-five per cent were diagnosed as psychopathic personalities. Twenty-five per cent were feeble-minded. Sixty-nine per cent were guilty of theft. Twenty-five per cent were guilty of offences definitely influenced by alcoholism.

A similar problem arose in England in the years following 1918, more serious in proportion to the total population but involving, apparently, a smaller percentage of the men mobilized. Prison authorities noted an abnormally high proportion of first offenders among convicted soldiers in those years. In 1919-20, 6,461 demobilized men were received in prisons, 3,411 of these being first offenders and only 1,388 such as could be called habitual criminals. In 1920-21, 9,580 ex-soldiers were sent to prison.[13] The governors of various prisons spoke of the emergence of a "new stamp of offender." The governor of Durham prison stated that "men and women of respectable antecedents and parentage, in regular employment, and in no respects associated with the criminal class, are taking to serious crime (embezzlement, fraud, false pretences, housebreaking, and robbery) with astounding facility." [14]

At the end of World War II the crime rate among our veterans should be expected to exceed that among American veterans of World War I. The war itself has been infinitely worse, and the men have seen much longer periods of service. But if the rate of criminality among our veterans does not exceed that of World War I, we should expect at least 60,000 of the mobilized men to be sent to prison for serious crimes in the years immediately following the war. Past experience tells us that many of this group will be physically handicapped as a result of the war and many will be mentally unbalanced.

. . . But Everything Worth While Takes Time

The demobilized soldier has a furious craving to live, but he is

[13] M. A. Hobhouse and A. F. Brockway, *English Prisons Today, Being the Report of the Prison System Enquiry Committee.* London, Longmans Green, 1922, pp. 23-24.
[14] *Ibid.,* p. 24.

geared to a demoniacal restlessness. He does not know where or how to begin to live. Everything worth while takes time. The veteran has long since forgotten how to wait for the satisfactions of civilian life. The war has been a sort of suspension of life, a waiting for the end until life could begin again. Then all at once the butchery is over and he is free. He finds life full of inexplicable delays and postponements, conditional successes, qualified defeats, debatable benefits—he wants to live but he can't. In short, he learns that life is will and therefore frustration.

Real living takes time. It is a matter of slowly getting a start and rising to the top of a profession through hard work and careful planning over a period of years. It is a matter of publishing a book and waiting until people find out about it, meanwhile surviving somehow those delays of print which tarnish truth. It is a matter of meeting a woman, experiencing the slow ripening of a relationship—a matter of the endlessly slow but irreversible processes of parenthood. It is a matter of gradually acquiring the hard-won respect of neighbors and colleagues and friends, of savings scraped together bit by bit, of the slowly accumulated pounds about the middle. It is a matter of learning to accept a world in which one rarely gains a reputation until he has ceased to deserve it.

The soldier has no time for all these things so long as he is in the army. The veteran has all the time there is—the rest of his life. But he cannot immediately get the fevered pulse of war out of his ears, nor can he believe that the time he is living in is real; it is borrowed time and does not count. Having no time for the real satisfactions of life, the soldier has to accept the ready-to-serve substitutes that are easily available, furtive amourettes with quick and easy women, gambling, fighting, alcohol. He feels that he must use short-cuts to such happiness as he can find. The veteran cannot easily get used to the long hard road—to learning, to professional success, to marital happiness.

While he was in the war, it seemed to the soldier that anything would be possible once he had returned to civilian life. The blind cannot believe that a seeing person could possibly have any problems. They think that if they could just see, everything would be all right. The soldier believes that everything will be solved for him when the war is over. Anything and everything will be possible. He is going to travel. Every soldier intends to travel. For the ambitious, the most grandiose purposes seem attainable, as so often happens when people break their habits and get out of their accustomed social milieu. The ambitious will make millions, rise in politics, write great books. Others will just be satisfied with a moderate job, a home, and comfort.

Civilian life looks easy to the soldier. It is actually very hard for the veteran. There is the waiting, and the starting at the bottom. There is the fighting down the restless urge to give things a push, to hurry them up, to play fast for high stakes. There is the urge to do something spectacular, and thus to make up for lost time. There is the attempt to revive one's dulled sensibilities. There is the bitterness to overcome. There is the learning that the frightened old people are right, and one must make such terms as one can with the universe. There is the learning that one has been living all the time in the army and out of it, the learning to give up glamorous ambitions, and the bringing one's self to accept a little dull job and to marry a woman who is just a good ordinary woman and to buy a suit of clothes with two pairs of pants.

The Veteran
Must Adjust
To Family Living

B EFORE the veteran can become a civilian again, he must find his place in society and settle down in it. He must get established in the economic world, and he must learn to accept the kind of job that he can get. He must once more adapt his personality to the life of the family and the local community. Perhaps he must go back to school. Each of these adjustments contains its own inherent difficulties.

In many ways war is like a masquerade. In fact war *is* a sort of gigantic masquerade, and this fact furnishes our best clue to all the things that happen to our moralities when war takes hold of the country. School teachers dress up in brilliant uniforms and become handsome young officers; business men strut and pose a while as bureaucrats; the harmless postman becomes a hard-boiled sergeant; doctors of philosophy supervise the manufacture of munitions; an obscure garage mechanic or a man from a cross-roads town becomes a national hero; the housewife drives a taxi or runs a lathe. Everybody pretends, everybody moves out of his customary orbit, in order to win the war.

As in a carnival or masquerade, the sexual impulses of men are released in war. This powerful drive, as we know, is ordinarily kept in check and forced to do the work of the world by the most terrible inhibitions that the human mind is capable of absorbing. And the sexual expression of individuals is watched over by a whole series of institutions that punish violators with Draconian severity. In war all this is changed. The habit systems of individuals are shattered and their morality is dissolved. Institutions of control lose their power to keep human beings in line.

There is a great release of sexuality in conventional channels. In the period of preparation for war, marriages, births, and divorces all increase as in any period of economic prosperity. Writing in mid-1943 of the years of war and preparation for war, Professor Ogburn says:

> During this period the marriage rate per 1,000 population increased in almost unprecedented degree. This was due in part to economic prosperity; but around the period of the passage of the Selective Service Act in September 1940 and for a few months after the attack on Pearl Harbor on December 7, 1941, the marriage rate rose steeply and may be attributed to the war.
>
> The birth rate per 1,000 population followed, ten months later, the course of the marriage rate, except that the swings of the birth rate were not so great as those of the marriage rate.
>
> The divorce rate per 1,000 population increased by slightly less than 10 per cent per year, which is somewhat greater than the increases in most periods of prosperity.
>
> In the First World War, after the preparation as such was over, both the marriage rate and the birth rate in the various warring countries fell very greatly and stayed down until the close of the war, the birth rate lagging about a year behind the marriage rate.
>
> In the three post-war years following World War I, in the various combatting countries, the marriage rate went up a good deal higher than in pre-war years, and the birth rate also increased beyond normal in most of the countries. The peak of the marriage rate was one year after the war, and of the birth rate one year later.[1]

War Brides of World War II

We have heard and read a great deal of "war brides." Of these Ogburn says:

> [The period from December, 1941 to April, 1942 was] the period of the "war brides." The newspapers and magazines of the early months of 1942 contained much discussion of the question as to whether or not young women should marry in

[1] William F. Ogburn, "Marriages, Births and Divorces," in *The American Family in World War II*, The Annals of the American Academy of Political and Social Science, Sept., 1943, pp. 20-29. See also: J. H. Bossard, "War and the Family," in Howard Becker and Reuben Hill, *Marriage and the Family*, Heath, 1942; and Willard Waller, *War and the Family*, Dryden Press, 1940.

haste when their beaux were about to go overseas and might never return. This point is of some interest in the present volume, which deals with the family. It may be questioned whether war marriages establish a family or not. By definition, a marriage marks the inception of a new family. But if the couple live together only a week or so and have no children, they can hardly be said to have set up a family. But the husbands of many of the war brides will return and the couples will found a family in the full sense of the word.

It is interesting to speculate on how many war brides there were. It is possible that there were about 150,000. This estimate is reached in the following manner. The war-bride marriages are defined as those occurring in December, 1941 and the first four months of 1942, over the number that occurred the previous year. For the eight states, with eighteen million population, for which data on marriages are available at the time of writing, there were about one-third more marriages during these five months than in the previous year. For these five months, then, about one out of four brides may be said to be war brides. For the United States as a whole, there probably occurred in these five months 600,000 marriages, one fourth of which, or 150,000, were war brides, or about 1,000 war brides per day. After we had been in the war for more than five months there may still have been war brides, but, as the term is popularly understood, the war marriage excitement occurs at the beginning of a war.[2]

It is interesting to note that many of these war brides, determined to be with their husbands as long as they can, become camp-followers—of a respectable sort—and trek wearily from one training camp community to another. The life of these girls in those dreary, overcrowded, and money-mad communities is far from enviable. They must pay frightful rents and live under degrading conditions. They are much alone, many of them away from home for the first time. Most of them have nothing whatever to do. When they have their G.I. babies, which happens with alarming frequency, the children must begin their lives under very unfavorable conditions, and the problems of the mothers grow exceedingly complex. Whatever else such arrangements for life and love may be, they are not marriage. The groups of human beings so

2 Ogburn, *op. cit.*

established, however great the mutual affection which binds them together, are hardly families.

Passage of the conscription act in 1940 also produced a flurry in marriages. There were a certain number of true conscription marriages, that is, marriages effected in order to dodge the draft. In some instances, determined draft-evaders clinched the draft exemption by immediately having a baby, which was sometimes cynically spoken of as "draft insurance." It should be noted that the formula, "Pre-Pearl Harbor father," covered such persons perfectly with its protecting mantle, until the manpower quotas forced the drafting of a certain number of fathers. A study of a confidential nature was done under the supervision of the writer by a graduate student of Sociology during this period. It revealed that such "conscription-marriages" could readily be found at the time, and that the attitudes of the persons involved in them present their own peculiar problems, which will certainly be accentuated when the soldiers return and the husbands are branded as slackers. The little joke of the matter is that practically all the men involved in such marriages would most likely have been rejected anyhow for reasons of psychoneurosis.

The greatest release of sexuality, however, is not in such conventional channels.[3] Wherever men and women meet, some of them join in illegitimate unions. In the front-line brothels established by some of the European armies, soldiers stand in line for hours in order to enjoy a few moments with a prostitute. In the resting-station brothels, there are more conveniences, but the entire atmosphere is scarcely less swinish. There are, of course, separate brothels for officers and for men. In thousands of other places sexuality flourishes. Clandestine prostitution springs up in occupied areas; women at home consort with prisoners of war; the capital cities of nations become dens of vice; hospitals are also the scene of many erotic affairs. Sexual expression, for large sections

[3] A great deal of information on this subject is contained in Magnus Hirshfeld, *The Sexual History of the World War*, Panurge Press, 1934. In spite of serious defects, which were probably not the fault of Hirshfeld or his collaborators, the book is a valuable source. The material covered is mostly the sort of thing that does not get into historical records, since the behavior described is for the most part illicit and covert. Therefore, the method employed by Hirshfeld is necessarily unsatisfactory, but is perhaps the best one possible for utilizing the available information. Such books, unfortunately, are often put to the uses of pornography, but this one should certainly not be so regarded.

of the population, becomes a sort of roistering pleasure like drinking or gambling.

The Veteran Doubts His Ability to Love

Among the emotional lacks which candid introspection so often
reveals to the veteran is an incapacity to love, at least in the ordinary sense of the word. Love, as we in America use the term, love
between the sexes, implies a fusion of the spiritual and the physical.
A derangement of the capacity for this kind of love often involves a
split between the physical and spiritual elements of that highly
complex sentiment. The soldier understands lust. The depriva-
tions of army life intensify it. The soldier also understands
idealized love, and that, too, is probably intensified by war. But to
get these things together and to express them toward the same
person is difficult. Lust, bargaining, exploitation, the trading of a
quid pro quo disguised at best by a pretense of affection in some
transitory relationship—such is sexuality in wartime. As some
critics have noted, one of the achievements of Hemingway's books
is that he repeatedly takes characters who have just such attitudes
and transforms them before our eyes into persons capable of ideal
affection.

The disorganized man wants a woman. Almost any woman will
do. All women serve the same purpose for him. As Hemingway
puts it:

> Vaguely he wanted a girl but he did not want to have to
> work to get her. He would have liked to have a girl but he
> did not want to have to spend a long time getting her. He
> did not want to get into the intrigue and the politics. He did
> not want to have to do any courting. He did not want to tell
> any more lies. It wasn't worth it . . . Then sooner or later
> you always got one. When you were really ripe for a girl you
> always got one. You did not have to think about it. Sooner
> or later it would come. He had learned that in the army.
> Now he would have liked a girl if she had come to him and
> not wanted to talk. But here at home it was all too com-
> plicated. He knew he could never get through it all again.
> It was not worth the trouble. That was the thing about French
> girls and German girls. There was not all this talking. You
> couldn't talk much and you did not need to talk. It was simple

and you were friends. He thought about France and then he began to think about Germany. On the whole he had liked Germany better. He did not want to leave Germany. He did not want to come home. Still, he had come home.[4]

The veteran himself recognizes very well the difficulty of attaining once more a normal attitude toward sexuality. Remarque's analysis of his questionings is typical.

Drops of rain fall glittering from the trees; I turn up my collar. I often long for affection even now, for shy words, for warm, generous emotions; I would like to escape the crude monotony of these last years. But what if it actually came to pass? What if all the gentleness and variety of those other days drew around me again? If someone actually did love me, some slim, delicate woman, such as the one there with the golden toque and the slim ankles—how would it be? Even though the ecstacy of some blue, silver night should gather about us, endless, self-forgetting in darkness, would not the vision of the fat whore come between us at the last moment? Would not the voices of the drill sergeants suddenly shout their obscenities? Would not memory, scraps of talk, army jokes, at once riddle and destroy every decent emotion? In ourselves even now we are still chaste, but our imagination has been debauched without our being aware of it; before we knew anything of love at all we were already being lined up and examined for sexual diseases. The breathless wonder, the impetuousness, the night wind, the darkness, the questionings —all those things that were still with us when, as sixteen-year-old boys, we would race along after Adele and the other girls through the flickering, gaslit wind, these never came back. Though the time was when the woman was not a whore, yet it did not come back; though I believed it might still be otherwise, and though she embraced me and I trembled with desire, yet it did not return . . . Afterwards I was always wretched.[5]

The soldier is often keenly aware of what is happening to him, and worries about it even while he is a soldier. Cuber reports,

[4] Ernest Hemingway, "Soldier's Home," in *The Short Stories of Ernest Hemingway*. Modern Library edition. Reprinted by permission of Charles Scribner's Sons.

[5] Erich Maria Remarque, *The Road Back*. Little Brown, 1931, p. 209. This passage is of suggestive interest to those of a psychoanalytic turn of mind.

in his study of changing courtship and marriage customs in World War II, that "not a great many men are initiated into prostitution when they are in the army . . . by and large the patrons in the army are the same patrons when at home, although the patronage seems to be more frequent and more open in the army situation." [6]

Are War Marriages Really Marriages?

If the soldier happens to have contracted marriage during his term of service, as so many thousands have done, he must make his adjustments within the invisible but confining walls of the marriage institution. Not all war marriages, of course, are destined to be unsuccessful, but they have their peculiar hazards, and the percentage of failures is certain to be high. These peculiar problems are well illustrated in a case reported by Cuber.

> "We were college 'steadies' for six months with no mention of marriage ever made between us. We were not prudish in our erotic behavior though I did remain a virgin. . . . Then he was drafted. I promised to write him twice a week and he promised to write as often as he could. Gradually his letters became more and more ardent. And soon he proposed. Before I could collect my wits for a reply he was home for a furlough. We weren't alone for an hour before he was pressing the marriage issue with all the high pressure tactics I had heard of plus a few more. . . .
>
> "I liked him very much. We did seem to have much in common. I doubted that I was in love but couldn't prove it. We were both emotionally tense after months of separation. I don't know just how it happened but I suddenly realized that I was no longer virginal. The seven-day furlough was almost over and the pressure to get married was now greater than ever. . . .
>
> "We were married on the sixth day of the furlough. Then I received a letter from him stating that he had found a room for me near the camp and that he had made arrangements with his commanding officer to have his week-ends free. I could surely find a job there. So overnight I packed a few belong-

6 John F. Cuber, "Changing Courtship and Marriage Customs," in *The American Family in World War II,* The Annals of the American Academy of Political and Social Science, Sept. 1943. See also John F. Cuber, "The College Youth Goes to War," in *Marriage and Family Living,* Feb. 1943.

ings and boarded a train for another part of America where I had never been before. And there I lived for three months a semi-prisoner. One and a half days each week were deliriously happy; five and a half were dismally lonely, like a prisoner in a foreign land. . . .

"Then he received orders to move and I went back to my home community because in his new situation it was impossible for him to live with his wife. At first I was lonely, but soon the exhilaration of being 'among my own' again readjusted me. I moved in my old circle of friends. . . .

"One day someone suggested that I go on a 'date'—a purely platonic date, of course, with a fraternity brother of my husband. And the date was platonic to the point of brutality. Both of us were so anxious that it remain platonic and that there be no infidelity that the whole affair was funny or tragic depending upon how you look at it. There being no harm on that date there was another and another and suddenly they weren't so platonic. Gradually I began to realize that I was falling in love with this man and he with me. And accordingly we broke off the relationship, abruptly.

"Soon thereafter I discovered that I was pregnant—by my husband, of course. (The other affair had never gone that far.) When I wrote the news to my husband he was very disturbed. Though solicitous of my welfare he couldn't help revealing the fact that the rôle of father was incomprehensible to him under the circumstances. I could understand him because I felt the same way. We had never really been truly married and both of us knew it. If we had had a normal home life we could perhaps have fallen into some kind of normal love relationship even after marriage. But the sum total of our married life was seven week-ends in that not-too-pleasant room in a foreign culture.

"Meanwhile I was haunted by my recently discovered relationship with the second man. I cannot justify it ethically but I feel it emotionally. A week ago I learned that my husband has gone overseas. I shall not see him now for the duration at least. The second man, like me, finds it difficult to call our relationship off, even though he knows that I am pregnant and I strongly wish to remain loyal to my husband. . . . I haven't the slightest idea how it will all turn out, but I must confess, being as rational as I am, that I can see many possible outcomes but none that is satisfactory."

This is the essential story of a war marriage between two

persons, one 22 and one 24 years of age, both college graduates and both professionally trained. The case has been quoted at length because so many aspects of the war courtship and quasi-marriage are revealed through it: (1) the hurried nature of many marriages between two persons not emotionally quite ready for marriage, or, stated otherwise, aborted courtship; (2) some of the effects of prolonged separation for married and unmarried pairs; (3) the problems of a quasi "home"; (4) the subtle and important influence of the ever potential third person in that kind of marriage, and (5) the wartime nuptial pregnancy.

For the future stability of many of these marriages the best prognosis was probably given by the woman: "I can see many possible outcomes but none that seems satisfactory" as a basis upon which to build a good family life for man, woman, and child.[7]

In Cuber's case, the problem of the baby is typical. The love-starved, not necessarily sex-starved soldier does not quite know how to accept a baby. It may of course be that his fundamental normality carries him through this crisis, and parenthood then helps him to make the other adjustments. Some of the most pathetic and touching stories of the present war deal with the young mother suddenly surrounded by a group of soldiers who take her baby away from her and tend it for her. Among the soldiers in the South Seas there is an "I've never seen my baby" club, whose honorary president is the father of twin girls now approaching their second birthday. Such stories seem to indicate powerful parental drives in the soldiers which will help them to adjust in the post-war years.

The attitudes with which people sometimes enter upon matrimony in time of war are illustrated by the young woman who declared to the writer: "I don't love him. I've told him I don't love him. But he's an aviator and he says I should marry him anyhow and give him a little happiness. He says he knows he'll be dead in a year, he hasn't any chance of living through the war. But if he should still be alive when the war is over, and I still feel the same way, he says I can divorce him and it will be all right." Very few people, and particularly very few young people, realize that no agreement to permit divorce has any legal or moral validity.

7 *Ibid.* See also Willard Waller, *op. cit.*, for other cases.

Chances of Success of Post-War Marriages

If the war marriage is full of uncharted dangers, it is equally hazardous for the veteran to marry immediately after his return to civil life. Calvin Hall has demonstrated this on the basis of American figures for World War I.[8] The years 1919 and 1920 appear to have been especially ill-fated for marital happiness. For at least eleven years thereafter, marriages contracted in those years revealed a disproportionate number of divorces. The evidence is so consistent that there can be little doubt of its meaning: Marriages contracted in the post-war period are in fact unstable. Marriages contracted in 1917, 1918, and 1921 showed the same characteristics in less pronounced form. Hall's explanation of his figures seems to add something to our discussion:

The most plausible [explanation] is that the unstable post-war marriages were an effect of the war itself. The argument for this hypothesis can be developed as follows: During a war-time period and especially when there is more or less universal conscription among certain age ranges, many young men and women who would normally contract marriage are forced to delay this act. Such a delay period, spent in partial segregation between the sexes, serves to intensify the normal desire to participate in matrimony and this intensified desire has the effect of reducing even the customary rationality which men and women display when they agree to contract marriage. Furthermore, the hysteria attendant upon the close of a major conflict undoubtedly acts as another inhibitor of rational processes. There is also a third factor operating to make for unstable marriages as a result of war. Presumably many couples anticipating a delay agreed to and did marry as soon as the war was over. War, however, is a notable breeder of personality and physical changes and many of those engaged couples who had been compatible before the war were so changed, psychologically and physically, that there was no longer any compatibility. And yet because they felt bound by their previous betrothals they entered into an unsatisfactory connubial relationship. Thus heightened desire, post-war hysteria, and personality or physical changes, operating singly or together, can account for the instability of post-war marriages.[9]

[8] Calvin Hall, "The Instability of Post-War Marriages," in the *Journal of Social Psychology*, Vol. V, pp. 523-530.
[9] *Ibid.*

Many who do not marry commit other follies less irrevocable in nature. Some veterans report turning from one sex affair to another, trying, no doubt, to discover in the relationship of the sexes the meanings that war and army life had taken from their lives. "My life used to be full of everything," says a Hemingway character. "Now if you aren't with me I haven't a thing in the world." To which the girl replies teasingly, "Othello with his occupation gone." And so they go about, as another writer puts it, forever knocking at all the doors of their youth, hoping they may be admitted because they are still so young and wish so much to forget.

Upon his return to civil life, the soldier finds the system of prescribed relations between the sexes in various ways altered from the pre-war pattern. The most important change could be summarized by saying that women have gained equality as human beings but have lost much of their sexual bargaining power because of the scarcity of males as well as for other reasons. In addition, moral standards of the entire population have been relaxed, and a very disorganized generation of post-war youth has come upon the scene. All these things make sexual license possible for the veteran and facilitate the follies to which so many devote the post-war years.

In war, woman gains her rights, because a nation cannot fight a war without its women, and, as Bossard says, "When the man is away the woman must play—at being a man." [10] The strides made by women in recent wars are well known. World War I brought votes for women in England and America, opened to women workers a great many doors that were never closed thereafter. World War II has brought even greater changes. Apparently, all wars have produced similar phenomena. Some observers believe that the Civil War altered the position of women, especially in the South; [11] others, that the Punic Wars altered the position of women in Roman society.[12]

While woman has gained in one way she has lost in another. After a war, marriageable men are scarce and women are correspondingly plentiful. (A phenomenon which Nature, in some

10 Bossard, *op. cit.* The reader will find Bossard's entire chapter helpful.
11 John Andrews Rice, "My Father's Folks," in *Harper's Magazine*, Sept. 1940.
12 Willystine Goodsell, *A History/of the Family as a Social and Educational Institution.* Macmillan, 1915, p. 131.

mysterious way, corrects by producing a surplus of boy babies.)
The veteran's sexual bargaining power is therefore high. Ogburn
has shown that a slight surplus of males produces the highest proportion of married persons in the population; in general, this is
conducive to conformity in matters of sex morality. With such a
surplus of females as war usually produces, the market value of
women usually falls rapidly. It does not take a large surplus to
induce active competition for the young, unattached males. At the
end of World War I, there were approximately two million extra
women in Germany in the twenty-to-forty age group, or five women
to every four men in the entire group. In France the situation was
similar, about six women to every five men in that age group in
1921. Included among the surviving males were many disabled
who were incapable of family life. Most of the surviving males
were already married. There was, therefore, a very great surplus
of unmarried women over unmarried men. The situation of the
woman was worsened by the fact that she had to compete with
younger women as well as her contemporaries.

There were thus a great number of women in post-war Europe
who could not live within the mores, and a great number of men
who did not want to. When the women cannot live within the
mores and the men do not want to, the entire family system is shattered. The veteran who does not marry has an unusually good opportunity for cultivating dalliance relationships. Dalliance relationships, unfortunately, do not help him to get domiciled in society.

Like the ripples raised by a stone in a millpond, the effects of
war upon human personality slowly die away. A considerable proportion of veterans manage to establish satisfactory family relations and to rear healthy and normal children. Others never do. Let
no one suppose that the effects of the present war upon human
personality will disappear in a single generation. Psychoanalysts
and social workers of the year 2050 will still be liquidating the
more remote effects of the present conflict. Some veterans will undoubtedly inflict their pathologies upon their children and their
children's children.

The effects of the present war will not quickly disappear, but
there are things which we can do to help the veteran readjust in
society. We cannot, of course, repeal the laws of causality; we can-

not undo what has already been done, but we can try to behave intelligently and humanely in the presence of the great problem of veteran readjustment. To a considerable extent, we can remedy the physical damage of war, to some extent even the mental damage. We can assist the veteran to get on his feet financially. We can teach him to make the best use of his remaining assets, help him to overcome his undesirable attitudes. To do these things, we must begin by understanding the veteran. The question of what we can do to help the veteran readjust is discussed at greater length in Part IV of this book.

The Veteran Must Adjust To Our Class Economy

MOST of the skills that soldiers acquire in their training for war are irrelevant to civilian life. Some few men learn useful trades that they practice in later life. In general, however, the picture is one of men who struggle very hard to learn certain things and to acquire certain distinctions, and then find that with the end of war these things completely lose their utility. When the war is over, the sergeant's stripes, the lieutenant's bars, and even the aviator's wings open fewer doors than people suppose. And as for those humbler skills, such as that of digging a fine fox-hole or throwing hand-grenades with dexterity, they are utterly valueless.

Men who do the maintenance work and the paper work of the army sometimes acquire useful trades and helpful administrative experience. A modern army is like a great city that must be constantly supplied and maintained. It must often train its own technicians for certain jobs. Sometimes—not very often—those technicians are able to support themselves in later life by the practice of trades learned in the army.

The specialist in the paper work of the army has a little better chance of making use of his army experiences later on. There are two armies, the army of men and the army of marks on pieces of paper. Whenever a man moves about or does anything in the army of men, someone makes the appropriate notations in the paper army. When a man draws a new blouse, gets a leave, goes on sick call, learns to shoot, swim, drive a truck, or send Morse code, when he goes AWOL, when he eats his breakfast, when he does not eat his breakfast—somebody must make an appropriate record of such events. Battles are fought on paper, campaigns won or lost before a single shot is fired. The ubiquitous typewriter follows the soldier wherever he goes. Where goes the typewriter go the typist and the man who directs him. Orders must be typed and an infinite number of copies must be prepared. Reports must be filled out and sent back in neat sheaves of, say, eight copies. When Sevastopol was falling and the Germans were showering every kind of missile including railroad iron on its crumbling defenses, typists in a cave beneath the city were still busily pounding out the endless paper work of the army; how men ever fought before typewriters were invented is a mystery. Now it happens that army paper work is not very different from the paper work of civilian government, big business, or any other bureaucratic organization. The person who has specialized in this paper work, and especially the person who is responsible for the work of an organization, becomes a sort of administrative jack-of-all-trades and has some chance of capitalizing on his experience in later years.

The Veteran Must Usually Start at the Bottom

Most soldiers, however, must start anew, and that means they must start at the bottom. A few fortunate ones can make capital of their military career but most veterans must begin civil life in some rather humble capacity. They have grown older while in the army; no matter, their economic position is determined by their skills, which are those of the young boy who entered the army. War matures a man quickly, in peculiar ways, to be sure, and at an uneven rate in various aspects of personality, but the economic status of the veteran is that of the unmatured boy.

It is difficult for the veteran who has had so much discipline in the army to accept the disciplines of business and industry. Many veterans grow so sick of being ordered about that they build up a lasting resentment against it. But at the same time the ex-soldier needs and expects definite orders and instructions; often he has lost some of his capacity to act on his own.

A complicating factor in the veteran's rebellion against the discipline of industry is that this discipline must be imposed upon him by civilians, and his army training has predisposed him to resent civilians. The boss, who hires and fires him, writes recommendations for him, raises or lowers his pay, and otherwise disposes of his destiny is nothing but a soft civilian. The foreman thinks he is tough, he thinks he has a sharp tongue, but the veteran has seen and listened to hard-boiled sergeants and chief petty officers. While the veteran was risking his life for his country, the boss and the foreman were having an easy time of it and getting rich. The veteran can not help reflecting that a smash of a gun-butt, or even a well-directed blow at the bridge of the nose—This Judo is marvelous!—might easily dispose of such a man forever.

Probably the veteran has offers of jobs. And such jobs! He has a chance to keep the books of a dingy little furrier's shop on a back street. He can work in the box-factory, forever pounding little nails into orange crates. He can be a clerk for the railroad, working in a great room with several hundred others under the watchful eye of the boss whom the little clerks fear as if he were the Red Death itself. He can deliver groceries, press pants, solicit laundry business, sell subscription books. He can start a little garage or a filling station with his demobilization pay and probably lose it all. He can get a job selling insurance; he can sell things on commission, and either of these openings will give him the privilege of licking the boots of civilians. It is hard for the veteran to realize that this bleak economic prospect was what he was fighting for.

The prospect of thirty years of ill-rewarded work at a dull job is not alluring to a man who has lost his habits of work. For among his habits which have been sloughed off by the army is the complex constellation of habits, skills, and attitudes which normally reconcile the wage-slave to his drudgery. There is work in the army, but there is also a great deal of idleness, and the work is not motivated in the same manner as that of the civilian laborer; therefore the veteran lacks the central part of the toiler's equipment, the motivation to work. Indeed, as we have seen, army life, where everything is provided without charge, is antithetical to the very idea of working for one's living.

He Feels That His Country Owes Him a Job

The soldier's predatory attitude toward property, and his feeling that others owe him something because he spilled his blood or risked his neck have something to do with the veteran's insistent demands for pensions and preferments. Romains has sketched this complex of attitudes skillfully in the following passage:

Yesterday when I was passing a fruiterer's stall I suddenly realized that I was thinking (you mustn't take this too seriously), "He ought to think himself damned lucky that we don't relieve him of his pots of jam and his vegetables." (Probably the memory of the three days' fast had something to do with it.) But there's something in that whole attitude that is pleasurable and stimulating. Isn't that exactly what went to make up the sense of belonging to a noble caste in the days of aristocracy? The noble fought, let himself be killed, but, apart from that, didn't do a hand's turn. He expected the villein to bring him the tithe of his crops, a proportion of the yield of his wretched industries, the virginity of his female children. My men don't think of themselves as aristocrats, don't address one another as Sir Knight or baron . . . because in their eyes those terms have a glamour of age which disguises their real significance. But they are passing through a comparable stage of evolution. Many of them will feel badly let down when one of these days, they are asked to take up once again their base, mechanic trades. All will accept as their right a pension which shall assure them a means of life when they're beyond work. Put yourself in their place. They've entered into a compact with the nation and that compact has two main clauses, no less binding for being unspoken: "You must protect me, even at the cost of your life," says the nation. "All right," replies the soldier, "but in that case you must make yourself responsible for my life so long as it continues." The trouble is that there are too many of us, whether it's merely a question of our pride or of the privileges which we claim from the future. It's difficult to be overweeningly proud of a state of life which one shares with millions. It's difficult to expect the nation to keep its warriors indefinitely, when those warriors are no less than the nation in arms. Aristocracy is only an effective doctrine when it is applied to a limited number. The ennobled should not amount to more than a hundred thousand.[1]

To this discussion we should add that defeat in the ordinary processes of economic competition greatly re-enforces the veteran's

1 Jules Romains, *Men of Good Will*; Vol. VIII, *Verdun*. Knopf, 1940, pp. 437-438.

idea that the rest of the world should support him. But it is doubtful that the veteran can lay much claim to the status of aristocrat. He becomes rather a sort of privileged beggar.

The problem of the veteran's economic status cannot be separated from the question of his place in the class system of society. Concerning the standards by which one's social position is measured, the veteran has some right to be confused. He has seen men's worth computed by three sets of standards in rapid succession, first by the standards of civilian society, then by army standards, and at last by the standards of the post-war period.

One's rank in civilian society depends upon ancestry, wealth, occupation, or profession, moral status, and evidences of culture and refinement. Of all these criteria, wealth or income level is the most important, and all others must give way to it. The upper classes tend to be composed of persons who have at least a moderate amount of wealth for a few generations and who enjoy high professional and cultural position. A social class is a group of people set off from others primarily by similarity of life chances. On the mental side, the class system is simply a system of upward-looking and downward-looking attitudes.

From Army Caste System to Peacetime Class System

When a young man joins the army, he brings with him civilian standards of class and the attitudes that go with them. The army has its own characteristic hierarchy but, even in the democratic nations—perhaps especially in the democratic nations—one's position in that hierarchy tends to correspond to his class position in society. The commissioned officers are the elite of the army, and tend to be taken from the upper classes or at least from the educated group; formerly commissions could be purchased on behalf of a young man who had a suitable family background. Hereditary status plays an important part in every officer *cadre*, but various considerations sometimes force a lowering of these bars, so that persons of any social class who have demonstrated their military capacity may become officers. One of these considerations is efficiency. If an army is to be really effective, it must give positions of leadership to talented men of whatever rank in society; this is the logic of Napoleon's maxim concerning *la carrière ouverte aux talents.* The army that has best met this criterion in World War II is probably the Russian and the next best job has been done by the German army. Or it may come about that the need for greatly expanding the officer corps or for replacing casualties forces armies to open their commissioned ranks to competition, an eventuality that occurs frequently in modern war.

When, for whatever reason, army positions are opened to competition, men of military capacity rise to the top. If this competition takes place in war, there is a rapid testing that brings promotion to the men who can fight and eliminates those who cannot. In time of war it is possible to distinguish a Grant, a Sherman, or a Stonewall Jackson from a Burnside or a McClellan. Grant, the drinker and unsuccessful business man, can obtain supreme command when the times call for hard, stubborn fighting. Nathan Bedford Forrest, trader in human flesh whom the best families of the South could never quite accept, no reader of books or theoretical tactician but a killer and a man born for war, wins battles because he gets "thar fust with the most men," comes at last to be recognized as almost the equal of Stonewall Jackson.

While these great men are winning high place, many thousands of lesser men are finding their way to less spectacular promotion. This man who has been a sergeant in the regular army, who has taken advantage of his opportunities and obtained a college degree, comes up from the ranks and becomes a major and then a lieutenant-colonel. Others come in from civilian life at the time when the army needs officers, and, since competition in the early stages is far from severe, go up rapidly. But while this shoe-salesman becomes a lieutenant and that unemployed schoolteacher a beloved captain, a brilliant young philosopher remains a private, perhaps being promoted to the grade of corporal after a couple of years. One cannot say, exactly, that the bottom rail is on top; it is not, always, or even usually. But when war comes men must sell their talents in a different market, and some abilities that formerly brought a high price are worthless, while other capacities that were formerly worth but little now come very high indeed.

The military caste of every nation, the corps of professional soldiers who are the officers of the peacetime army, does everything it can to protect itself against those soldiers who rise from the ranks and those who come in from civil life. Professional soldiers never quite accept these outsiders, however necessary they may be in time of war. To the professional officer, such men are "temporary gentlemen," or "gentlemen by Act of Congress." Every attempt is made to assure that their military rank will be cancelled at the end of the war. Even today the gulf between the Army of the United States and the United States Army is only less wide and deep than that between the reserves and the regular navy.

The common soldier is hardly in a position to understand the revaluation of men which takes place in the officer ranks. What he does see is that he and his comrades are living in a world where their worth, and therefore their social standing, are determined by criteria alien to civilian society. Physical strength, bravery, skill in dealing with the physical facts of life and with the harsher aspects of social reality count for much in the army. A farmer, a taxi-driver, or a policeman may well be a better man than any Doctor of Literature. Privates feel, of course, that their subjugation to their officers is temporary, and hope that some day their positions will be reversed. One of their most frequent comments is, "I hope I meet that guy in civilian life."

The end of the war terminates competition of the military sort, and subjects the veterans to another revaluation of their abilities. They are restored to the civilian competitive system, and the system itself is somewhat altered. Some are able to return to a status assured by inherited wealth and family background. Most veterans must find their own way on the basis of their own abilities and the luck that comes to them. Those who come out best in this new competition are not always those who have been the best soldiers.

When soldiers meet again after a few months of civilian life, they often find much of their old comradeship gone. Remarque notes this, conjecturing that "profession and family and social standing, like so many wedges, have split us asunder." [2] Competition has also played a part in this severance, in that it has oriented each man to the task of looking out for himself and living for himself. There is this difference between the competition of the army and that of civilian life: That competition in the army is emulation directed toward the common good, while competition in civilian life is each for himself. When comrades meet after some months out of uniform, they often find the clash of class conceptions dis-

[2] Erich Maria Remarque, *The Road Back*. Little Brown, 1931, p. 198.

tressing. In the army all are just plain soldiers; they share everything. When they return to civil life, one looks at the other in a patronizing manner and calls him, "My man." [3]

Particularly distressing is the situation of the "ranker," the "temporary gentleman," when he returns to civilian life. Many of these, of course, return to a higher status in civilian life than they occupied in the army, but many others never again rise as high, hold as much power, or touch as much money as during the war. A veteran of the Rainbow Division tells of his great pleasure in meeting his former captain who had become a shoe clerk in a bargain basement. One can hardly begrudge him that pleasure; no doubt he had his reasons for feeling as he did. Still, one cannot help thinking about the captain.

[3] *Ibid.*, p. 180.

Some Veterans
Return to School

A PROGRAM of rehabilitation through schooling has many advantages. The school can be adjusted to the veteran better than any other institution. Education can be tailor-made to his measure. Educators are accustomed to treating the aberrations of youth with a wide tolerance; teachers can afford to make allowances where employers cannot. An educational environment, in America, is traditionally one in which social pressures are not severe; under the light yoke of education the veteran has a chance to work out his emotional readjustments. Education is, furthermore, the shortest route to real rehabilitation, whose goal must be to enmesh the soldier once more in the communicative process of society, and to restore him to his rightful place in competition. Education can do these things as nothing else can. Certainly for the younger soldiers, a few years in some educational institution would be the best possible bridge from the army to civil life.

Schooling, even college training, was in fact furnished to a great number of disabled veterans after World War I. At that time the program was limited to the disabled, of whom 329,969 registered for vocational training, 179,515 entered training, and 118,355 were classified as rehabilitated and employable by reason of training.[1] While the results of this program were not altogether gratifying, it set a precedent for the use of education as a rehabilitating agency.

Veterans: A Very Special Type of Student

Many veterans find the reversion to the status of pupil, with its assumption of immaturity on the part of the student, somewhat repugnant. They do not like to be told that every theme must be

---

[1] Cf. Gustavus A. Weber and Laurence F. Schmeckebier, *The Veterans Administration, Its History, Activities and Organization.* Brookings Institution, 1934.

folded once, lengthwise, and must have the student's name and the class and the date on the back, in the upper left-hand corner, three inches from the top. They do not readily accept supervision of their hours, amusements, and morals. They resent the dean of men and his use of landladies as spies. They have managed to take care of themselves in various corners of the world, have given a good account of themselves at certain disputed barricades, and they do not enjoy having their lives regulated by bespectacled professors who are, for the most part, the softest of soft civilians.

While the veteran resents the assumption of immaturity, it would be an error to suppose that he is actually mature. War has aged him and developed some aspects of his personality, but it has prevented him from growing up in other ways. The veteran is not immature in the same way in which the ordinary college boy is immature. He knows more about sex, perhaps less about love. He knows how to fight, but is less likely than the college boy to have had a satisfactory work experience. In academic work, the boy who goes directly from school to college has a great advantage, but the veteran has a greater sophistication and a wider experience of people, especially outside his own social class. Both the college boy and the veteran are shockingly uninformed on political affairs. The veteran who has become a commissioned officer or a non-com has some organizing ability; he knows how to run things. What is certainly indicated is that, if the veteran returns to school or college, *some way must be found to capitalize on his experience and to remedy its lacks.*

The veteran has lost much of his interest in studies. Very likely he began to lose interest before he joined the army. It is hard to memorize eighteenth century poetry when interruption of studies is momentarily threatened and death within a few months is highly possible. Then came the war, and an end of studies, and the withering away in one's mind of all that the studies stood for. One learned to live for the moment, looking forward to the soldier's hectic holidays, and resorting to comic books for intellectual stimulation. It is a long way from there to Parnassus, and who is interested in mountain-climbing anyhow? What does one get when he has climbed Parnassus? A medal?

The thought of returning to my theological studies, interrupted three years earlier, flitted through my mind occasionally. The idea plunged me into a most somber mood. No doubt it would provide a tranquil existence after the tumult, but the war had implanted a restlessness in my spirit which filled me with an inexpressible contempt for the uneventful drudgery of everyday life. I did not crave adventure, but subconsciously, I suppose, I had expected something phenomenal to happen upon the return home, some great change, a new start. There had been a thunderstorm and the atmosphere had failed to clear. It was the same petty, monotonous, joyless, suffocating world of three years before, only now I was more intensely aware of it. Faces and voices of old acquaintances looked and sounded familiar, and yet we did not understand each other. Something had come between us.[2]

In school, as elsewhere, the veteran, who has had his belly full of discipline, rebels against authority. Teachers, accustomed to their own strange world in which they maintain without too much trouble their ill-defined authority over a room-full of fraternity men, foot-ball players, nonentities and big men on the campus, do not quite know how to cope with this surly and unpredictable fellow who comes back from the wars, who sits apathetically through a dozen good lectures and then reacts with violence to some casual remark. To the veteran, the professor is just another civilian who has not been anywhere or seen anything, who does not know war and therefore does not know much. But the teacher who can establish a favorable relationship with the veteran finds in him a confused and bewildered boy in need of help. When such a relationship arises, there is no longer any question of authority.

The moral atmosphere that the veteran establishes on the campus is hardly conducive to serious study. Vera Brittain notes that her war generation upon return to civilian life continued to be obsessed by the "desperate feeling that life was short." They had brought with them from the trenches the philosophy of eat, drink, and be merry, for tomorrow we probably get our heads blown off. And over them all hovered an "inexplicable sense of urgency" which led "to a greedy grasping of the second-rate lest the first-rate should never materialize."[3] The description is accurate, but the sense of urgency is not inexplicable. The transition from short-term to long-term adjustments is most difficult. Ordinarily we can

2 Pierre Van Paassen, *Days of Our Years*. Hillman-Curl, 1939, p. 91.
3 Vera Brittain, *Testament of Youth*. Macmillan, 1933, p. 498.

overcome the reckless hedonism of the young by means of our elaborately organized moral system of threats and bribes. War changes all that with its gladiator psychology, its *morituri* mentality, its state of mind of those about to die. That state of mind dies hard. "Extraordinary creatures, you young people," says a character of Remarque. "The past you hate, the present you despise, and the future is a matter of indifference."

Their Difficulty in Adjusting to School

Return to school brings the veteran into contact with a younger age group. The fellowship of veterans and of post-war youth is not altogether congenial. Post-war youth is worse than indifferent to the veteran; it resents him and is antagonistic to him. The veteran cannot understand that these younger men are jealous because they have been cheated of their war, or that they are disorganized because they grew to maturity under the confusing conditions of war. He does not share the normal interest of college boys in the undergraduate culture. He cannot get as excited as they do about football, fraternities, freshman rules, hell week, or dunking people in the pond. He has few convictions concerning the best kind of fraternity rushing. In short, it is next to impossible to treat the veteran socially as an undergraduate. Post-war youths, in their turn, find it quite impossible to understand veterans, with their apathies and their intensities, their strange jokes which are not funny at all, and their deep and inexhaustible wells of bitterness. The two generations just do not mix.

Some of these points are illustrated by the following life-history document:

"In the Summer of 1919 I returned to college after an absence of a year, a part of which I had spent in the service. The soldiers were then straggling back to college, and by that time there were some hundreds of us at our midwestern university.

"As I looked about me, I found a number of the boys whom I had known before. There was Leslie N., big and eloquent, destined for the law if he ever managed to complete his college courses. Years before he had confided in me his regret that everything worth saying had already been said. He was sorry there was no room for any more eloquence in the patriotic line which was his specialty. He was very young, but he volunteered for the army and went to

France. He saw some action and got a whiff of gas. When he returned to college, he was still the same jovial, self-confident fellow as before, but with an under layer of hardness and cynicism that had not been visible in the earlier days. He went out for football, and found himself in poor condition. He called the coach aside to explain that he had been in France and had been living high. 'I see,' said the coach, 'all the vices with the possible exception of homosexuality.' Only the coach did not call it homosexuality. I believe Leslie was finally dropped from the squad, and I am sure he did not care very much. I know he did little school work that year.

"The group with which I was most *en rapport* was composed of two other veterans, a non-veteran, and myself. There was Walt, who had been an aviator. He had been in France and had crashed a couple of times. He had all the usual yarns about the Paris seen by the young aviators, some French post-cards, and a few magazines. That year he was a restless and uneasy instructor in mathematics; his salary was quite small. Then there was Tom, the disabled soldier. He had picked up a piece of shrapnel in his leg because he guessed wrong and walked on the wrong side of the road. Army doctors had already performed seventeen operations on him but his leg was not well. He walked with a limp and had an open sore from which pus came out occasionally. Just a freshman, he was intellectually the least developed of the group—but this child had been in hell. As an infantryman, he had seen a great deal of the war. He had also been in many government hospitals; he had little to say of the more serious aspects of hospital life, but he loved to tell of his conquests among the nurses.

"There was Martin, the civilian. He had tried after graduation from college to get into some branch of the service, but all had turned him down because he was too light. Highly intelligent, sensitive, literate, quick and sure of himself, he had mastered his environment and solved his problems, but at the cost of suppressing his ambitions. He was content to be a small-time teacher, or so he maintained. To him, ambition was a snare and a delusion. He was taking work toward an M.A. in Education, although he regarded it as unspeakable balderdash. He fancied himself as a roué; he thought he was hard and sophisticated on the subject of women, but actually he was extremely susceptible to nice young girls. His expressed aim in life was to get married, buy a seven passenger automobile, and have enough children to fill all the seats. He never managed to make it quite clear what pleasure he expected to derive from this life-plan, but it was one way of expressing his contempt for the world. Then there was myself, a Senior and by no means sure just what I wanted to make of myself.

"No one had ever told us about the Lost Generation, but all of our little group belonged to it. All of us tried to manage our affairs in such a way as never to be caught studying, and yet we all got good grades. To be caught studying was thought to be a disgrace. Only saps worked; only morons need to study. It was better not even to buy text-books. A very occasional trip to the library was permissible, provided that one did not overdo the matter. Writing letters or term papers was also permissible. On Sundays we all got together and walked to a hotel a couple of miles away for a dinner a little better than usual, away from the collegiate atmosphere. Then we would all go to Walt's room and talk.

"We all agreed that if a person could have everything he wanted for a couple of years, and then die painlessly, and if possible unexpectedly, from a bullet in the brain, that would be a splendid bargain; we talked of this possibility a great deal. We used to ask one another whether, for say ten thousand dollars, we would kill the harmless gentleman walking on the other side of the street, and the answer was always yes of course we would. Half-seriously we planned crimes such as bank-robberies. The hitch was that we were all intelligent enough to realize that it would be necessary to make a very good haul in order to profit from a crime; otherwise it would just not pay. We also realized that we knew nothing of the technique of crime, which was a specialized business which we hesitated to enter just as we should have hesitated to go into the automobile business without knowing more about it, and so our criminality remained a pleasing phantasy.

"As I see it now, we were trying like so many others of the Lost Generation to find some way to avoid the piece-meal sale of our lives—bodies, minds. We were trying to avoid the sordid day-by-dayness of the ordinary career by making one gigantic sale all at once. And since we had learned that the ideals for which our generation had been asked to sacrifice its arms, legs, eyes, lungs and peace of mind were the utmost nonsense, and the men who had sold us those ideas were crooks and frauds, it was an interesting idea to try to make our one big sale to the devil himself.

"Work, in the ordinary sense of the term, we abhorred, although most of us enjoyed using our minds. In spite of our inclinations in that direction, our little group went on no sprees and staged no debauches. We were all poor. Tom, with his disability pay, was probably the richest of our group. We had never heard of Freud's famous advice to young men, 'Be continent, but under protest,' but we followed it to the letter. I was much attached to those boys. We got together once after leaving school. After that one reunion, I never saw any of them again.

"We soldiers at the university thought we should organize. We had many meetings at which we made speeches concerning the desirability of organizing and having regular meetings. I do not remember just what the advantages of organization were supposed to be but I know I made quite a number of speeches on the subject. At these meetings there was no talk about our successful crusade to make the world safe for democracy. If anyone had dared to talk such rot he would have been hooted down. When the Legion came along, we all joined it. It cost a very small sum at the time.

"As students, we veterans made life unpleasant for some of the well-meaning gentlemen who taught us. It happened that I was in the one class in the university which caused more trouble than any other. The teacher was small, pot-bellied, and was beginning to lose his hair. There were about fifty or sixty ex-service men in his class, and he made the mistake of attempting to bully us.

"He began by inquiring about our home towns. He intended to assign each of us a project concerning his home community. Then he made supposedly humorous comments concerning those communities. The class began to become restive. He felt that this would be a good time to throw in a little fight talk.

" 'Now if any of you fellows think you are going to get by with anything, you're going to be fooled,' he said, walking up and down in front of the class and strutting a little. 'You fellows have got to work in here just the same as anybody else. I won't let any of you get by with anything. I'm the teacher, and I can flunk the whole class if I have to. Just buckle down and do what I tell you and everything will be all right.'

"This was just what we were looking for, a fight. I mentioned a common barnyard mixture which often figured in our conversation in those days, mentioned it quite loudly and without moving my lips, as I had learned to do in the Navy. The class roared. From then on, he never had any control over us. Every class was a pandemonium. The whole time was spent in a futile attempt to maintain order and to restore his sadly damaged dignity. He kept threatening to flunk the whole class. We knew he could never get by with that. Anyhow, we had been threatened before. People had threatened us with violence and sudden death, with court martial, imprisonment, dishonorable discharge, and execution at sunrise. We just couldn't get much worried about his threats. Then he made a great tactical error. He offered to organize another class, a tutoring class, in which for a consideration he would teach us enough to pass the course in about five hours. Instantly we took advantage of this error. Letters appeared in the college paper pointing out that something was wrong with a professor who could teach a subject in five hours, for extra pay, but failed to teach it in forty-eight class hours in return for his regular salary. We made things very unpleasant for the unfortunate man, and felt very virtuous about it. In the end he had to pass everybody.

"I have since come to believe that the university authorities were anxious to get rid of us. This was certainly a reasonable attitude on their part. They were most generous in the granting of credits for military service, and they relaxed other rules to the best of their ability. The university must have been sadly disorganized anyhow, what with the loss of the faculty and the difficulty of obtaining replacements through the war years, the insane period of the SATC, (Students' Army Training Corps,) and finally the influx of unmanageable ex-soldiers. I obliged the authorities by taking my degree and leaving at the end of the term."

The above story has some significance because it shows that the schools and colleges, if they are to handle the veteran successfully, must make special preparations for his return. There must be some adaptation of the curriculum and other requirements in order to give veterans the kind of training they want and can profit from. Teachers and administrators must learn something of veteran psychology, if they are to avoid such mistakes as those chronicled above. Dean John L. Bergstresser, of the College of the City of New York, has pointed out that many of the younger faculty members will also be veterans who bring with them certain problems of their own.[4]

Estimates as to the number of veterans who will return to school or college after the war vary greatly, but there will doubtless be hundreds of thousands. If the schools are willing and able to make the necessary adaptations—as they probably are—we may be sure that the educational environment is the best place for many, if not most, of the younger veterans.

----

[4] In a paper presented to a four-state conference of college administrators and guidance workers at Columbia University, April 22, 1944.

Types of Veterans: Disabled, Professional, Normal

W AR does different things to different men. It disables one, unbalances the mind of a second, pauperizes a third, and makes a fourth write great literature to ease his tortured soul. Every type of veteran has his own characteristic problems of adjustment.

The Disabled: Society's Greatest Responsibility

The disabled veteran is the man for whom the war never comes to an end. He is the bitterest veteran, and the one whose claim upon society is greatest. More than any other old soldier, he is in danger of pauperization.

The war never ends for the disabled veteran because he carries a reminder of it in his body. His arm, leg, or eye is gone, and he wages an unceasing struggle to live without it. He must inevitably shape his life and adjust his personality to his disability. In everything he does or thinks or dreams he must remember his handicap.

The shock visited upon the wounded soldier is the greatest which the human body is ever called upon to resist or the human mind to endure. At one moment a man is at the peak of his physical powers, a hardened young athlete capable of running miles with a heavy pack, going without food, sleeping in a fox-hole, or killing his enemy with his bare hands. At the next moment, he is a hopeless cripple wedded to pain and condemned to live with his deformity the rest of his life. Laurence Stallings tells of a wounded captain. He was pulling a lanyard when he was struck and he woke up in the hospital addicted to morphine. He was never able to find out what hit him.

Naturally the disabled veteran is the bitterest of all. He is the

159

one who has paid the price of war. It began with his pain, which was his and his alone, which no one could take from him or share with him. Many writers on war have told of the bitter look of wounded men, and of their pessimistic words. We read of the miracles of modern medicine that save all but a few of the wounded and we forget that every wounded man must still experience a great deal of intense suffering, that pain must be his companion for weeks and months on end. The disabled veteran is not a fool; he knows that his society sent him on a dangerous mission and his quite personal agony is a result of that mission. Many a disabled veteran knows very well what life holds for him. Aware that he can never again lead a normal life, he refuses to deceive himself about it. He knows pain will never quite leave him, no employer will ever have him except for pity, no woman but for pay. No little baby will pit its tiny strength against his fingers, because there is only a hook on the end of his arm. No child will ever love him; there will be no child. Nasty, brutish, short—his life, his breath, his temper.[1]

The disabled veteran has always had a hospital experience. Having suffered some months of pain and helplessness, he has seen and been a part of a great deal of human misery. A military hospital can never be a pleasant place. After the horrors of the dressing station whither the bleeding stumps and remainders of men are carried, one must endure the hospital where those pieces of men fight the long battle against putrefaction and try to emerge with as large a stump of arm, as much of a leg, as good an eye as circumstances permit. Hospitals are better now than they once were. During the Civil War, the dressing stations were little more than butcher shops and the hospitals hardly different from pest-houses. The Civil War doctors, who loved to amputate, sharpened their knives on the soles of their shoes, stood in blood, worked with their arms spattered with blood up to their elbows, and stacked the amputated limbs in neat piles outside the door. Doctors knew nothing of antiseptics in those days, and so the wound almost always infected, and the patient lay in the hospital with a few hundred others while letting nature take its highly odoriferous course.

---

[1] Note the frequency of violent and lawless acts by disabled veterans. Current newspapers carry the story of an attempted assault on John L. Lewis by two disabled veterans. Crime statistics show a high percentage of disabled veterans who become criminal.

Many writers have described life in a hospital. The patient's field of attention is narrowed, being dominated by pain and minute awareness of the state of his body. Social contacts are few but intensely meaningful. One adjusts to invalidism and learns the tricks of getting by. If he pretends not to know or understand about morphine, he gets it to ease his pain. He knows that the doctor talks to him in a certain way when he is about to insert a probe. He comes to evaluate and resent the professional cheerer-uppers who walk along the aisles, the "hedge-rows of misery," and demand great, big smiles.[2] In the long months of pain and uncertainty, one acquires patterns of thinking and feeling which gradually become inflexible. The disabled veteran is more emotionally intense and unstable than other veterans, a condition that probably begins in the hospital.

The task of readjustment for the disabled veteran is that of reestablishing normal social and occupational relationships in spite of handicaps. The community accepts him readily enough, but family and job relationships are problematical. Understandably enough, the disabled are at a great disadvantage in relations with women. Many are completely unfitted for family life both in physique and in attitudes. Others are abnormally sensitive about their handicaps and establish sex relationships with difficulty. Psychological and psychiatric guidance could probably help in such matters, in so far as any help at all is possible.

The rehabilitation program for disabled veterans after World War I was supposed to help them attain occupational readjustment. The fundamental idea was sound: to retrain the veteran in an occupation in which his disability would not be a handicap.[3] He must be retrained in other ways as well. It takes skill to walk on artificial legs and to make the most of a piece of an arm. The badly disabled must make a sort of profession of living with their disability. Necessarily, life adjustments revolve around it.

A part of the adjustment of the disabled veteran consists of acquiring social rôles, attitudes, and rationalizations clustering around his disability and having the function of helping to make it bear-

2 One of the best hospital stories was written by Laurence Stallings. See "Vale of Tears," in *Men at War*, edited by Ernest Hemingway, Crown, 1942. Stallings' satire of the YMCA man is vicious, but it reflects an attitude shared by many at the time. It is part of the soldier's attitude toward men of talk.

3 The shortcomings of this program are analyzed elsewhere. See below our chapter "Some Spectacular Failures in Helping Veterans."

able. Inferiority feelings may easily arise around such things, especially if the person had a previous tendency in that direction. This may lead to over-compensation, and to the insufferable, uncertain combination of pride, insecurity, and aggression so often seen in the crippled and the deformed. If, however, the defect does not give rise to psychological compensation, but merely to acceptance of the handicap at its face value as a disabling injury, it may lead to pauperization.

It is undoubtedly better for the disabled veteran to develop a compensatory drive, and to develop a structure of attitudes and rationalizations to minimize his handicap. Part of the process of helping him to adjust is to show him what he can make of his life in spite of a handicap and to suggest plausible rationalizations. This involves the formation of social rôles that enable one to make the most of what one has and to fend off pity. That is the function of the cripple's smile, which interposes a hard, bright cheerfulness between him and the person who might otherwise offer him useless sympathy. The smile also, of course, gives the last touch of pathos to the cripple's appeal, though one cannot say whether or not the cripple is usually aware of this.

McGonegal and Gibson: Two Remarkable Veterans

Charles McGonegal, one of the great disabled veterans of World War I, now spends much of his time in helping the disabled of World War II to overcome their difficulties. He has no hands, only bright steel claws, but he can do incredible things with them. *Time* magazine recently printed a character sketch of McGonegal, and described his methods with the disabled.

In December 1917 Private McGonegal left Hoboken with 12,500 others aboard the Leviathan, seabound on her maiden voyage as a transport under the American flag.

So McGonegal, of North Dakota, who had known only prairies, horses, steam engines and a whirl through training camps, went to France. He arrived in the Toul sector on January 19, 1918, where his outfit relieved some Moroccan soldiers near Beaumont. On a clear day the American could see the city of Metz. They said to each other that sooner or later they'd knock the damn place down.

McGonegal's one bother was what to do about a diamond ring he wore on his left hand. If he got killed, it should go back to his family. It had been his meal ticket on critical fiscal occasions. McGonegal made a small leather pouch, sewed the ring in it, and hung it around his neck against his dog tags. Then he felt better.

On the morning of February 3, 1918, McGonegal went out as a grenadier opening the way for wiring parties. The Germans signaled back for a barrage. As McGonegal fumbled for another hand grenade, shrapnel struck his head. He sagged down. When he rallied he tried to prop himself on his hands, to rise. But he found his arms were gone just below the elbows.

Later, at Field Hospital No. 13, they found he had eight teeth missing, a bad mouth wound, a fracture of the skull, both knees splintered and 102 other small wounds, cuts and burns.

The doctors gave him the leather pouch with the diamond ring.

When he got out of the hospital, with two artificial arms, he took a business course and started selling insurance. He worked in a lumber yard, drove a truck, did clerical work in Los Angeles, worked for a utilities company. For four years he was postmaster of Bell, California. Now he is national field secretary for the American Legion, is married, with a couple of sons, and has a ranch.

Last week he went out to Walter Reed Hospital, in Washington, as he goes around to many hospitals where sit young ex-soldiers without hands, and without much hope. He did a a few of the things he is used to doing nearly every day. He did them with ease. He took a box of matches out of his pocket and lit his cigaret. He used a telephone. He wrote a good hand, in pen and pencil. He handled a pack of cards. He showed the goggle-eyed boys how to do these things. He talked to them all.

"But say," said one of the boys who had lost an arm, "what about when you go to dance with a girl? Do you put a hand like that around her?"

McGonegal's eyes flashed. He called in a nurse and did a few turns around the floor with her. It looked fine.

"You must come to understand," said McGonegal to the boy, "that warmth comes from the heart and not from the hands anyway."

He will go to six more Army and Navy hospitals between now and April, and spend a week with the boys at each of them. His elder son is overseas now.[4]

4 *Time*, Feb. 14, 1944.

A further story is told of McGonegal and his methods. A boy was invalided home without arms. He sat at home, alone and bitter. His mother tried to talk to him, but failed to draw him out. The boy attended one of McGonegal's meetings. That night he dressed in his best, and got ready to leave the house. With considerable emphasis, he said to his mother, "I'm going out and don't you ask where I'm going."

He was going to see his girl.

Billy Gibson is another disabled veteran who has persuaded a great many crippled young men that they can lead a normal life in spite of a handicap. Before World War I, Gibson was a song and dance man whose specialty was an imitation of George M. Cohan. He lost his right leg in the Argonne. He became so expert in the use of his artificial leg that he was able to return to vaudeville and do all his old impersonations. Later he worked for a manufacturer of artificial limbs. At present he spends his life cheering up crippled soldiers in the hospital wards. First he goes through his dance routine and then he shows the patients that he has an artificial leg. Sometimes he organizes a little tour of the night clubs for the convalescents whom he has trained.

The readjustment of the disabled veteran does not depend entirely upon himself. He must acquire skills and adjust his attitudes, but the world must also be ready to receive him. Industry, particularly big business, has apparently made some progress in this direction. Studies have been made to ascertain what sorts of duties a man can safely and effectively perform after he has lost an arm, a leg, or an eye. Scientific job analysis should be able to accomplish great results in this work. Early experiences with such placements are apparently encouraging.

A piece of a man may do very well for industry, but not for a woman. A crippled man has a problem in his erotic relations. If, like such men as McGonegal and Gibson, he has an unusually attractive and outgoing personality, he may be able to overcome this handicap, but for every one who has such an asset there are a dozen who do not. A physical handicap detracts from a man's bargaining power in relations with women. Very likely there will be a considerable number of veterans who will never be able to make normal family adjustment and will therefore resort to commercialized relations.

In planning our policy for the treatment of disabled veterans, we must also remember that some kinds of disabled men constitute a public health problem. We may expect our veterans to bring back with them some strange diseases, and difficulties may arise in preventing the spread of these diseases. Experience indicates a need for special care in the handling of tuberculous veterans; it is clear that we must make some modifications in present procedures.[5] Cases of tuberculosis among veterans of World War I have remained at a high figure since 1919. Hospital admissions in 1942 numbered 9,658, while $40,000,000 was paid out to 63,000 veterans who suffered partial or total disability because of tuberculosis. The problem is to keep the veterans hospitalized until they are cured. Of the 9,854 discharged from hospitals in 1942, only three per cent could be classified as "medically rehabilitated." Tuberculous veterans go in and out of the hospitals with astonishing ease; there have been 300,000 admissions since World War I. Some veterans have left the hospital and been readmitted as many as twenty-four times, while six to eight admissions are not uncommon. There is no way of forcing or inducing veterans to remain in the excellent hospitals for a full cure, especially since the disability payments provide an extra $50 a month for the wife or other person attending a patient who elects to be treated at home. But as long as the tuberculous veteran remains uncured and at large, he is a menace to the health of the community, and some way must be found to induce him to undergo the treatment necessary for full recovery.

The Veteran Who Is Psychoneurotic

It is perhaps justifiable to group together all those who in one way or another have broken down psychologically as a result of war. These are the ones to whom the term, shell-shock, used to be applied; a somewhat misleading but useful term. It is obvious that many different kinds of cases, in fact most of the nervous disorders known in civilian life, are included in such a category, and each kind of disorder has its own prognosis.

We have not as yet perfected our understanding of these cases, and we do not know how to treat them as effectively as we treat

---

[5] Louis Dublin, "Function of the Health Officer in the Control of Tuberculosis," in *American Journal of Public Health*, Dec. 1933, pp. 1425-1429.

the physically disabled. The facts that we can set down with any assurance about such cases are rather few.

According to current estimates, the armed services were discharging psychoneurotic veterans at the rate of 10,000 cases a month in late 1943 and in early 1944. The army alone has discharged 216,000 veterans for psychoneurosis at the time of writing.[6] By the end of the war this figure will probably be increased by many hundreds of thousands. Neuro-psychiatric breakdowns constitute about thirty per cent of all casualties, but the rate varies from one theatre of war and one military organization to another. If our experience of World War I is repeated, great numbers of psychoneurotic cases will be added to the rolls in the post-war years. Although anxiety states predominate in the current conflict, the neuroses of war are much like the neuroses of peace.

Our past experience with such cases has been discouraging. Of the 67,000 beds in Veterans Administration hospitals, almost half are still occupied by the psychoneurotics of World War I. We have spent a billion dollars on such cases, their cost being sometimes computed at $30,000 a case. Therapy in this field has lagged far behind the rest of medical practice. It is clear that the readjustment of the psychoneurotic is fully as much a social as a medical problem, and the social aspects of the problem have been neglected.

The basis of psychological breakdown in war is ordinarily some pre-existing weakness in the personality. Some attempt has been made to screen out obvious misfits in induction, but suitably trained psychiatrists are few, the needs of military life not too well understood, and the attempt has not been highly successful.

Because the basis of a breakdown is usually a pre-existing weakness, it follows that the prognosis is poorest for those who have the least reason for breaking. For example, the man who cracks up in combat has a better chance of recovery than the one who breaks in training. The writer has often talked with shell-shocked veterans of World War I, and it seemed clear enough that the stresses and strains that broke them would not have harmed the ordinary man.

The circumstances of combat have much to do with the incidence of psychoneurotic casualties. When, as on Guadalcanal or the

6 Statement by Col. William Claire Menninger, as reported in *Time*, May 29, 1944.

Anzio beachhead, the same troops are kept for long periods in a severe and apparently almost hopeless fight, when the men get the idea that they have been sacrificed or forgotten, the number of breakdowns is large. The leadership of a military unit also has a profound effect upon the incidence of mental breakdown. Jittery officers can send men to the hospitals in droves. Good leadership, such as that furnished by Carlson to his Gung Ho raiders—a highly selected group, to be sure—can keep the rate of breakdown minimal, even in spite of severe combat conditions.

Where men of previously stable personality break under the strain of combat, their condition may be diagnosed as traumatic war neurosis. Kardiner, in his authoritative work on the subject, notes that the symptoms of true traumatic neurosis vary according to the time when they are observed.[7] He differentiates between acute, transitional, and stabilized forms of symptoms. Symptoms of the acute period include such things as: shock and manifestations of terror, coma, mania, delirium, paralyses, and disturbances of the senses. In two or three weeks the transition is made to the stabilized form, which is usually similar to one of the well-known types of neurosis or psychosis.

Although these stabilized neuroses or psychoses can assume almost any of the forms known in time of peace, most of the traumatic neuroses, according to Kardiner, have a constant core of symptoms which are readily recognizable. The individual becomes fixated on the trauma, and alters his conception of his self and the outer world. He has a typical dream life; he re-lives his terrible experiences in dreams. There is a contraction of the general level of functioning, irritability, and a proclivity to explosive aggressive reactions. Those who have had experience with such persons will have no difficulty in identifying these symptoms. The tendency toward explosive aggression sometimes gets the psychoneurotic veteran in trouble with the law; of this tendency the current newspapers furnish many examples.

For cases of traumatic neurosis, early diagnosis and treatment are most important. But under combat conditions, early treatment is often difficult if not impossible, and in the period intervening between breakdown and treatment the symptoms, like other habits, become rigid and stabilized; we say that they are fixated. The

7 Abram Kardiner, *The Traumatic Neuroses of War*. Hoeber, 1941.

difficulty of giving early treatment is greatly increased by our failure to foresee the number of psychiatric breakdowns that would be produced by the conditions of modern war. If after this war we follow our traditional policy toward veterans, which is to neglect the disabled for several years, hundreds of thousands of psychoneurotics will be ruined beyond hope of cure.

The Choices in Dealing with Psychoneurotics

A principal difficulty in the readjustment of the psychoneurotic is the public attitude toward him. While the physically disabled veteran is in general kindly regarded by society, our attitude toward those broken in mind is far less sympathetic. There is a stigma connected with psychological breakdown, even a suspicion of malingering.

The notion that psychoneurotics are malingerers is probably wholly false. Medical science has progressed sufficiently to be able to weed out such cases effectively. Few deliberate malingerers get by, but the layman is to some extent justified in his suspicion of the psychoneurotic. It is true that such breakdowns result fully as much from a man's own pattern of attitudes as from the exigencies of war. The ethics of the matter is obscure.

Pensions for the psychoneurotic present a nice problem. On the surface, it seems reasonable to suppose that society has just as much of an obligation to the man whose mind has broken as to him whose body has been maimed—and in some cases it undoubtedly has. But the pension for the psychoneurotic may give him a psychic and social gain from neurosis that will make recovery more difficult. To put the matter rather crudely, it may come about that a man makes his living by having a war neurosis; it is his means of gaining distinction in the world, his excuse for not subjecting himself to the struggles of life. Pensions may thus do positive harm to the psychoneurotic. Furthermore, if there is an extensive development of pensions for psychoneurotics after the war, this will certainly create ill-feeling, because the public will realize that most of these men have made only the slightest of contributions to the war and that a great many of them would have broken anyhow. Institutional care, as an alternative to pensions, also involves risks and disadvantages.

The best solution would seem to be some development of social case work which would give help where it will aid recovery and withhold it if that will aid recovery but still recognize the need for relieving human misery wherever it exists. Anyone who can invent a successful social therapy for the psychoneurotics of war will rescue many lives from ruin and save the nation billions of dollars.

In some respects, the popular attitude that regards the psychoneurotic veteran with some suspicion is partly justified. They are probably poor marriage risks. Circumstances alter cases, and the veterans themselves differ greatly, but the odds are against them. Similarly, for certain jobs, especially in the field of human relationships, and for jobs that involve great psychic strain, psychoneurotics are suspect. Employers report, however, that where a psychoneurotic veteran is reemployed *at his former job* he usually performs very satisfactorily.

It is well to remember, also, that there are psychotics and former psychotics and neurotics beyond counting, who escape diagnosis in ordinary life. Much of the work of the world, and much of the very best work, is done by persons not in the best of mental health. It would be most unfortunate for the veteran if he were made the victim of discrimination simply because his case has been diagnosed.

Pauperized Veterans: Society's Handiwork

The pauperized veteran, a well-known social type, is a person who capitalizes on the pathos of real or supposed military service to obtain charity. Well known today, the soldier-turned-beggar is a familiar historical figure.

Some veterans, of course, would have become paupers if there had been no war. There are others who become paupers because they find the transition to civilian life difficult, learn the technique of begging, and become pauperized.

The basis of such pauperization is often some real trouble, a minor disability that makes it hard to earn a living or an injustice that sours a man and makes him quit trying. While struggling with his problem, the veteran gets no help, or not enough help, or the wrong kind of help. He learns that he can live acceptably on his small gains from appeals to charity, and henceforward makes his living in that way. He loses his self-respect as a worker and producer, and gains status and self-respect in the world of panhandlers and grifters, and then works no more. "Only saps work."

A specific example of a pauperizing situation is the following: In 1919, the soldiers were turned loose with sixty dollars dismissal pay—at that time enough to buy a suit of clothes but no more. They received little effective help in their quest for employment. Many real disabilities went uncompensated. There was no way of doing justice to the veteran in those days, but there were many charities and there were many kind-hearted passers-by. This was a perfect recipe for producing pauperism. When it becomes known, as it did in 1919, that the veterans have not been treated fairly, and that many of them are necessitous through no fault of their own, great pathos attaches to the veteran's plea. "Buddy, I just got discharged from the army and I ain't got a job. Can you spare a dime for a cup of coffee and a roll?" This is the situation most favorable for the would-be panhandler.

It would not be difficult to prevent such a situation from arising. All we need to do is to give the veteran adequate help in the period immediately following a war. Such is certainly no more than his due. While adequate help, intelligently given, will not pauperize, the lack of such help, as experience has shown a thousand times over, will pauperize. The kind of help the veteran needs, and wants, is the kind that helps people to help themselves. Unfortunately, veterans have not usually received it.

Those Who Make a Career of Being Veterans

There are certain men who, after a war, make a kind of profession of being veterans. Their stock in trade is their war experience, their greatest asset their ability to appeal to the sentiments of fellowship among veterans.

Status as a veteran is useful in politics and in certain businesses and professions. It is valueless to the farmer, who depends upon the bounty of nature and is but little beholden to other men. The politician, however, may use his veteran status by running for office with the backing of the powerful veterans' organizations, or a school administrator may depend upon veteran status as a means of gaining and keeping favor. In such businesses as insurance, where there is little price competition and everything depends upon social contacts, it is a great advantage to be a veteran. It is natural that such men, in their public relations, should make a great deal of being veterans and should organize their lives around that aspect of personality.

Frequently, the professional veteran is disabled. In such a case his honorable wounds and disabilities, however great a personal handicap, become a professional asset. Such a man is McGonegal, who has made a profession of helping other cruelly wounded men. Such a man was the famous Corporal Tanner of G.A.R. days who had lost both legs in action and thus made, as Powell remarks, "a pathetically impressive appearance as a veteran." Tanner was for a time Commissioner of Pensions under President Harrison, and though he soon had to be dismissed, he was in office long enough to make good on his promise to drive a six-mule team through the Treasury in the interest of the veterans.[8]

There is no earthly reason why a veteran, especially a crippled one, should not turn his war record to advantage if he can. Often the manner in which he does this is entirely praiseworthy, as when a disabled veteran spends his time in helping others. Unfortunate political results sometimes ensue when the professional, in order to consolidate his leadership, persuades other veterans to demand things that they do not need.

"The Lost Generation": Professional Veterans

The writers of the so-called "lost generation" were also professional veterans in their way. They capitalized on their war experiences by writing books against war.

The term, "the lost generation," was supposed to have been originated by Gertrude Stein, referring particularly to Hemingway, and it is one of history's little jokes that a woman of whom the general public thinks only in terms of her contributions to gib-

---

[8] James Tanner (1844-1927), better known as Corporal Tanner, was a famous figure among veterans in the last century. At Second Manassas he received a wound necessitating the amputation of both legs just below the knees. He learned to walk with artificial legs and he studied stenography. He was summoned to the house where Lincoln lay dying, to take notes on the examination of witnesses of the assassination. He became a lawyer, office-holder, perennial candidate, and a particularly active lobbyist on behalf of veterans. He was very active in the Grand Army of the Republic.

berish should have coined the best descriptive phrase of the decade. The term came to be applied to a whole group of young writers who wrote prolifically about their war and post-war experiences. Representative of the group were such men as Hemingway, Dos Passos, Stallings, E. E. Cummings, Graves, Sassoon, Gibbs, Aldington, and, among the Germans, Remarque. Vera Brittain told the woman's story of the war.

Profoundly disillusioned about war, these veterans wrote to declare the truth insofar as it had been given to them to see the truth. They cried out *de profundis*, wrote their books "with their heart's blood." Many of them went to war while still quite young, and lost their youthful idealism in the blood and muck of battlefields and hospitals. They beheld horrors and those horrors shocked them into writing some great literature. Several of them were wounded or maimed, a reminder that tragedy for the individual is sometimes the good fortune of the race.

Cynicism pervaded the work of the lost generation. That was because they started out as idealists; for the cynic, their kind of cynic, is merely the disillusioned idealist. They taught that war is a great crime, a fraud upon the innocence of the young, a plague, a holocaust, a desecration, a pointless slaughter, a meaningless catastrophe, and that after the war came nothing good. "The conditions are that the winner shall take nothing." But when they had said that they had told all they knew. Their wisdom carried them no farther.

It is significant that so many of the American representatives of the Lost Generation became expatriates. They were that relative rarity, refugees from the United States of America, refugees not from persecution but from boredom. They were bored with their native land and frustrated by it because war had destroyed their zest for life, they were tired of virtue because virtue had betrayed them. They did not escape boredom by living in Paris or by cultivating, as so many of them did, the flowers of evil. The lack was in themselves. They needed a cause to give meaning to their lives, but they were disillusioned about causes, as all members of that wasted generation had a right to be, and so they made a sort of cause of not believing in causes and bored themselves in the attempt to be earnestly not in earnest about anything.

The reaction against war among veterans of World War I was

strong for a time. The writers of the lost generation symbolized and spearheaded that reaction. Even in Germany there were those who rallied to the slogan, "Nie Wieder Krieg." (Never war again.) The League against War and Fascism, led by the French veteran Henri Barbusse, once claimed millions of American members. But this group of sincere war-opposers was never more than a minority in any nation, albeit a very vociferous minority, and a great many members of that minority were among the first to fall in line when the drums began to beat a second time. The members of the Lost Generation hated war, but certainly not in the way in which the Quakers hate it. Hemingway, after his early works debunking war, devoted himself to sex, death, and sadism, and finally came around in *For Whom the Bell Tolls* to the point of glorifying a war of which he approved. When the time came for the next crusade, most of the other writers reversed their pacifistic position of the 1930s. To the best of our knowledge, Vera Brittain is the only member of the group who is a war-objector in the present conflict.

Hemingway and the other lost but very vocal sheep made a life adjustment of publicizing their maladjustment and that of their generation. They were nevertheless sincere, and they spoke for a great many who lacked their gift of tongues. They spoke for all "whom the storm-winds battered."

The Majority of Veterans Readjust—In Time

The great majority of veterans work out a fairly good adjustment, usually after a considerable lapse of time and often at considerable cost. They are acutely maladjusted for a time, then they build up habits and sentiments of civilian living, and after a while cease to feel maladjusted. But probably habit comes first, and the realization of the habit later.

Veterans who have had combat experience are very likely to display some psychoneurotic symptoms at first. Many veterans tell of their evil dreams in the first few months after demobilization, when all the horrors of the battlefield, successfully exorcised in the daytime, come back to haunt them at night. Many have pronounced startle reactions and jump violently at sudden noises. After World War I many veterans had a strong tendency to fall to the ground when they heard noises that sounded like shells.

By displaying an abnormal apathy or an unexpected intensity of emotional reaction, the veteran may show himself out of touch with his environment, a very general type of maladjustment even among those without front-line experience. A soldier who had served only a few months in a training camp returned to his home and the next day went down to the railroad station of the small town in which his parents lived. While he was there, he saw an old man and a little boy start to drive across the tracks in their horse and buggy just after a freight train passed by. Suddenly the express train roared down on them from the opposite direction. It struck them. The civilians screamed and ran about excitedly. The soldier, emotionally detached from a situation in which he was powerless to help, calmly and curiously observed the spectacle, then observed himself and wondered what manner of man he had become. Many veterans complain of this failure to find in themselves the proper emotional reactions, or of finding emotions much too intense for the occasion.

Bernard De Voto tells the following story:

"One afternoon in June of 1919 the parents and the younger sister of an ex-soldier met the train that was bringing him home from Yaphank. He came slowly down the Pullman steps—there he was—he had the same number of arms and legs—he had no scars—there were strange symbols on his sleeves and shoulders—and in that heart-pulverizing moment the war was over at last. There followed the tears, the half-syllables, the kissing and hugging and handshaking which could not even try to express the inexpressible. The family knew that there were no words for what was in their hearts and yet, all the way across town in the family Ford, they were tensely waiting for him to say something—for this magic to be distilled in speech. But he had nothing to say. He merely sat stiffly, choked with a silence that rapidly grew more frightening to his family. Then at a certain corner he stirred a little. The family's breath caught, they strained forward, and the soldier said —accusingly, belligerently, in the tone of one used to giving orders— 'Good God, hasn't Bill Gleeson painted his drugstore yet?'

"That is one ex-soldier's memory of homecoming. The words meant nothing but he has come to understand how and why they were discharged in irrational anger at these strangers who sat in the Ford with him, at the foreign town he found himself in, and at all the aliens he had encountered since he had marched up Fifth Avenue with his division in a blizzard of torn paper. The words had no significance at all. Except that somewhere between Apremont and the eastern fringe of the Argonne Forest he had lain for some hours in a shellhole with a recently wounded man and two men long dead, while German artillery fire moved up and down and round about, reaching for him personally. Lying there, he had vividly remembered how the paint was scaling from Bill Gleeson's store front and how often Bill had said he was going to clean it up. While the counter-barrage searched for him he had decided that a decent regard for the opinion of mankind required Bill to keep that promise. But Bill had not kept it—and peace, the home town, America had let that soldier down.

"He has lived to understand also why he was never able to explain that trivial irritation to those whom it shocked." [9]

Work helps the soldier to readjust. He forms habits of work after a time, and these become a basis of self-respect and dignity. Work necessitates social relations and slowly restores the soldier to the communicative process of society.

The family plays a most important part in readjusting the veteran. Family members make allowances for his mental states and help him to find the road back. If he marries—and is fortunate in his marriage—the experiences of marriage and parenthood enable him to put his military experience behind him.

In all of this, it is probable that the veteran works out his adjustment on the habit-level first, and only later—often much later—realizes that he has become a thorough-going civilian. Justice Holmes—the soldier whom the elder Holmes tried so hard to find after he had been wounded in one of the battles of the Civil War—certainly made a success of his adjustment to civilian living, but he is said to have thought of himself also as a soldier throughout his life.

[9] Bernard De Voto, "Older than God," in *Woman's Day*, June 1944.

Veterans Stick Together in The Post-War Years

A N informant has supplied a story concerning the strange behavior of a young man newly returned from a war:

"It was some time during the winter of '37 when I got word that Joe was coming home from Spain, where he had been fighting with the Loyalists for over two years. Although he and his wife had never been intimate friends of mine, I had been tremendously impressed by the heroic idealism of this young man, who had given up a very good job, a wife whom he loved dearly, and possibly his professional career.

"I went down to the dock with some other friends to see him as soon as the ship got in. Our greetings were short, at that time, because we were all aware of the desire for quiet that he must have had—and also for privacy with his wife. However, although at the time I was surprised beyond words, his wife, who is a psychiatric social worker, invited the group of us over to their apartment later that very evening. (I realized later that a group of comparative strangers was, in some degree, a necessary buffer to absorb the high tension and hysteria which must have existed between the reunited couple.)

"They lived in an apartment in Chelsea—one large room with a screen at one end, behind which was the kitchenette. When I entered, there were about twelve or fifteen people in the room. But I did not see Joe. I asked his wife, Rose, where he was. She pointed vaguely to the screen. After a few minutes, I went over to the screen, pushed it aside. There, to my surprise, was Joe with three other Battalion veterans. They were still dressed in somewhat military clothes. (I don't think that the Abraham Lincoln Brigade had real uniforms, but I may be wrong.) The one piece of apparel which was uniform was the dark beret that they all still wore—in the house, mind you.

"Their conversation was all: 'Do you remember when,' and

'Do you remember the guy that . . . ' And all these men had just disembarked together. This was Joe's first evening at home in over two years. They stayed huddled behind the screen for the entire time I was there, indifferent—or frightened by the civilians in the living-room proper. At no time was there any feeling of gladness at seeing any of the people who had gathered there to greet Joe. As a matter of fact, he never came out from behind the screen. They stood cramped between a serving table littered with empty coca-cola bottles and withered bits of bologna and a sink loaded with dirty dishes.

"It seemed to me at that time that Joe's world was the world behind the screen, that all of us waiting to see and talk to him— his wife included—were completely unreal to him, terrifying, unimportant. This was particularly impressive because Joe had always been a most out-going man, the type who had always been charmingly gay, a man who could always be depended upon to keep the mood of a group on an enjoyable level.

"These men were all radicals, idealists. They had not been drafted into a war about which they did not know very much. They had a high degree of political awareness, so much so that they had all been willing to risk everything to go and fight for the democracy of a country which meant nothing to them personally. And still, even they felt so cut off from the country and the people they had left here."

They Feel at Home Only with Other Veterans

From the point of view of his wife and his former friends, Joe's behavior was most eccentric. It is, however, easily understandable on the basis of what we have learned about veteran psychology. Almost by definition, the soldiers of the Abraham Lincoln Brigade were men who reacted with unusual violence to ideas and who were therefore willing to sacrifice their lives in order to win freedom for a foreign land; they could resist Fascism, but they could not withstand the impact of the soldier mentality. Joe and his companions stuck together because they still felt the old solidarity, the comradeship of men at arms, and that feeling outweighed all other obligations. They knew and trusted one another, but they had little of either liking or respect for civilians; even these former talkers and idea-lovers had forgotten how to talk to civilians. It is largely this feeling of comradeship toward veterans, combined with strangeness tinged with hostility toward civilians, that causes veterans to stick together in the post-war years.

Other factors contribute to cause the veteran to depend on other veterans for human companionship. Often he feels that he does not receive the recognition he deserves for his military service. Naturally, he has expected to be something of a hero upon his return. He did not conceive this idea without encouragement from others. It has been carefully implanted and tended in his mind. To some extent, the community makes good on its promise to honor the veteran. The first soldiers to return receive excellent treatment. There are parades and fine speeches for the benefit of the young men who have suffered and bled in the training camps. But uniforms soon become commonplace. There are many heroes, and not enough hero-worshipers to go around. By the time the last of the soldiers come home—those who have done the real fighting—their deeds have already been forgotten, or so it seems to them.

A hero of the 1918 A.E.F. tells the following story of his return to New York City:

> When I came back I had all kinds of stripes on my uniform, service stripes, wound stripes, and the insignia of the Fighting Sixty-Ninth, Rainbow Division. I thought everyone would look at me, the great hero. I'll never forget that first ride in the subway. I expected people to show recognition. My uniform told the story of my acts. Well, everyone was busy reading the paper and no one even looked up. I was really disappointed. You see I was with the army of occupation and the war was over for six months when I came back. We had a parade but it was nothing like we had seen in the movies. The guys who didn't see action got the great applause. By the time we got back, the country was fed up with these war heroes. . . . I remember I met a girl I knew and I thought she would treat me like a hero. She acted as though she had seen me the day before.

"Patriots," says Vera Brittain, "especially of the female variety, were as much discredited in 1919 as in 1914 they had been honored." And she adds that perhaps the post-war generation was right in believing that "patriotism had nothing to it, and we pre-war lot were just poor boobs for letting ourselves be kidded into thinking it had." [1] Other returned soldiers tell approximately the same story.

Even while the war continues, the social status of the soldier begins to decline. At the beginning of hostilities, he is welcome everywhere; nothing is too good for him. As time goes on, the relations between soldiers and civilians become embittered. Civilians come to feel that soldiers are an irresponsible and dangerous element in the population—which indeed they sometimes are. Soldiers resent the civilian attitude and circulate the bitter myth about the park with the sign, "Soldiers and dogs keep off the grass." [2] The soldier in training camp cities or the great cities where he spends his furloughs is often thrown upon the lower elements of the population, the fringe of the underworld. These half-world characters cheat him, and he becomes increasingly antagonistic toward civilians. By the end of the war this alienation of the military and civilian elements of the population has gone a long way. Then the soldier becomes a veteran—a "civilian" himself—and returns to his home, bringing with him the soldier's attitude toward civilians.

The fact is that there is no settled and secure place for the veteran in American society. In some primitive societies, a boy does not become a man until he is also a warrior. In ancient Rome and in Sparta every citizen was a warrior and every warrior a citizen. But in our society the returned soldier has good reason to be dissatisfied with his status. He can re-enter the economic order only at the bottom, or on the fringes, like a boy of seventeen or eighteen. If he returns to school, he must become a pupil again, and be subjected to the teacher's whims. In his own family, and in other families, his status is problematic, and his elders at least try tentatively to regulate his habits and his morals. Very possibly the soldier who is a veteran of hard campaigns is still too young to vote. Glory compensates for some of these things, but after a while the supply of glory runs short.

Or it may happen that the veteran returns to a community where the old and young are already at odds, and this fact accentuates

1 Vera Brittain, *Testament of Youth*. Macmillan, 1933, p. 490.
2 Vagts notes that "Even after 1815, under a regulation dating from the days of Charles II, soldiers remained excluded from public parks and gardens in London." Alfred Vagts, *A History of Militarism*. Norton, 1937, p. 155.

his difficulty in building a satisfactory set of social relationships
with persons who are not veterans. In many American communities, the different generations wage unceasing warfare on the subject of recreation. In our society we condone vices only in the old
who can get no pleasure from them. We forbid the young to
cultivate them. But the restless young, who have not as yet gained
a stake in the moral order, demand to be amused, and they constantly find amusements of which their elders disapprove. Into
such a situation the veteran returns with his frantic search for
pleasure. He joins the unassimilated and ungovernable younger
group in rebellion against the elders. The split between the war
generation and the older age groups may persist for years. After
World War I this cleavage was symbolized by widespread disapproval among older persons of the goings-on at American Legion
conventions. Now that Legion members have grown older, their
conventions have become rather tame affairs, to which members
take their wives, and there is no longer any popular disapproval.

Veterans Are Immigrants in Their Native Land

The task of assimilating the veteran into the community is one
of reincorporating him in the communicative process, placing him
economically in such a way as to make the best use of his abilities,
tying him down by membership in the family and other groups,
and arranging for him to take his part in the political deliberations
of the community. When the veteran returns to the civilian world,
his situation is much like that of the immigrant. In fact, the
veteran is a sort of immigrant in his native land. He is like the
immigrant because he has no sure and settled place in society
and because he derives many, if not most, of his social satisfactions
from the company of others of his own kind; partly because he
prefers their society and partly because he does not fit in anywhere
else.

The analogy with the immigrant suggests that the tendency of
veterans to stick together for a time is not altogether unhealthy.
Paradoxical as it may seem, the best way for veterans to establish
relations with the rest of society may be for them to cling to their
own group, to cleave to their own kind, *for a while*. The society
of veterans will thus furnish a sort of causeway leading to normal

social relations, and the veterans will most quickly attain the goal of normal community relations if they make haste slowly.

Our experience with immigrants demonstrates clearly that groups of aliens tend to be assimilated together, and that it is best that it should be so. Early students of immigration were often concerned over the fact that many immigrants cling to their native culture, settle in their own cultural islands, develop their own institutions, have their own banks, schools, churches, social and business associations and even their own newspapers. In this way they seem to resist assimilation. Many persons still believe that it would be better if these immigrants gave up their old culture at once and immersed themselves immediately in the main currents of American life. However, studies of immigrants have repeatedly shown that a period of clinging to the old culture is useful, and that the associations of the foreign-born with each other supply a bridge to American society. It is obviously better to have a foreign language paper in which the foreign-born can read about American political struggles and become familiar with other American ideas than for the native-born to be completely unable to communicate with the immigrants. Furthermore, these foreign colony institutions lessen the degree of personal disorganization in the immigrant. The priest and the elders of the community must speak to the immigrant in his native tongue if they are to reach him at all, and even his economic adjustment may be easier if he makes it in the company of his countrymen.

The analogy with veterans is clear. We must attempt to assimilate the veterans in groups as well as individually. If veterans form their own organizations, which they have a great penchant for doing, then those organizations can be incorporated into the pattern of community life and the veterans with them. Opposition to the veterans' organizations, which has arisen so often in the past, will not prevent those organizations from existing but it may alienate the veteran group from the rest of society.

A further clue furnished by the immigrant analogy concerns the importance of participation in assimilation. We have learned that the key to the assimilation of the immigrant is participation. Here the contrast between European and American methods of assimilation is illuminating. In Europe embittered struggles have taken place for many generations over just one issue, Who is to oppress whom? When one nation has conquered and annexed another, it has often tried to annihilate the culture of the subject people, that is, to assimilate the conquered people by force to the people of the conquerors. If one thing is clear from the study of history, it is that such methods do not work. The Poles have been Germanized and Russianized for many generations, but they remain Poles, the Czechs are stubbornly Czech no matter what the language of their conquerors. In America, none of that. No force. Opportunity. We allow our immigrants to be as foreign as they wish, but we insist that their children be educated and we permit them to send their children to the public schools. If aliens desire to do so, they may become citizens and vote in our elections, but no one forces them to take this step. If immigrants organize themselves into associations, our politicians will bargain with those associations and thus persuade a whole new group of foreign-born to participate in American life. And so it comes about that a free country —albeit corrupt and materialistic—accomplishes without planning or effort what European despotisms have always been unable to do.

With the veteran also, participation is the royal road to assimilation. Let him organize! Let him make his demands and suggestions! No doubt he will sometimes be unreasonable—as who is not?—nevertheless he will have begun to argue and to participate. The ideal outcome would be a gradually widening sphere of participation for the veterans and their organizations. Starting with themselves and their own concerns, such as veterans' relief and the care of the disabled, the veterans would naturally tend to widen their interests through the years, and would soon find themselves participating in wide areas of civilian life. This is the method of assimilation through participation, the method of a free and democratic society.

Entr'acte: Politically, the Veteran Is a Damoclean Sword

ACTION and reaction are equal and opposite: What the veteran does to society is the natural consequence of what society has done to him. The veteran is politically dangerous because army life has given him attitudes that are inconsistent with participation in the normal sort of political life.

Politics is conflict. Every state is at all times an arena of conflict, a struggling confusion of parties, classes, interests, religions, races, and cultures contending for power. The boundaries of the state are determined in conflict; a state may in fact most properly be defined as merely a discrete power system. The uses of state power, the limits of state power, the precedents of justice are all decided not by principles, in the last analysis, but by force or the threat of force. All politics is power politics: there is no other kind.

Conflict the soldier can understand, as can the veteran. It is easy for the veteran to hear, with Justice Holmes, the roar of bargain and of battle.

Politics is conflict—and compromise. Not often in politics do we pursue an advantage to the uttermost. We temper the exercise of power with concessions on the part of the strong to the weak; as the Chinese have it, we try not to break the other man's rice bowl, and we sometimes say it is *politic* to behave so. Justice is not merely, as Thrasymachus believed, the interest of the stronger, but the interest of the stronger in interaction with the interest of the weaker. We usually stop short of ruthlessness because we need the other person; we need his labor and his good will. Hence we do not attempt to destroy him completely but merely to bend him to our uses: we compromise with him. And therefore politics, with its derivatives of law, justice, charters, and constitutions, nearly always involves compromise. In normal times, the art of politics is largely the art of compromising or accommodating conflicts in such a way as to satisfy as large a number of persons as possible. A politician is merely a person who is expert in making such arrangements.

Compromise is hard for the veteran to comprehend or to practice. Especially in the lower ranks, army life does not allow wide latitude for compromise. Tolerance of certain very minor differences, possibly, but no compromise between groups or interests, no bargain, no give-and-take between the soldier's will and the army's commands.

Veterans Believe in Action—Not in Talk

Most of all, politics is argument. Argument is fighting with words, with symbols of morality and of principles. Argument is winning a man's consent by the manipulation of verbal counters, beating down his resistance with words and logic. Politics is argument, the endless talk, talk, talk, of the parliamentarians, the talk that delays action and atrophies the muscles of the executive arm. But it is talk in which everything gets considered, the needs of the many along with the desires of the few.

For argument, the soldier, even the highest soldier, is often incapacitated. In the army world, it is not necessary to win a man's consent by talk or argument; only the words of command, and those stylized into unrecognizability, are necessary in a military system. Argument is taboo; one cannot argue about orders. The soldier cultivates the pure act and loses "the habit of the word."

History is full of great soldiers who lacked the faculty of using words in argument. Moses, though keen in military matters, was slow of speech, with the result that he had to depend unduly upon Aaron, the civilian expert in public relations. Grant was taciturn, Haig notoriously inept in speech. Vagts notes that "Foch used to express himself 'by vehement discharges, like machine-gun explosions, riddling the interlocutor with a hail of short phrases, violently elliptical and one might say apocalyptical.' Akin to him was Kitchener, with his 'rambling and cryptic discourses,' and Manteuffel, the Chief of the Prussian Military Cabinet, of whom it was said 'his knowledge is extremely small, but the little he knows he knows for certain.' " [1] Even the great Napoleon, on the 18th Brumaire, stammered and hesitated before the assembly that he had come to dissolve and had to be rescued by his brother Lucien, the parliamentarian, a phenomenon which Vagts explains by saying that "The only words at the instantaneous service of the officer being those of command, he is not facile in speaking from the platform." [2] In fact the military man has lived too long in the world where the private will of the individual does not count, where no one consents or wins consent but everyone takes or gives orders, and he no longer remembers, if he ever had an occasion to master them, those arts by which one gains the support of others by winning them to one's own way of thinking. That was why Wellington, when he became Prime Minister, was found to be, as Guedalla notes, "defective in the minor art of persuasion."

Officers and soldiers feel themselves above argument with its un-avoidable delays and compromise with its necessary hypocrisies. It is action that counts for the soldier; in war it is often better to do something foolish than to do nothing at all. The soldier learns to act somehow, and quickly, even though what he does may be wrong. Again and again, all through the ages, one reads of the soldier's opinion of politicians, who must live and die by another code: Politicians are talkers not doers, mere time-wasters; they are hypocritical and dishonest because they do not say what they mean or do what they say. For compromise and argument, which are the essence of politics, usually involve some pretence and hypocrisy. For these things the soldier has no talent and with them no patience.

It is difficult for the veteran to comprehend the utility of the long discussions of civilian politics. Clemenceau once attempted to explain the matter to Boulanger: "Since it is necessary to tell you, these same discussions which astound you constitute our honor. They prove above all our eagerness to defend the ideas which we believe just and fertile. These discussions have their inconveniences, but silence has more. Yes, glory to the countries where one speaks! Shame to the countries where one is silent!" [3]

When the veteran, the army-made man, returns to civilian so-

[1] Alfred Vagts, *A History of Militarism*, Norton, 1937, p. 327.
[2] *Ibid.*, p. 326.
[3] Quoted in *ibid.*, p. 325.

ciety, he understands conflict perfectly, compromise less well, discussion and argument hardly at all. He wants action, dislikes talk, distrusts talkers. He is intolerant of the hypocrisies without which politics is impossible. That is enough to make the veteran politically dangerous, but there are yet other reasons why veterans so often disturb the peace of society.

Let us admit that the veteran, this man disgusted with politics and impatient of argument, has a real, a just grievance—indeed, a whole series of grievances. Without that admission we cannot properly understand, evaluate, or predict the veteran's behavior. He comes to believe that he has been swindled, and that belief is rarely without some foundation in fact. We have induced him to risk his neck for patriotism, but allowed others to get rich from his sacrifices. A nation like ours wages war on the basis of an unspoken truce; while the men are fighting we suppose there will be a truce in all our little wars of classes and interests and races and religions and political parties. But there is never any ceasing in these wars and thereby the soldier knows he is betrayed. We have imposed upon the soldier's innocence and generosity; we have taken his youth and given him the memory of horrors; we have taken everything from him and left others at home to get along the better because he is away. To get his consent to be a soldier, we have promised everything, but usually given very little. As a measure of the swindle perpetrated on the soldiers, we should remember that the United States has never yet taken adequate care of the disabled in the years following a major war, and it has never given its recently demobilized soldiers of any war before the present one any real help in the task of readjusting themselves to civilian life. As the veterans said in 1919, "They said when we went away that when we came back nothing would be too good for us, and when we came back that was just what we got, nothing."

They Can Become Politically Dangerous

The veteran is dangerous to society not only because he is embittered but because, through circumstances over which he has no control, he lacks a stake in the social order. Like the I.W.W. of former years, he is, upon his return to society, the jobless, womanless, voteless man. He has no job; he has lost his habits of work;

he has developed attitudes that unfit him for many occupations; and he has not even the civilian's adjustment to his own standard of living. Family, wife, children, neighbors, local community, lodge, church, and school have less hold upon the veteran who has long been away from them than upon ordinary men. Possibly very much to his regret, the veteran lacks the attitudes that would make such things meaningful to him in the usual way.

By reason of his military service, the moral and political ideas of the veteran differ from those of the balance of society. He is disillusioned about words and men of words; he is immune to many of the words to which civilians respond and thus beyond the control of those who make their living by using such words. He is not interested in certain of the finer moral distinctions, although he admires forcefulness and bravery and loyalty.

The veteran is politically dangerous because he has a great deal of hatred to work off. By making him into a soldier, we have carefully cultivated his sadistic-aggressive impulses, taught him to fight and to kill without mercy, and then done him a series of injustices—should we then be surprised that he fights back? The veteran is accustomed to direct action but not to discussion; he has a pronounced aversion to discussion. He feels intensely but not intelligently, intensely because he has suffered, unintelligently because his political education stopped when he entered the army. He is not afraid to take risks; he has been shot over. He is hard enough to do whatever he feels he wants or needs to do, to beat up pacifists and radicals, lynch Negroes, or assassinate the men who made the peace of which he disapproves.

In a post-war period, the major political force is the veteran's anger. He is full of anger, needs something to hate, something to fight, something to protest against. Hatred, as we know, is of all the emotions the most easily transferred from one object to another. Therefore many people try to tell the veteran whom and what he should hate. The politicians struggle for the privilege of riding this whirlwind. When it has been decided whom the veteran of this war shall hate—labor, capital, radical, reactionary, Jew, Catholic, Negro, immigrant, isolationist, internationalist, pacifist, militarist, imperialist, Anglophile, Russophile—when it is decided which of these he shall hate, then it will be possible to write the political history of the next twenty-five years.

Full of danger for him—and for the world—is the fact that if the veteran fails in the competitive process of society he has a perfect excuse for his failure, and the worse his failure the better is his excuse. From the nature of the case, a great number of competitors, whether soldiers, veterans or life-long civilians, must fail in the competition of life. If the veteran fails he can put the blame on his military service. The more of a failure he makes, the greater becomes his claim upon society. That is the why of bonus armies and of demands for adjusted compensation and pensions and veterans' preference on the WPA.

Demagogues Will Try to Make Them into Stormtroops

Veterans are highly organizable. Organization takes place spontaneously if it is not planned. Veterans understand veterans; they need one another. They yearn to talk of exciting incidents by flood and field and to tell sad stories of the deaths of heroes. They have lost their sense of solidarity and of comradeship, their cause, and they are eager to recapture them. They need a cause in which to lose themselves and find their souls, but they are politically uneducated and therefore often unable to discriminate between good causes and bad ones. They are accustomed to identify themselves and their interests with the larger group and are inclined to believe that whatever veterans want is good for society. They have suffered real injustice, and can easily bring themselves to believe that they are entitled to anything they can get.

For these reasons the veteran is the ready tool of the demagogue who talks against talk and promises direct action. Often these demagogues who lead veterans are exceedingly cynical men to whom pity and humanity are abhorrent. Spendius, Matho, Catiline, Röhm, Göring, Hitler, Mussolini—there is no accident in the fact that these men have been the leaders of veterans.

The veteran can be the tool not only of the demagogue who talks against talk, but of the "undercover" demagogue as well. According to the New York Post's "Undercover Reporter," the Ku Klux Klan "has already started a campaign to win the support of a formidable army of returning servicemen." The May 16, 1944, issue of The Post describes part of the Klan's procedure. Although it was forced underground because of its menacing activities in

Detroit during the early days of World War II, and was officially disbanded in March, 1943, the Klan continues to operate from its secret headquarters in an apparently deserted building in Detroit. Harvey Hanson is reported to be the "organizer and brain of the underground Klan."

Significant in this connection is the technique of appealing to the returning soldier. According to the "Undercover Reporter," the campaign is based on the following plan. The Klan offers a free employment service for veterans, presumably with the cooperation of personnel directors of certain Detroit industrial plants. Those veterans whom the Klan succeeds in placing (as well as others) are solicited for membership by means of the printed "creed" of the United Sons of America, the organizational name under which the Klan openly operates. The creed advocates not four but eleven freedoms, including freedom of collective bargaining, and freedom from persecution because of race, color, or creed. "Several articles of this creed are designed to appeal strongly to men who have fought in this war. Any ex-soldier could honestly subscribe to every word of this creed, not knowing that these professions of Americanism and Christianity are just the window-dressing of an organization that has taken over the Klan oath, the Klan's symbol of the fiery cross, and the Klan's vehement hatred of Negroes, Catholics, Jews, and aliens."

The fact that a newspaper has sought out and exposed the machinations of one anti-democratic organization, does not mean that this organization will suddenly cease functioning or that no other organizations of a similar color are actually at work in an effort to capture large numbers of veterans. There are doubtless more than a few groups busy today with plans of their own, aware that the veteran, because of what he is and what he has gone through, can be easily captured. And he can indeed be easily captured by demagogues if society fails to capture him first for the uses of peaceful democratic living.

The veteran is always a powerful political force, for good or evil, because others cannot protect themselves from him. He has fought for the flag and has absorbed some of its *mana*. He is sacred. He is covered with pathos and immune from criticism. This pathos is enhanced by the customary period of neglect and mistreatment in the years immediately after a war; the sufferings of the deserving enable the undeserving to collect rich rewards later. The most transparent frauds get by, because no one dares to speak against the veteran—even to prove that he is not a veteran. Congress suspends its rules and bylaws to pass legislation in the veterans' behalf. All this is by no means limited to modern America. Remember that even Cicero stayed his tongue when speaking of Sulla's veterans who had joined Catiline's conspiracy.

The amount of disturbance created in society by the veteran varies with the nature of society and of the veteran's relation to it. Veterans are most dangerous when society itself is most disorganized. In a solidly integrated and stable society, the veteran problem need not be severe. In a society that is in flux or in transition, the veteran is certain to be troublesome. The problem is worse in a competitive than in a non-competitive society, and it is probably worse in a free society than in a despotism. The veteran is unquiet and disturbing in proportion to the degree of injustice done to him. The mercenary soldier probably makes the least troublesome veteran, if he receives his pay, but modern nations are forced to rely principally upon citizen soldiers.

When a rapidly changing, even unstable, and highly competitive society like the United States practices the *levée en masse* as we have, when there is such injustice in the waging of the war as there inevitably has been, when politicians cannot wait until the war is decently buried to begin competing for the veteran vote—who can say what will ensue? America has been very fortunate in its veterans so far. They have raised up no Catiline and no Hitler. Their worst exaction has been a little petty larceny graft.

We have been fortunate, so far, but will that good fortune continue? Let us suppose that at the end of the war the soldiers do not find their promised land, the Beulah land flowing with milk and honey, but find instead unemployment and neglect. Let us suppose that some of the veterans must go hungry, must beg on the streets, must sell their Purple Hearts and other medals, must wear their army uniform until it dissolves in rags, must walk the streets in wind and rain and snow to look for work and to be told there is no work by sleek civilians who have obviously done well for themselves during the war and have collected a great deal of money; and let us suppose that these civilians can still eat and drink and dance in the expensive night clubs while the hungry soldiers watch them from the outer darkness. . . . If then there comes a suitable demagogue to lead these veterans and to tell them what many already believe—that politicians are swindlers and their followers are born fools—if there comes a demagogue who tells them they have been suckers and talks against talk with overpowering eloquence and he leads these sullen soldiers in a fascist crusade, may not our democratic structure which even now totters at length collapse? Will the veterans of World War II turn into Storm Troopers who will destroy democracy?

Our Past Attempts

— and Failures —

to Help the Veteran

Veterans' Organizations
Assist Him
To Readjust

I T is natural for ex-soldiers to form associations to perpetuate the memories of their war, to care for their disabled, and to watch over the widows and orphans of fallen comrades. There have been hundreds of such organizations in the United States and Europe. On the American scene, the three most important veterans' organizations to date have been the Grand Army of the Republic, the Veterans of Foreign Wars, and the American Legion, each of which in its time has exerted great influence upon our national life.

Why Veterans Want Their Own Organizations

The newly returned veteran is of the race of Ishmael. "And he will be a wild man; his hand will be against every man, and every man's hand against him; and he shall dwell in the presence of all his brethren." Civilians do not understand the veteran. They do not sympathize with his strange resentments or approve of his rough and violent manners. He has become an alien.

There are things about the soldier that only soldiers understand. The soldier comes home, is happy to see his family, talks to his mother and father for a while, enjoys his mother's cooking, luxuriates in a soft bed, rises late with a feeling of sybaritic self-indulgence—and then finds to his surprise that what he really wants is to see his comrades once again.

Because he has been so long cut off from the communicative process, the ex-soldier is mentally isolated from civilian society; he no longer knows how to take his part in it, since he has come to lack the necessary emotions, habits, and words. Talk of politics irritates him; gossip bores him; newspapers, except for the sports section, and the comic strips, leave him apathetic. With all these things he has lost the sense of identification and the feeling that such things matter. In morality the veteran displays the same differentiation of tastes. He is used to lusty pleasures.

Because they feel at home with one another—and because they do not feel at home with anybody else—ex-soldiers naturally form groups. Here they find solidarity, and live over again the significant experiences of their lives. For others, the war is over. For the veteran, the war is never quite over. He has left his youth in it. Besides, the army is in his blood, and he has a need for "belonging" and for regimentation, that he never outgrows.

Probably nothing could prevent ex-soldiers from forming small, like-minded groups to cultivate the verdant growth of memory. It is a safe bet that the veterans who stormed Jericho and the members of Gideon's band had their annual reunions, with parades and the blowing of rams' horns. It is equally inevitable that such groups should sometimes be formalized by organization. Small groups of veterans have probably always arisen spontaneously, although the emergence of large, national organizations had to wait for the development of the idea of mass honor, which was largely a notion of the nineteenth century.

Some kind of organization of veterans is inevitable because human beings are always reaching out to find something that might save their lives from utter meaninglessness. The need for such fellowship is so great that people will form associations to commemorate almost anything: the event does not need to be significant. There is an association in New York to cultivate the memory of the blizzard of 1888, and it held a meeting in 1944 at which a famous Arctic explorer told how to avoid death in a snow-storm. The great blizzard was a little touch of nature, which made the whole world kin, it gave people a feeling of solidarity, and the survivors organized so that they would not lose their hold upon this thing that added richness to their lives.

When, for whatever reasons, an association has been formed, certain consequences ensue from the fact of organization. The persons who belong to an association have some trait or interest in common. The natural consequence of organization is to give very special importance to the common trait.[1] The trait that veterans

---

[1] An interpretation suggested by Frank Tannenbaum's analysis of the prison community.

have in common is that they once defended their country by force of arms. The trait that comes to the fore in veterans' organizations is patriotism, not the patriotism of the advanced thinker but the patriotism of the common man; not the patriotism of the person who loves all mankind and is a patriot of every nation but his own. It is the soldier's patriotism that these organizations catch up and institutionalize, and the soldier is a man who loves his country as it is and fights to defend it from harm. It is natural that such organizations should turn out to be foci of militant and patriotic conservatism, that they should be more interested in defending the Constitution than in understanding it, and that the man who has fought to defend the country from external enemies should often end by defending it from change.

Certain ills characteristically attack organizations and to these ills the organizations of veterans are by no means immune. Individuals sometimes use organizations as a springboard to their own personal advancements. Members of the group may come to think of their organization as a sort of conspiracy for the advancement of their own interests at the expense of non-members. Members may hold too tightly to the original purpose of the organization when that purpose should be modernized, or they may forget their purpose while it still has a living meaning. Organizations may compete, each fighting to become the biggest and best, and the real interests of members may be injured in such a scramble. And schemers, of course, may pervert any organization to their own uses.

Positive gains for society, on the other hand, are inherent in nearly every kind of formalized association. When a group has attained formal organization, it must make its compromises with the society that tolerates its existence and sanctions its activities. Thus the sect becomes a denomination, the gang a sort of political party, the cellar club a harmless association of adolescents. These compromises bring to the fore a socially acceptable, compromising sort of leader. As the group widens its participation, its members participate groupwise in the life of the community, thus at once forcing and being forced, pushing and being pulled, in the process of readjustment to society.

This is the rationale of veterans' organizations. Veterans will form their societies and organizations whether civilians approve them or not. They always have and they always will. Such groups respond to the veteran's inner needs. They help him to find the road back to normal social participation. Tolerate, recognize, and guide such groups and they become socially useful. Oppose them, alienate them, antagonize them, force them underground—and they become dangerous.

Some Earlier Veterans' Organizations

The Order of the Cincinnati was formed by American officers in April, 1783, with the approval of the highest authorities of the army. It was composed of officers of the Army and Navy, and was originally intended to carry hereditary distinction, the title passing to the eldest son. French officers who had fought with the Americans were eligible for membership. Lafayette and von Steuben were active and popular members.

The original plan of the Cincinnati aroused widespread criticism. Benjamin Franklin made fun of it in his own inimitable way, taking the hereditary principle apart in a famous letter in which he set forth arguments later copied by the writers of the French Revolution; Franklin even took time to pay his respects to the eagle. Samuel Adams also attacked it severely, and John Adams thoroughly disapproved it. The legislators of Massachusetts passed a resolution against the organization, and Rhode Island disfranchised its citizens who were members. There was also great opposition in South Carolina. Popular feeling against the Cincinnati as a self-constituted nobility became so intense that the hereditary principle had to be abandoned.

But the political influence of the order remained great throughout the lives of its members. It set an example for its successors by pressing the demands of the veterans for pensions and other benefits. Since its members were officers, its influence was on the side of aristocracy. In fact, monarchical sentiment and other counter-revolutionary tendencies were strong in the Cincinnati. It may be significant that this least tolerated and most opposed of American veterans' organizations was the most undemocratic in its policies.

After the Napoleonic wars, British officers of both army and navy founded the United Service Club in 1817. Organizations of common soldiers came later,—not until the extinction of feudalism had made it possible for the idea of mass honor to emerge. The Prussian government in 1842 authorized the formation of *Kriegervereine* or Warrior's Societies. These proved an important adjunct to Prussian militarism, being dominated by conservative classes and thus contrasting sharply with the *Schutzvereine* or Riflemen's Associations, which carried on the ancient traditions of the militia and were more democratic in nature. In Japan organizations of veterans were even more closely integrated into and controlled by the military system.[2]

The Grand Army of the Republic (G.A.R.)

The Grand Army of the Republic, an organization of Union veterans founded directly after the Civil War, held its first meeting in 1866. It was an organization of all the soldiers of the Union, privates as well as officers. General John A. Logan, an early G.A.R. commander-in-chief, stated the purpose of the organization, to "commemorate the gallantry and sufferings of our comrades, give aid to bereaved families, cultivate fraternal sympathy among ourselves, find employment for the idle, and, generally, by our acts and precepts to give the world a practical example of sincere, kindly cooperation."

When the student of history thinks of the G.A.R., he usually thinks of pensions, for it was the G.A.R. that gave the first demonstration of the feasibility of raids on the Treasury by veterans' organizations. At first the organization did not prosper, and for a time it even seemed to be in danger of extinction. When, in the seventies, it began to campaign actively for pensions, it caught the interest of the veterans, though it counted only some 60,000 on its rolls. The Arrears Act of 1879 helped the pension drive to acquire momentum, and stirred the veterans' interest in the G.A.R. From 1881, a standing committee of the organization sat with Congressional committees. Soon the G.A.R. reached a point where it could state its requests to Congress as demands; it did not need to come begging, cap in hand. A gag rule was enacted that prevented posts in disagreement with the official policy of the organization from expressing their disagreement publicly. When, in 1893, the Noah Farnham Post Number 458 of New York protested against pen-

2 Alfred Vagts, *A History of Militarism.* Norton, 1937, pp. 386 ff.

sion grabs, the post was disciplined and its members were subjected to scurrilous attacks. Official propaganda of the organization was put forward by the National Tribune, edited and controlled by George E. Lemon, a Washington pension attorney.

The G.A.R. reached its membership peak in 1890, when it had on its rolls 409,000 members, or more than half of those eligible for membership.[3] This was twenty-five years after the end of the war. In 1880, fifteen years after the end of the war, its membership was only 60,654. After 1890, membership slowly declined, but the organization retained a political power out of proportion to its numbers. Like other such organizations, it had its assorted auxiliaries through which it carried on certain activities and both extended and prolonged its power.

The natural affinity between pensions and high tariffs became most apparent in the years following the Civil War. The tariff policy of the Republican Party produced a treasury surplus, which might have been disturbing in its political and economic effects if some genius had not had the idea of paying out the surplus moneys to the veterans. The veterans, naturally, favored this scheme and were ready to give their support to the party which so befriended them.

The position of the Republican Party, and of the pensioners, became very strong. It was the party of the Union, the party that championed the soldiers, entitled in every election to wave the bloody shirt, bloodied and torn, of course, in the process of putting down the "Democratic Rebellion." The veterans not only voted for the Republican Party, but protected it from the danger of ever having a surplus in the treasury. Over both veterans and politicians the owners of protected industries watched with a benignant eye, while William Graham Sumner, breaking his bitter old heart in the struggle to convince people that the tariff was a tax that made everybody poor and enriched no one correspondingly, turned at length from the study of Political Economy, which assumes that human beings are rational, to the study of Sociology, where no such assumption is necessary.

3 Gellermann's figures, in William Gellermann, *The American Legion as Educator.* Bureau of Publications, Teachers College, Columbia University, 1938. General Alger, one-time Commander in Chief, stated that "On June 30, 1890, the Grand Army of the Republic numbered on its rolls 458,230 men, that it had 7,175 posts."

Driving "a Six-Mule Team Through the Treasury"

The climax of the drive for Civil War pensions came in the late Eighties. In 1888, there were 419,763 active pension awards for the Civil War; five years later, in 1893, the number had risen to 935,084, which was near the peak. Harrison campaigned for the presidency with the felicitous slogan, "Now is not the time to weigh the claims of old soldiers with apothecary's scales." Harrison made good on his promises to the veterans by appointing the famous Corporal Tanner, a professional veteran, as Commissioner of Pensions. Corporal Tanner was a veteran who had lost both legs in action. An active proponent of pensions, he had gained prominence in the organization in the early seventies. When he was made Commissioner, he announced that he was going to "drive a six-mule team through the treasury," adding, "God help the surplus!" He granted pensions and increases with such a free hand that he had to be removed in 1889, after only a few months in office, but he was not removed until he had made good his designs on the treasury surplus, nor were the pensioners added during his regime ever stricken from the rolls.

Whatever the results of these policies upon the economy, they furnished rich pickings for the pension agents. At one time there were more than 60,000 registered pension attorneys, their permissible fee for each case being originally ten and later twenty-five dollars. George Lemon, publisher of the pro-pension National Tribune, was probably the most successful of these agents. In 1885, years before the high point of pension claims, he admitted that he had in his files 125,000 pension claims.

The G.A.R. practiced pressure politics long before the term became popular. It had its way of defeating officials who opposed the demands of the veterans' bloc, as Grover Cleveland learned to his sorrow. But in spite of its most persistent efforts, the G.A.R. did not succeed in obtaining any really effective guarantee of veterans' preference in the civil service system of the United States. Powerful committees lobbied with great persistence until 1903, Lemon's Tribune thundered and threw mud, and in 1900 some 1287 posts sent petitions to Congress—all without avail. Congress never became convinced that the majority of the members of the G.A.R.

wanted veterans' preference in the civil service.[4] The G.A.R.
was, however, successful in obtaining veterans' preference laws in
many states, and in fact probably obtained the results it desired
in the federal service through its political power, which gave it
control over many appointments.

Though no doubt its major concern was pensions, the G.A.R.
did not entirely neglect its other objectives. In accordance with
the standards and customs of the time, it gave its support to institutions caring for the orphans of deceased veterans. In Pennsylvania there was, from 1864 on, a great proliferation of these institutions, for which, according to a contemporary writer, the G.A.R.
deserves much of the credit:

> In resisting the narrowing and belittling of the undertaking,
> while no set of men can claim the exclusive honor, the soldiers
> of the late war may justly demand a preeminence. Especially
> is this true of the Grand Army of the Republic, an organiza-
> tion composed of the honorably discharged veterans of the
> war for the suppression of the rebellion. To perpetuate the re-
> membrances of that struggle, to keep alive the friendships
> which were formed amid common hardships and dangers, and
> to cherish a love for the Union of the respective States for
> which they fought and bled, are some of the objects of its
> existence. And among other obligations of mercy, the mem-
> bers of this brotherhood are pledged to extend aid, when
> necessary, to the unfortunate families of their comrades who
> were slain and crippled in battle. Fidelity to their vows, quick-
> ened by a remembrance of the dead and a regard for the liv-
> ing, have placed these banded warriors foremost in the sup-
> port of that system which provides a home and a school for
> those whom they are obligated to defend and protect. By
> their numerical strength, and by their social and political
> standing, they have been enabled so to shape legislative action
> as to obtain favorable results. Not only has the Grand Army
> been ready to exert its powerful influence in favor of securing
> ample appropriations for the support of the schools, but it has
> also heartily favored every enlargement of the State's liberality
> to the orphans.
> It is largely due to its influence that provisions have been

---

4 *Cf.* Paul Joseph Woods, *The G.A.R. and Civil Service.* Abstract of a
Doctoral Dissertation at the University of Illinois, Urbana, Illinois, 1914.

made to aid the pupils, after completing their term at the schools, to continue their studies at the normal schools of the State. Members of the order, as well as those who had immediate charge of the children, had repeatedly been pained by seeing earnest and promising students, on arriving at the age of sixteen years, sent away and their student-life suddenly ended, too often never to be resumed . . . Deeply impressed with this fact, the members of the organization deemed it a duty to see that some provision was made for this class of orphans. They accordingly made known their wishes to the Superintendent, who, heartily concurring in their views, asked and obtained of the Legislature in 1872 an appropriation of two thousand dollars to assist a limited number of the most worthy pupils, who had completed their term at the orphan schools, to further pursue their studies at the State normal schools. It is also largely due to the same influence that the normal school fund was subsequently increased and made permanent.[5]

By the end of 1876 admissions to these Pennsylvania schools totaled 8,277, of which 2,772 represented children still in institutions. While we do not now regard institutional care as the best solution for the problem of dependent children, we should not forget that these institutions were a great advance over previous methods of child care, and that they were conducted in accordance with the best practices of the time.

The attitude of the Union soldier, and of the G.A.R., toward the Confederate soldier went through a series of transformations, changing from the curious kindliness of the years of combat to vindictiveness in the post-war years, then at length mellowing, if not to friendliness, at least to something much more positive than forgiveness in the 1880s.[6] In 1884, Oliver Wendell Holmes, Junior, described the war-time attitude of the soldiers as follows:

You could not stand up day after day in those indecisive contests where overwhelming victory was impossible because neither side would run as they ought when beaten without getting at least something of the same brotherhood for the enemy that the north pole of a magnet has for the south—each

[5] James Laughery Paul, *Pennsylvania's Soldiers' Orphan Schools*. Harrisburg, Penna., 1877, pp. 150-151.
[6] This story is well told by Paul Buck in *The Road to Reunion, 1865-1900*. Little Brown, 1937, Chap. X, "The Veteran Mind," pp. 236 ff.

working in an opposite sense to the other, but each unable to get along without the other.[7]

But in the years immediately after the war this attitude changed; perhaps, one may suppose, because the veteran's inevitable bitterness had in this case been re-deflected against the enemy. Grant, after giving generous terms to Lee, changed to harshness toward the beaten South; other veterans also forgot their sympathy with the Confederate soldier as soon as he ceased to be an enemy. For years the G.A.R. maintained watch and surveillance over all that pertained to the war. It supported committees to examine school textbooks, especially in history, to eliminate textbooks that failed to present the war in its true light, and to deplore the absence in some of the books of words like "treason" or "rebellion."

In the 1880s veterans of both the Blue and the Gray began to mellow. In 1882 the G.A.R. held its annual encampment in Baltimore, where it was well received; Confederate veterans marched with them that year. In the eighties these "Blue and Gray reunions" became frequent. The greatest of these was probably the twenty-fifth anniversary of the Battle of Gettysburg, when the men who had tried to kill each other twenty-five years before, met as friends and comrades, an event not often paralleled in history since the rape of the Sabine maidens. When Grant died, Confederate generals served with Union officers as pallbearers at the funeral. Such gestures, in which veterans took the lead in reconciliation, did much to heal the wounds of the Civil War.

Confederate soldiers were less free to organize, being under suspicion for some years, and therefore no organization appeared equal in scope to the G.A.R. They organized, of course, but on a local and restricted basis, and they dominated such secret societies as the Ku Klux Klan. Not until 1889 did the Confederate veterans found the inclusive organization, the United Confederate Veterans.

7 Quoted in *ibid.*, p. 236, from the Boston Advertiser, May 31, 1884.

The American Legion
Of World War I

A FTER World War I, a great many organizations competed for the favor of the veterans. The American Legion early emerged as the most successful competitor, its nearest rival being the older and somewhat more exclusive organization, the Veterans of Foreign Wars. The Legion now claims to be the largest veterans' organization in the history of the world. Since limitations of space do not permit discussion of all contemporary veterans' organizations, we shall concentrate on the Legion and omit the others, while conceding that these other organizations have considerable importance.

The purposes, programs, and activities of the Legion have been subjected to a minute and usually suspicious scrutiny, and it has often been condemned, but it has been a dominant force in American life for two decades. Most of what has been written about the Legion has been either panegyric or exposé. Neither is justified. The Legion, like any other human institution, is neither all good nor all bad.

The American Legion was founded at a three day caucus in Paris, beginning on March 15, 1919. Among the leaders of the group were Colonel Theodore Roosevelt, Jr., Colonel Bennett Clark, Colonel William J. Donovan, and Captain Ogden Mills. These men were and are conservatives. They have never made any secret of their intention to found an essentially conservative organization.

From its inception, the Legion was non-partisan; both officers and men were enrolled without distinction. Membership was open to anyone who had served in the armed forces during World War I, and it has now been opened to veterans of World War II. Unlike its great rival, the Veterans of Foreign Wars, the Legion did not exclude the training camp veteran.

The preamble of the American Legion constitution states the purpose of the organization:

For God and country we associate ourselves together for the
following purposes:

To uphold and defend the Constitution of the United States
of America; to maintain law and order, to foster and perpetuate a one hundred per cent Americanism; to preserve the
memories and incidents of our association in the Great Wars;
to inculcate a sense of individual obligation to the community,
state and nation; to combat the autocracy of both the classes
and the masses; to make right the master of might; to promote peace and good will on earth; to safeguard and transmit
to posterity the principles of justice, freedom, and democracy;
to consecrate and sanctify our comradeship by our devotion
and mutual helpfulness.

Certainly no democratic American can quarrel with these objectives. Nor can anyone doubt that the overwhelming majority
of the members of the Legion sincerely believe in them. Many
question the right of the Legion to determine the interpretation
of the Constitution, or Americanism, or the public good. It is at
this point that controversy begins.

Gellermann [1] found that the Legion, up to the time of his study,
reached its highest membership, relatively and absolutely, in 1931.
The 1,153,909 members of that year represented twenty-seven per
cent of the potential membership. Four years later the Legion enrollment dropped to twenty per cent of its potential membership.
The onset of war terminated the period of decline. In recently published literature, the Legion lays claim to more than 1,150,000
members enrolled in 11,800 local posts. Its claim to being the
largest veterans' organization in the history of the world is probably justified.

Gellermann's study of the Legion has shown that its members
are for the most part in comfortable circumstances. A survey made
for the Legion in 1935 showed that 33.5 per cent of the members
owned their own businesses. Employed by others but in relatively
good positions were another 29.7 per cent. Workers, white-collar

1 William Gellermann, *The American Legion as Educator.* Bureau of Publications, Teachers College, Columbia University, 1938. Gellermann's book was
quite hostile to the Legion, and went so far as to call the Legion fascist and
unpatriotic. Many of Gellermann's criticisms, however, were based upon the
liberal philosophy of the Thirties, and would now have to be revised in the
light of events that have vindicated such Legion policies as preparedness and
nationalistic education.

workers, and miscellaneous workers constituted 29.7 per cent, while 7.1 per cent were unemployed, retired, or on relief. As Gellermann puts it, "The average Legionnaire is a business or professional man whereas the average American is a wage-worker." Gellermann also quotes an estimate by the American Legion Monthly of the year 1927, placing the average yearly income of the Legionnaire at $3,031, in contrast to $1,933 for the year 1920. These indications clearly place the great majority of Legion members in relatively comfortable circumstances. The dues, however, are small, and we should bear in mind that the lower economic groups are not organizable, or can be organized with great difficulty. Community studies have consistently shown that members of the lower economic groups are not joiners, while the middle and upper groups are relatively gregarious. Even the labor unions have been most successful in organizing the more favorably placed and successful workers.

The top leadership of the Legion, as Gellermann has shown by an extensive analysis, is supplied by a group of well-to-do men. National commanders have averaged a little older than other Legionnaires (average age 36 in 1918). Most of them had previously held high commissions in the army.

While members of the business classes have been very active in the Legion, they have not had the field entirely to themselves. The organization has had a considerable trade-union membership, with certain posts dominated by this group. The Legion has often been accused of being anti-labor, which was doubtless true of some local posts, but the national organization has maintained cordial relations with the American Federation of Labor. Leaders of the Legion and the A.F. of L. customarily appear as guest speakers at one another's conventions. Relations between the Legion and the C.I.O. (Congress of Industrial Organization) have probably been less friendly.

The organizational unit of the American Legion is the local post, which is usually named after a local soldier killed during the war, often the first to be killed. (No post may bear the name of a living person.) In 1937 there were 11,248 posts; there are now said to be 11,800. These posts carry on the local program of activities and send delegates to regional conventions, which elect officers and pass resolutions for the area. Only official delegates from the regional organization are able to vote at the national convention, but many others attend. The organizational set-up is such as to afford dissenting posts little opportunity to register their disagreement. Like almost every other organization in the world, the Legion tends to be ruled by a small group of persons who have been intensely interested in its internal affairs and its politics over a period of years. In this respect the Legion does not differ from a church, university, political party, or labor union.

The Varied Program of the Legion

The veterans' organization arises, as we have seen, because veterans come into civilian life almost as immigrants and need the society of ex-soldiers as a bridge to normal community adjustment. During the early period, the urge is strong to meet in small, face-to-face groups to talk over old times and new problems. During these years, the activities of an organization find a natural focus in the desire of the veterans to help their disabled comrades, to care for the dependents of the deceased and the disabled, and to assist one another in getting a start in the world. During this period, the memory of the war years is still vivid and the comradeship of men at arms still strong. After a time, the veterans begin to be better adjusted in society; consequently some of them lose interest in veterans' affairs. The organization must then cast about to find new causes and new bases of unity. As the drive for pensions revivified the G.A.R., so the desire to provide for the veterans of World War II is injecting new life into the American Legion.

In its early years, the Legion fought hard and successfully for the disabled of World War I. Legionnaires discovered shocking examples of neglect and mismanagement in everything that pertained to veterans. By 1924 they had achieved their objective and reformed the Veterans' Administration. The Legion did this job well. It forced the construction of hospitals and the establishment of the Veterans' Administration. As Culp remarks, "It is a tribute to the Legion as well as to the Veterans' Administration that the affairs of that government body have been handled since 1924 with a minimum of attention to politics and a maximum to the problems of the disabled." [2]

[2] Dorothy Culp, *The American Legion: A Study in Pressure Politics*. U. of Chicago Libraries, 1942, p. 8.

When Legion posts were being founded, members sometimes thought of them as mutual advancement societies. As a veteran who helped to found one of the leading posts recently explained to the writer, "When we first organized we thought that all of us fellows could stick together and do business with each other. We soon found out that didn't work. We had to give our business where we could get the best price and the best service." They discovered, in other words, that business is competitive and one cannot change the basis of competition for the sake of sentiment. However, some persons whose business is almost wholly a matter of contacts—young lawyers and insurance agents, for example—might well profit from membership in such an organization. This business advantage sometimes causes such persons to become professional veterans.

For some years annual conventions furnished a focus for the activities of the Legion. Brilliantly organized, planned and executed, they were like gigantic, spectacular college reunions. Like such reunions, they furnished a moral holiday for the aging veteran, an opportunity to recapture his youth, to claim once more the privileges of youth and irresponsibility by being "one of the boys" and to obtain a temporary feeling of youthfulness by the copious use of *spiritus frumenti*. While the national conventions were great business affairs for which cities competed vigorously, the state and regional conventions were also important. Very likely the Legion post of Tamaroa, Illinois, got as much pleasure from its "Rube Band" that paraded at state and regional conventions as other posts did from more expensive displays. The New York convention of 1938 was the high tide of the pre-World War II Legion. However, at the current moment hotel men no longer regard the Legion convention as a first-class prize. It no longer draws the free spenders; of late years it tends to become "a place where you go with a clean shirt and leave with a dirty shirt." All this will change again if the Legion enrolls a large group of the veterans of World War II.

Another focus of Legion activities has been the matter of benefits for veterans. There was the drive for adjusted compensation, sometimes called the bonus. It has been the custom of righteous citizens to hold up their hands in horror at the mention of the bonus, but the thousands of millionaires created by the war and the high wages paid to many workers gave the veterans a case. The campaign for the bonus supplied, in the early years, a very useful outlet for the veterans' bitterness; they might easily have done worse things—and in European countries they did. The scale of benefits was ridiculously low. The drive for the prepayment of the bonus, in which the Legion apparently participated reluctantly and only after its hand had been forced, was indeed a raid on the treasury. But it was mild compared to the raids made by the G.A.R., and we should not forget that such pork-barrel legislation is an old American tradition. To date the Legion has been much more moderate than the G.A.R. in its pension demands. It has never driven a six-mule team through the treasury, nor ever tried to do so.

The social and community services of the Legion have received less attention than they deserve. In addition to the services to needy veterans, which have always been a primary concern, their social efforts have often been outstanding contributions to community welfare. The child welfare program has been particularly good. The Legion began this work in 1925 with a campaign to raise an endowment to care for an estimated 30,000 World War I orphans. Child welfare work has continued to receive attention since that time. According to Legion figures, it has reached 5,900,000 children and has cost $50,000,000. Ninety per cent of the children were helped in their own homes and kept with their own mothers. The Legion has also supported some excellent child welfare legislation.

The authoritative Social Work Year Book of 1929 evaluated the Legion's child welfare program as follows:

> The program of the American Legion is radically different from that of any other order in its cooperation with existing social agencies and its broad assumption of responsibility for child welfare projects. Two of the Legion's state branches have very small institutions, but the order has no national institution. The national office employs a staff of trained social workers in five areas of the country, and local Legion posts cooperate closely with health agencies and social agencies of every kind in caring for the children of veterans. Support of welfare legislation is a major activity, and a relief fund of $100,000 a year is administered from national headquarters in Indianapolis as temporary aid to cases for which local posts are making permanent plans.[3]

[3] C. W. Areson, "Fraternal Orders," in *Social Work Year Book, 1929*, edited by Fred S. Hall and Mabel B. Ellis. Russell Sage Foundation, 1930. See also the *Social Work Year Book*, 1943, pp. 119 and 609.

According to Legion spokesmen, "beyond the care and protection of children of veterans of World War I or II, the American Legion is concerned with all children. Through its example and influence, many more family homes have continued to be maintained when death and disability remove the breadwinner. Aid to dependent children in their own family homes has been increased by Federal, State and County Government through the influence of the American Legion. Maternal and child health aid and services have been improved and increased for the benefit of mothers and their children. Community coordinated endeavor has been established to help remove the causes of child dependency, neglect, and delinquency." In addition, local posts have engaged in widely diversified activities, making gifts to their communities of public parks, playgrounds, and swimming pools, furnishing leadership for Community Chest drives, and otherwise making themselves useful.

Education has always been a particular concern of the Legion. In conjunction with the powerful National Education Association, the American Legion instituted American Education Week in 1921. The week idea took on, and by 1924 the Legion had enlisted one hundred and forty organizations in its program. At first devoted to intensely nationalistic programs, the emphasis was then shifted to social conformity in general; still later the content appears to have had little supervision by the Legion.[4]

When in 1933 the schools of the country were threatened by widespread cuts in the name of economy, J. W. Crabtree, Secretary of the National Education Association, appealed to the Legion for help. The Legion took a strong stand, and helped to save the school budgets.

Characteristically, Legion posts have been much interested in every feature of the school program that has to do with nationalism or patriotism. They have conducted ceremonies, donated flags, and subsidized essays and historical contests. Their "indirect approach" through sports and other activities has been particularly effective. Critics of the "indirect approach" would do well to reflect that Red Russia is also very fond of sports. In their cultivation of the rugged and the manly, Legionnaires have found a congenial activity in promoting boxing. Duffield, writing in 1931, noted that twelve states had changed their laws to permit boxing, largely as

4 *Cf.* Gellermann, *op. cit.*, Chap. VIII.

a result of Legion pressure, and that many Legion posts sponsor boxing matches. According to Duffield, in South Dakota, the Legion collects a percentage from all matches, while in Mississippi it has complete control of boxing. This Legion policy of promoting sports is, by the way, based on thoroughly sound psychology. Many military men have recognized the value of sports as preparation for war. Sports are, in fact, the great reservoir, as well as the means of expression, of the sadistic-aggressive element in our culture.[5]

The Legion and Academic Freedom

The Legion has on occasion interfered with the academic freedom of teachers. The concept of academic freedom was invented to protect advanced specialists in the publication of the results of research in their fields of study. This is still its most defensible function. Truth, relevance, and honesty are the best defences when academic freedom is threatened. One may question whether the cloak of academic freedom should cover the teacher or writer when he is dealing not with facts or research but with propaganda, admitting that this distinction is difficult to make in the concrete instance. One may also ask whether it should enable the member of a revolutionary party, obedient to the orders of party officials and somewhat callous to the promptings of his own conscience, to propagandize his party line from the vantage point of the public school. But here we should note that membership in such a party or religious sect, before it could affect the merits of a controversy, would have to be established in accordance with the strictest rules of evidence.

It is foolish to suppose that any community will for long support with public money a kind of education that undermines its established institutions. Regardless of what educators may think, the people who pay the taxes are going to have their say about what is

[5] To a great many readers this context will unfailingly suggest Wellington, Waterloo, and the playing fields of Eton. Wellington did attend Eton for a time, but before organized sports became a prominent feature of Eton life. According to Philip Guedalla, Wellington himself attributed much of his spirit of enterprise to the tricks he used to play in and about a broad, black ditch in an Eton garden. Guedalla remarks, "The tribute may be found unsatisfying by athletic purists and a shade disappointing even to Etonians, since their playing-fields appear only in the attenuated form of a ditch in a dame's garden. But such as it was, he paid it." (Philip Guedalla, *Wellington*, Harper, 1931, pp. 22-23.)

taught in the schools and who teaches it. If the citizens and tax-payers believe the earth is flat, it will probably go hard with the school teacher who openly declares that it is round, although certainly the rest of the country should send some suitable home missionaries to such a community to familiarize the members of the school board with the facts of geopolitics. Granting these facts of life, we must still say that local posts of the Legion have sometimes been tyrannical and unfair in their handling of teachers, which can be said of almost every large and powerful organization that has interested itself in education.

In its campaigns against textbooks and its interference with teachers, the Legion has had the support of majority opinion; and at least on one issue, preparedness, its position has been proved objectively correct. Doubting the prospect of permanent peace, the Legion has advocated a large army and navy. It has advocated education of the young in patriotism looking toward the possible defence of the country in time of war. When the Legion was studied during the thirties, by such liberals as Gellermann and Duffield,[6] this pessimism with regard to the prospect of lasting peace seemed a grievous fault to them and to their readers, but their strictures against the Legion on this charge seem ridiculous today. If it had not been for the activities of the Legion and similar groups in keeping alive the military spirit, if it had not been for the rudimentary military establishment that we maintained, we might not have been able to fight the present war at all.

The Legion's Military Preparedness Program

Unlike many so-called pacifists—pacifists that is, between wars—the Legion has been entirely consistent in its attitude toward war. The Legion belief has been that war would certainly come and we should prepare for it. Pacifistic critics of the Legion have been against preparedness and against the Legion because it believed in preparedness, until they woke up one morning hot for war and found they had no army. By contrast with the Legion, its critics enjoy the distinction of having done everything they could to make their country weak and to get it into war. The consistent opponents

6 *Ibid.* Also Marcus Duffield, *King Legion.* Cape and Smith, 1931.

of war, such as the Quakers, of course, were not guilty of this contradiction.

The Legion describes and defends its foreign policy in the following brief statement:

> It's a Fact
>
> That in 1919 the American Legion brought forward in the form of the National Defense act, the first National Defense legislation after World War I and this legislation became law in 1920. Had that law been fulfilled there would probably have been no global war.
>
> That in 1923 the American Legion insisted that the fortification of Hawaii, Wake, Midway and the Phillipines be so strengthened that invasion would be impossible. Had that been done, the Japs could never have taken the Phillipines or the East Indies.
>
> That starting in 1924 and continuing until Pearl Harbor the American Legion insisted upon the fortification of Guam. Had this been done the Japs would have been forced to attempt a campaign there before attacking Pearl Harbor.
>
> That the American Legion in 1923 demanded a Navy strong enough to patrol and control both the Atlantic and Pacific Oceans and has each year since that time insisted upon such a Navy. Had that Navy been provided the loss at Pearl Harbor would not have been so great as to occasion the loss of the Phillipines, Wake, Guam, and the East Indies.
>
> That in 1922 the American Legion proposed the Universal Service Act which, had it been enacted, would have made the Manpower Commission, the OPA, the WLRB and other similar governmental agencies unnecessary, thereby saving billions of dollars.

The American Legion, like the G.A.R. before it, has practiced pressure politics. Culp characterizes the Legion's legislative committee as the epitome and model of pressure organizations.[7] Measures inspired by the Legion are introduced by friendly Congressmen. While the bills are in committee, the Legion committee states the attitude of the organization and tries to win support. The Legion lobby keeps in close touch with Congressmen, bringing doubtful ones in line by means of an avalanche of letters and telegrams from home. The Legion exercises similar power over the state legislatures.

[7] Culp, *op. cit.*

But for the most part the Legion has used its power for worthy purposes, and it is difficult to understand why the organization has been so generally and so roundly damned. Its members are mostly in comfortable circumstances, but that is not a crime. The Legion is conservative, but on friendly terms with the American Federation of Labor, and it has attacked Hamilton Fish and thus dissociated itself from his brand of conservatism. The Legion's activities on behalf of disabled veterans have been unselfish, the more so because Legion members belong to the economic group that pays heavy taxes. The Legion has pioneered in various welfare fields, but, except among professional social workers, has received little credit for it. The Legion favored the bonus, but did not take the lead in pressing for the prepayment of the bonus. The Legion kept the spirit of nationalism alive in the piping times of peace, for which it was greatly censured; but as it turned out this was probably a public service. Now that war has come, and not through their agitation, Legionnaires are working for adequate care for the veterans of World War II. In this work, the Legion has a great task ahead of it. It may be that because of the Legion's interest in this matter, we shall not neglect our soldiers after this war. If the Legion helps to obtain just and intelligent treatment for the veterans of World War II, it will have amply justified its existence.

What Veterans' Organizations Contribute to Society

Many persons regard the veterans' organization as an unmitigated nuisance, a sort of thorn in the side of society. The truth is that such an organization performs many socially useful functions.

If it were not for such organizations, the veteran might be a very troublesome individual. The founders of the American Legion recognized this fact, and designed a social machine that has proved extremely effective in containing and redirecting the hostilities and aggressions that the veterans brought home with them. If there had been no American Legion, this energy might very well have spent itself in destructive ways which would have brought no benefit either to the veterans or to society.

Quite aside from any programs it may advocate, a national organization of veterans which ignores the cleavages of religion, class, politics, and nationality background performs a great service to national unity. One of the greatest evils of a post-war world is the persecution of minorities; if veterans join in this activity the democratic process suffers greatly. But if the veterans are organized in such a way as to minimize these differences, if they mingle with members of other cultures, classes, and religious groups at the meetings of their local posts, there is less likelihood that intolerance will flourish among them. Here a very clear line of policy is indicated for veterans who are members of minority groups. If they wish to combat prejudice and intolerance, they should not withdraw into their own organizations, but should become active participants in the inclusive organizations. The same reasoning seems to apply to labor groups.

From the point of view of the individual member, the contribution of the veterans' organization is magical. By its alchemy, the organization transforms an experience that would otherwise be most destructive into a social asset. The ex-soldier has lost his years, his youth, and he brings back the memory of nameless horrors. There is no place for him in civilian society. The veterans' organization gives him a place of honor. His fellow soldiers understand him. They value his achievements. They do not tire of listening to him so long as he is willing to listen to them. When, like all the heroes of the past, he is in danger of being a bore, the society of his fellows saves him from this fate so much worse than death. Through the organization the veteran gains a stake in society. Some honor is due him for his military service, but he must belong to an organization if he hopes to collect it. There has to be an occasional parade and he must march in it. In this manner he learns to be proud of his status as a veteran and to love the country which, with only a little nagging, does him honor for the services which he once performed in response to only a little compulsion . . . !

More, apparently, than other veterans' organizations, the American Legion has attempted to turn the veterans' energies into socially useful channels. Stimulated by the Legion, veterans have in the past twenty years been much concerned with community welfare. Doubtless the social intelligence of the veterans has not always kept pace with their good intentions, but then, an occasional Julius Rosenwald excepted, no one has really found the secret of intelligent philanthrophy. All people who mean well are bound to be mischievous sometimes. But think how much more harmful they might be if they did not mean well!

An unfortunate aspect of the veterans' organization is that it organizes one age group against the rest of society. This age group, protected by the pathos that surrounds the veteran, is able to prolong its domination of society for a long time. The G.A.R. ruled the country for nearly forty years after their battles were over. The pension rolls show to what an extent they used their dominance in their own interest. In the end the veterans were a small minority of the population, but their power to touch the public moneys was not diminished. Every veteran had his friends and relatives who voted right, not merely because their sentiments were right but because they did not want to see Grandpa Jim or Uncle Jasper lose his pension. Every political machine works on more or less the same kind of patronage principles. As always, when one age group prolongs its power unduly, there came a time when the ideas of the veterans of the Civil War were no longer adequate to the new world around them and the entrenched veterans stood in the way of progress. The same fate may befall any such organization which is not constantly rejuvenated by transfusions of young blood.

For various reasons, it is inevitable that most veterans' organizations should display a pronounced conservative trend. The common trait of the members of these organizations is that they have once been soldiers. War accentuates in-group feeling, the soldier is the symbol of this feeling. Soldiers fight to defend things as they are; military men of all ranks tend to be conservative. A veterans' organization is usually formed just after a war by men who do not understand or sympathize with the war-induced changes in the civilian society with which they lost contact when they entered the military service. For these and other reasons, veterans' organizations are nearly always conservative in tendency.

Liberals will gain nothing by criticizing them on this account. They will accomplish little by dropping out of such organizations and fighting them from the outside. If liberals, intellectuals, labor union members and representatives of the less common shades of opinion wish to influence veterans in the next twenty-five years, their best chance will lie in joining the veterans' organizations, participating in their activities, compromising with them, and helping to form their policy in free and democratic discussion. If they do this, they may also find that they have taken an important step in their own education.

Attempts To Help
With Pensions
And Other Relief

AMERICAN ingenuity has fathered a great many devices to better the condition of the veterans of our many wars. These have included pensions for death or disability or simply on account of service, land grant bounties, care at soldier's homes, vocational rehabilitation, life insurance, adjusted compensation, retirement pay, and medical care. The total money cost of these measures was approximately twenty-five billion dollars up to 1942. Veterans also enjoy considerable preference in the state and federal service. States have also given bonuses, tax exemptions, and a multitude of minor concessions. Minor benefits extended by the federal government include such things as burial at the public expense and the furnishing of a flag for a veteran's funeral.

Pensions and Other Relief Before World War I [1]

Our system of veterans' relief had its roots in English practice, from which it has slowly evolved to its present form. The American colonies, beset by constant wars with the Indians, early established pension systems, partly as inducements to enlistment. The Pilgrims at Plymouth passed such legislation in 1636. Virginia provided for veterans in 1644, Maryland in 1678, New York in 1691, Rhode Island in 1718. The money necessary to pay these pensions was not always available. George Washington championed the cause of the veterans of the French and Indian War. He was later to play a

[1] For materials in this section we are heavily indebted to an excellent study by Gustavus A. Weber and Laurence F. Schmeckebier, *The Veterans Administration, Its History, Activities and Organization.* Brookings Institution, 1934. This study is wholly factual and attempts no evaluation. The earlier study of William H. Glasson, *Federal Pensions in the United States,* Oxford U. Press, 1918, is also very useful.

most important part in originating and fixing in tradition the policy of pensioning old soldiers.

Our treatment of the soldiers and veterans of the Revolutionary War was characterized by shameful injustice, which the subsequent payment of lavish rewards to persons who had nothing to do with the war did not redress. The Revolutionary army was a miracle of poor organization. Because its supply system was undependable, its soldiers lacked food, clothing, and shoes. Pay was meager and often in arrears; when the soldiers were paid it was in depreciated currency. Changing conditions of enlistment, poor record-keeping, and fraud gave rise to many grievances. Morale was low. There were some serious mutinies, which were sometimes handled by appeasement and sometimes treated with a liberal dose of nitre. It is thought that promises of pensions and other rewards had much to do with keeping the army together.

The Continental Congress provided for half-pay for disabled soldiers in 1776. Two years later it passed unanimously an act granting half-pay for seven years to all commissioned officers who should serve until the end of the war. Private soldiers, by this same act, were promised a gratuity—the magnificent sum of $80. In 1780 the half-pay for officers was extended to life. The Continental Congress, of course, had to depend upon the states for the fulfillment of its promises, and various states did in fact pass laws to provide for the needs of the disabled and to make good the commitments to the officers. In 1780, Congress provided half-pay pensions for seven years to widows and orphans of officers who died in the service, but made no provision for the dependents of enlisted men.

This tender concern for officers and disregard of enlisted men continued into the post-war period. When the troops, by then generally disaffected to the edge of mutiny, were disbanded in the summer of 1783, each man received, according to Van Doren, one month's pay in specie and three in certificates. "This," Van Doren continues, "was the last recompense many of them ever got, except praise, for their years of hardship and privation." [2] The certificates, of course, were quickly sold to speculators for a small percentage of their face value.

Commissioned officers fared much better in that callously class-conscious age. Their half-pay for life was changed in 1783 to five

[2] Carl Van Doren, *Mutiny in January*. Viking Press, 1943, p. 237.

years' full pay. Some 2,480 officers were found to be eligible for "commutation certificates," which rapidly began to depreciate, since there was no provision for the payment of either principal or interest. These certificates, too, were bought up by speculators at extremely low rates, and when the claims were paid, the speculators profited handsomely. The officers received only a fraction of what the government paid out on their account.

The first United States Congress in 1789 took over the burden of pensions for the disabled of the Revolution. Then ensued a long series of increasingly generous laws relating to pensions for soldiers of that war. In 1818 pensions began to be granted to veterans and their dependents without regard to cause of death or disability. As a result of this liberalization, pensions for the year 1820 cost $2,766,440—more than had been expended in the entire period from 1789 to 1817.

The decision to pension all veterans was to be a momentous precedent in our history. Pensions were at length granted to widows on very liberal terms, which ultimately did not prevent remarriage. The last widow receiving a Revolutionary War pension, one Esther S. Damon of Vermont, died in 1906 at the age of ninety-two. Simple arithmetic shows that she was not born until the war had been over for thirty years, and she must have been some fifty years younger than her husband. The last of the pensioned veterans of the Revolutionary War died in 1867. Certain other pensions on account of the Revolutionary War continued to be paid until 1910. Approximately $70,000,000 in all was paid to pensioners of the Revolutionary War. In addition, 16,663 bounty-land warrants were issued, carrying title to 2,666,080 acres of land.

Until 1871 pensions to veterans of the War of 1812 and their dependents were granted only because of death or disability incurred in service. In 1871 these provisions began to be liberalized. Widows of such veterans were generously treated, and remained on the pay-roll until recent years—the last veteran pensioner died in 1905. One War of 1812 pensioner remained on the rolls in 1943, Esther Ann Hill Morgan, aged eighty-six, of Independence, Oregon. As the daughter of John Hill, a private in Clark's and McCumber's companies of the New York Militia, she received a pension of twenty dollars a month. Up to 1942 something more than $46,000,000 had been paid out in pensions for the War of 1812.

Mexican War veterans and their dependents received pensions only for death or service-connected disabilities until 1887. After that date the provisions of the pension laws were liberalized in the familiar manner. The last veteran pensioner of the Mexican War died in 1929, but 478 widows remained on the pension rolls in 1932, the value of their pensions being $279,000. About $61,500,-000 were paid to Mexican War pensioners up to 1942. The account, however, is by no means closed. There were still eighty-two pensioners in 1943, and they received $49,324.

Our many Indian Wars have also produced considerable numbers of veterans who have been able to claim pensions. Until 1892 such pensions were limited to cases of death or disability in service. In 1892 the door was opened to surviving veterans of certain specified Indian Wars between 1832 and 1842, and pension privileges were gradually extended by subsequent acts. In 1927 pensions were granted to disabled veterans whether the disability was service-connected or not. This legislation also granted benefits on the basis of age alone: $20 a month at age 62, $30 at age 68, $40 at age 72, and $50 at age 75. Up to 1942 we had spent nearly $89,000,000 on Indian War pensions. In 1943 we were pensioning 1475 veterans at a cost of $1,156,235.90 and paying another $1,252,618.21 to dependents of 3319 deceased veterans.

After the Civil War, pensions became a prominent political issue, and gave rise to pressure politics on a large scale. The drive for liberalization of conditions and increase in grants started slowly but gained great momentum about fifteen years after the end of the war. The "Arrears Act" of 1879 provided for collecting arrears of pensions in certain cases, and gave rich rewards to pension agents. In a famous veto message of 1887, Grover Cleveland called attention to the benefits received by the soldiers of the Civil War in the form of pay, bounties, pensions, civil service preference, and care in soldiers' homes, and stated that the veterans had "received such compensation for military service as has never been received by soldiers before since mankind first went to war." Although this particular veto was not over-ridden, the pension drive continued to function successfully. There were 2,213,365 soldiers who had served in the Civil War. The peak number of pensions was 970,352, a figure attained in 1901. The number of pensions was above 800,000 from 1892 until 1912. Since there was some mobility on the pension rolls, it seems likely that a very high proportion of the veterans ultimately made a pension claim or had one made for them.

Expenditures for Civil War pensions have to date been in excess of eight billion dollars. The account is by no means closed. As of June, 1943, we were paying pensions to 625 veterans whose average age was ninety-seven, the cost of these pensions being $4,870,564.63. Pensions were being paid to dependents of 32,552 deceased veterans at a cost of $15,682,850.46.

The story of pensions arising from the War with Spain, the Philippine Insurrection, and the Boxer Rebellion is much the same. The originally fairly strict pension provisions were progressively liberalized through the years. Up to 1942 we had spent almost two billions on this group. In 1943 we paid out $99,457,260.43 to 140,093 surviving veterans, and $23,531,288.05 to the dependents of deceased veterans.

In addition to pension provisions of a general nature, a great many pensions have been granted by special Acts of Congress, mostly to persons who do not quite qualify under the letter of the law, but whose cases were regarded as deserving. In many of these, extra amounts are provided to persons whose merits or circumstances seem to warrant special treatment. Such pensions are of course administered in the same manner as the others. Since 1862 artificial limbs have been supplied. Domiciliary care is given at the Naval Home in Philadelphia, (authorized in 1811, opened in 1831) at the Soldiers Home in Washington, at numerous Veterans' Administration Homes, and at various state homes.

Pensions and Other Relief for World War I Veterans

At the time of our entry into World War I, it was the intention of the government to avoid the pension evils that had arisen from other wars. After careful study, a system of service benefits not unlike workmen's compensation was enacted into law. The central feature was a system of voluntary, low-cost insurance, which the veteran could convert from term to some other form of insurance at the end of the war. Legislation also provided compensation for disability, and the compensation of families for death, allotments and allowances for dependents, medical treatment, prosthetic appliances, and vocational rehabilitation of the disabled. Though vocational rehabilitation was intended to be compulsory, it was never enforced.

This careful planning, however, was of little avail. The vocational training of the disabled was only moderately successful. About 180,000 veterans entered it, and 118,355 were believed to be rehabilitated and employable by reason of this training. The total cost of the vocational program was about $644,000,000. Claims for service-connected disability to the number of 1,141,206 were filed prior to June 30, 1932, and 541,000 awards were made.

Readers who regard World War I as incomparably milder than the present global combat may be shocked by these figures. It is true that only a small proportion of our mobilized men actually engaged in combat in World War I. Nevertheless, one fourth of our entire army subsequently filed claims for injuries alleged to have been incurred in the war. About half of this group (or one-eighth of the total number of soldiers) received compensation for service-connected disabilities.

By 1921 strong demands for additional veterans' compensation had crystallized. From that time on the veterans' benefits were a major issue of national politics. From 1921 to 1932 twelve general laws were passed relating to veterans, a principal feature of which was the liberalization of the interpretation of service-connected disability. Congress proved to be much more susceptible to veteran pressure than was the President, and there were many vetoes.

The 1924 Congress, dramatically overriding a presidential veto, passed the Adjusted Compensation Act. By this act veterans of World War I received a dollar a day for home service, and a dollar and a quarter for over-seas service, sixty dollars being deducted for the dismissal pay given earlier. Compensation was to be in the form of a twenty-year endowment policy of such an amount as could be purchased by the credit plus twenty-five per cent. Loans on these certificates, or policies, were authorized in 1927. Demands for immediate payment of the bonus led in 1932 to the ill-fated "Bonus Expeditionary Force," which we describe elsewhere. There was a great political struggle before the bonus was at length paid in full in 1936.

Immediately upon coming to power, Franklin D. Roosevelt made a determined attempt to cut the costs of veterans' expenditures.

The attempt was not highly successful. Nevertheless, the hard times of the past ten years have prevented any rapid expansion of veterans' benefits.

While there is as yet no general pension for all World War I veterans of a certain age, some pensions for non-service-connected disabilities are allowed. A veteran who served ninety days honorably, whose disability is total and permanent, may receive $30 a month if his income is not over $1000 if single or $2500 if married. There were 84,878 veterans of World War I drawing pensions for non-service-connected disabilities in 1943, at a cost of $37,879,290.87. This compares with three hundred and forty-one thousand five hundred and five veterans pensioned for service-connected disabilities at a cost of $165,865,297.31. About five hundred and fifty thousand veterans and dependents from World War I are on the pension rolls at the present time.

The total Federal expenditures for relief of veterans had reached an amount estimated by Buehler at twenty-five billion dollars by June 30, 1942.[3] Fifteen billions had gone in pensions. Another ten billions had been spent for adjusted compensation, insurance, and other benefits. Land grants of course were not included in this figure. Neither were expenditures by the various state governments.

Buehler has compiled two excellent tables (see page 223).

The Ethics of Pensioning Ex-Soldiers

There has been a great deal of argument about military pensions in the past, and no doubt the controversy will continue in the years to come. It may be worth while to attempt to formulate a few common sense principles on which we may judge such controversies.

Probably no one questions the justice of pensions for superannuated veterans of the regular military establishment. These men have given their best years to the army at a low rate of pay, one of the inducements being the pension system. They are entitled to their pensions.

The claim of the physically disabled veterans is clear but subject to certain qualifications. The pension is one solution to the prob-

3 Alfred G. Buehler, "Military Pensions," in *The Annals of the American Academy of Political and Social Science*, May 1943, on the subject "Our Service Men and Economic Security," edited by Robert H. Skilton, pp. 128-135.

	Total	Number of Pensioners June 30, 1942		Disbursements during fiscal year (in millions of dollars)		
		Living Veterans	Dependents	Total	Living Veterans	Dependents
Grand total	859,694	623,659	236,035	$431.2	320.3	110.9
War of 1812	1		1	0.0(a)	00	00(a)
Mexican War	95		95	0.0(b)	0.0	0.0(b)
Indian Wars	5,389	1,713	3,676	2.6	1.3	1.3
Civil War	38,689	975	37,714	19.5	1.3	18.2
Spanish-American War	209,833	146,886	62,947	125.7	102.7	23.0
World War I	550,929	432,409	118,520	263.9	199.4	64.5
World War II	1,246	93	1,153	0.2	0.0(c)	0.2
Regular Establishment	53,512	41,583	11,929	19.3	15.6	3.7

(a) $240.00   (b) $54,966.34   (c) $11,913.32

MILITARY PENSIONS, 1790-1942
(in millions of dollars)

Revolutionary War 70.0

War of 1812 .... 46.2

Indian Wars 88.8

Mexican War ....,........ 61.5

Civil War 8,007.1

Spanish-American War 1,792.6

World War I 4,619.5

World War II .... 00.0 (a)

Regular Establishment 223.6

Unclassified 16.5

Maintenance and expense 153.1

Total pension costs 15,078.9

(a) $200,000

lem of disability, but certainly not the best. If the disabled soldier can be rehabilitated, so that he is capable of full self-support, such an outcome is preferable for him and for society. And if he can be partly rehabilitated, that is better than a status of complete help-lessness. Compensation for disability must be of such a kind, and must be given in such a way, as not to destroy the desire to be self-supporting. Furthermore, disability is relative to one's accustomed occupation. An injury that unfits a man for manual labor might not be a great disadvantage to a lawyer, a banker, or a doctor. Nevertheless, all disabilities should be compensated in some way, in so far as they are actual economic handicaps.

The greatest abuses of disability claims have arisen with com-pensation for non-service-connected disabilities. The presumption of service-connection for disabilities developing within a specified period after the end of a war is dangerous. Even more dangerous is the tendency to establish pensions for all disabled regardless of the origin of their disabilities. The least justifiable pension is that which goes to all war veterans who have attained a certain age, their physical condition and financial standing being dis-regarded.

As for those disabled by reason of psychoneurotic breakdown, the case for pensions is less clear. They are, of course, sick persons, and as such entitled to care; but there is some question as to whether the care given to them should be based upon military service, and it may be that a pension would be the worst thing in the world for such persons. A pension, by giving them a secondary gain from neurosis—by making neurosis pay—may prevent many such persons from ever making a normal adjustment to life. We should therefore try to find some other mode of treating psycho-neurotics, perhaps some adaptation of psychiatric social work.

Similar gradations appear with regard to the claims of the veterans' dependents. Few would deny that when men are killed in war, the duty of supporting their widows and orphans devolves upon the nation. When a soldier is disabled, the state is respon-sible for him and his dependents. When a disabled veteran mar-ries and has a family, the obligation would seem still to hold. It would be obviously unjust to deny these wards of the state the privileges of family life, and probably their contributions to the population would be eugenically desirable.

A great abuse arises when a young woman marries an aged veteran on the road to the cemetery, and then draws a pension for the rest of her life on the basis of his service in a war that was over and done with twenty or thirty years before she was born. This sort of thing has happened a great many times in our history.

The veteran has also a valid claim to dismissal pay. If money, goods, and services can help him to readjust to civilian life, he has every right to get them. The principle of adjusted compensation—the bonus—is somewhat different. By reason of his military service, the veteran has been put at a disadvantage in competition with others. He has worked for $50 a month while others were drawing war-boom wages, and it is up to the state to make up the difference to him. There is more justice in this claim than scholars and pooh-bahs have usually been willing to concede, although the actual difference between the soldier's and the war-worker's pay is less than it seems when we consider only the crude, uncorrected figures. The only way to avoid such post-war problems would be to manage our wars in such a way that nobody makes any money from them. We may be sure that our soldiers would fight better, and feel better, if they knew that no one at home was getting rich from their sacrifices.

A tragic aspect of both pensions and bonuses in the past has been that sharpers and speculators have usually had the good of them. The Revolutionary certificates were in large part sold to speculators who reaped huge profits on them. Soldiers were also very often cheated of their bounties in land. The activities of the Civil War pension agents were scandalous; and some of their profits were huge. While in recent years there have been fewer loopholes, nevertheless some few persons, particularly certain lawyers, have made a very good thing of pressing veterans' claims. The activities of the veterans' organizations in handling veterans' cases free of charge have helped to minimize abuses of this kind.

It is also unfortunate that our aid to veterans, generous as it has been, has usually come too late to help them during their crucial years of readjustment to civilian life. We have spent immense sums on veterans, mostly after it was too late to do any good. If a veteran has not readjusted after ten years of civilian life, he probably never will readjust. The bonus of World War I, when it came, was too little and too late: too little for justice, too late to be of any help in readjustment. The money would have been just as well spent in attempting to rehabilitate the veterans of Pickett's Charge. A much smaller sum, spent wisely in 1919 and 1920, could have accomplished incomparably more.

If arguments for pensions, bonuses, and other subsidies are often fallacious, the arguments against them are rarely models of sound logic. We were told that the bonus of World War I would bankrupt the country, that we could never possibly pay it. But we were able to spend vast sums in rehabilitating German industry and in carrying through many other projects of equal wisdom. After World War II we shall no doubt hear all the same arguments. The fact is that no price would be too high if we could actually rehabilitate the soldier.

A much graver fallacy is that of regarding the question of pensions as the basic problem. Much—nearly all—of the literature on the subject reflects this misconception. We get nowhere by denouncing veterans for demanding pensions, by exposing the pension "racket," by writing books and articles against the veterans' exactions. The fact is that pensions—pension drives, bonus demands, etc.—are a symptom of a deep-lying maladjustment, and it is not sound policy to attack symptoms while disregarding the causes of symptoms. The cause of this particular set of symptoms is the veteran's maladjustment in society.

What Veterans on Relief Have Received

Many old soldiers who are not eligible for pensions or other Federal benefits fall upon hard times. State governments have passed a multitude of laws in order to help this group of veterans. Robert C. Lowe has summarized the provisions of this legislation as follows:

"Special statutory provisions for the care and support of veterans exist in practically all States. These provisions are of three types: direct relief (26 States), pensions (21 States), and care in State institutions (38 States).

"The majority of statutes providing for direct relief include the wives, widows and dependent children of veterans in the class of eligibles; over one-half of the statutes include other dependent relatives. Pensions are granted only to the veteran or his widow under the majority of State pension acts; a few provide for pensions to other dependent relatives. Care in state institutions is usually restricted to veterans and their wives or widows; only about one-half of the States provide for institutional care of other dependent relatives. Nurses who served in time of war are frequently designated as eligible for relief, pensions, and institutional care. Servants of soldiers are granted pensions under the laws of a few of the Southern States.

"Eligibility requirements for all three types of veteran assistance relate principally to residence, the war in which service was rendered, and need. Disability is a condition for receipt of such aid in a few States; some of whose statutes provide that the disability must have resulted from military service.

"The majority of State statutes providing for all three types of aid prescribe residence requirements . . .

"Veterans of all wars are eligible for direct relief in the majority of States making provisions for direct relief to veterans. However, legal provisions granting pensions to veterans of all wars exist in only three States (Massachusetts, New Jersey, and New York). Approximately three-fourths of the States providing for pensions grant them only to veterans of the Civil War, and most of these are Southern States which grant pensions to Confederate veterans. Minnesota does not provide pensions to any veterans except those of the Indian Wars. World War [I] and Spanish-American War veterans receive pensions under the laws of Maine.

"Nearly one-half of the States providing institutional care do not require service in any specific war but grant aid to all veterans of the armed forces of the United States. Approximately one-fourth of the States provide institutional care for Civil War veterans only, and these institutions are principally for the care of Confederate veterans . . .

"The statutes providing direct relief do not define need by specific terms but use such descriptive words as 'dependent,' 'needy,' and 'poor.' Ten of the twenty-one States granting pensions prescribe need as a qualification; seven State laws make disability a condition for receiving a pension without prescribing need; and the remaining four States authorize pensions on the basis of veteran status alone. Approximately one-half of the States which prescribe need as a condition for eligibility for a pension define need in terms of specific limitations on property and income . . .

"The type and amount of aid granted veterans varies widely." [4]

Pensions for Confederate soldiers, by the way, are often re-

[4] Robert C. Lowe, *State Public Welfare Legislation.* Works Progress Administration, Research Monographs, U.S. Government Printing Office, 1939, pp. 177-207.

markably generous. Alabama pays $600 a year, Florida gives $600 plus an extra $5 a month for those who lost an eye, foot, or hand in actual service. Georgia provides $360, South Carolina $240, and Arkansas $100. Kentucky, which did not secede, pays $600 to Confederate veterans. It is remarkable that these poor States, already burdened with the high cost of Federal pensions, should provide so generously for the warriors of the Lost Cause. The pensions are, of course, limited to cases of actual need.

Veterans' organizations usually participate in the administration of veterans' relief. New York State provides special relief for male and female veterans, for the families of deceased veterans, and for their dependent widowed daughters. The law provides that "A local unit of any of the following veterans' organizations is authorized to apply to the appropriating body of a town, city, or county for funds and to administer relief to veterans at public expense:

(a) The Grand Army of the Republic.
(b) The United Spanish War Veterans.
(c) The American Legion.
(d) The Disabled American Veterans of the World War.
(e) The Veterans of Foreign Wars of the United States.
(f) The Army and Navy Union of the United States.
(g) The Jewish Veterans of the Wars of the Republic, Incorporated.
(h) The Catholic War Veterans, Incorporated." [5]

A veteran may not be sent to an almshouse in New York. In Illinois, Oregon, and Washington he may be sent to the almshouse only with the consent of the commander of the nearest veterans' post. In this manner does the law attempt to protect the old soldier from this last indignity.

The sums spent for veterans' relief are considerable. A sample of 120 urban areas showed that in 1929 veterans' relief consumed between a fifth and a sixth as much money as general relief. From 1929 to 1933, however, veterans' relief increased much less rapidly than general relief. The figures follow:

[5] Elsie M. Bond, *Public Relief in New York State, A Summary of the Public Relief Law and Related Statutes.* New York State Department of Welfare and The State Charities Aid Association, Albany, 1936.

Expenditures from public and private funds administered
by public agencies in 120 urban areas, 1929-1933

Year	Veterans' relief	General relief
1929	$2,222,181	$12,133,856
1930	4,011,362	26,890,664
1931	7,726,884	53,452,819
1932	11,885,970	128,800,557
1933	12,840,909	239,313,607 [6]

Average monthly number of cases aided by
direct and work relief:

Year	Veterans' relief	General relief
1929	6,505	34,180
1930	10,719	73,244
1931	19,623	178,066
1932	36,731	463,157
1933	38,601	875,655 [7]

This same study made it clear that the veteran on relief in
urban areas in 1933 had no great financial advantage over non-
veterans. The following table of comparative expenditures brings
this out:

Average monthly relief per case in 1933

City	General	Veterans
Chicago—Three agencies	$30.55	$29.10
	28.13	
	25.32	
Boston	35.43	32.88
Detroit	25.66	14.03
New York	29.15	33.74
Saint Louis—Two agencies	12.05	23.24
	20.95	[8]

Veterans were well aware of this situation. A pathetic letter from
a soldier of the Spanish-American War, published in the New York

[6] From Table 7 in Emma A. Winslow, *Trends in Different Types of Public
and Private Relief in Urban Areas, 1929-1935*. U.S. Department of Labor,
Children's Bureau, Publication No. 237, U.S. Government Printing Office, 1937.
[7] *Ibid.*, from Table 8.
[8] *Ibid.*

Times on August 8, 1941, pointed out that veteran status was not
an unmixed blessing. Old-age pensions were difficult for a veteran
to get. Federal pensions for Spanish War veterans brought in $30
a month, which was less than an alien received on home relief.
A single man on home relief received $30 a month and food stamps,
while a veteran of 62 received $30 a month without the stamps. A
man and wife at 65 received $60 a month as an old-age pension,
which was just what a veteran with a wife would receive at that
age. A man with children and a wife might be better off on home
relief than on a pension. Other detailed comparisons brought out
the fact that veterans were no better off than non-veterans. What
had happened, of course, was that standards of general relief had
risen to and sometimes above the levels previously set for veterans.

In rural areas, however, the veteran on relief has a real financial
advantage over the non-veteran. In 1937, a sample of 385 rural
and town areas showed 54,771 persons on the general relief rolls,
the average monthly aid per case being $15.22. There were 2800
veterans, and the average aid per case was $24.33. To the well-fed
reader this difference may not seem large. To the person living
on $15.22 a month it probably seems enormous.

Bitter struggles were waged in the 1930s over the pitiful advantages to be gained by the status of the veteran on relief. Demands for veterans' preference greatly complicated the administrative problems of the alphabetical make-work agencies. Beginning
in 1937, Congress attached veterans' preference provisions to WPA
appropriations. Many veterans not eligible for other benefits were
glad to serve in the CCC camps. There were 130 all-veteran camps
in 1940, with a total enrollment of 27,000 men. The average age
of these veterans was 47 years.

Whether or not there are financial advantages in veteran status
on relief, there are certainly social and psychological advantages.
It must be a great deal easier for a man to take relief that is given
to him as a veteran than for him to accept something that is given
only for sweet charity's sake. And the veteran on relief has powerful friends and certain prerogatives, and it must be a comfort to
him to know that he can not be pushed around as easily as the
person who has never worn a uniform. For such excellent reasons
he clings to veteran status even when it is not financially profitable
to do so.

Veterans' Preferences and Other Benefits

Governmental largesse to veterans is not limited to pensions and relief. There are various other benefits for ex-soldiers.

The government life insurance is a valuable asset. The rates are low and the benefits high, because the government pays the overhead cost of the company. At one time many private insurance firms instructed their agents not to try to sell their policies in competition with government insurance, but to encourage all veterans to take the full amount of government insurance—a far-sighted policy which was probably very good business.[9]

Then there are the laws that guarantee the veteran preference in the civil service. Here the veterans of World War I accomplished quickly what the G.A.R. had been unable to do in many years; they achieved a really effective set of veterans' preference laws. The disabled soldier is particularly favored by them. That these laws work as intended is shown by the high proportion of veterans appointed to the Federal civil service. In the civil service of various States, veterans' preference comes near to being absolute, what with regulations that make it difficult for a non-veteran ever to outrank a veteran on the civil service lists.

Veterans' preference laws have often been criticized because they cause governmental employees to be selected on a basis other than efficiency. Indeed, one could hardly expect enthusiasts of civil service reform to endorse legislation that injures the structure which they have labored for generations to erect. We must concede that veterans' preference laws will probably lower the efficiency of the civil service. There is, however, one thing to be said for such laws: They recognize that the veteran has been damaged as a competitor and attempt to restore him to a favorable competitive position, and they help the veteran by giving him a chance to earn his living.

The underlying rationale of veterans' preference is that government can better put up with possible inefficiency than private employers. Private employers, if they hired disabled veterans at current rates of pay, would often be forced out of business by the competition of less sentimental entrepreneurs. Not so the government, to which the ordinary concept of solvency does not apply.

[9] Government insurance has been criticized with some justification because of the high rate of interest charged on policy loans.

In government, furthermore, efficiency is often not the first consideration; what is most important in many aspects of government is simply the just use of the irresistible power of the State. With respect to most of its functions, no one cares whether government is efficient or not if only it is just; inefficiency matters only as inefficiency means injustice. In other parts of government, such as the postal service, efficiency is desirable but a moderate degree of inefficiency does no harm. If, for example, the postmaster of a whistle-stop community is a disabled veteran minus an arm or a leg, he may be a little slow in getting out the mail, but that does no harm. Disability, however, does not always mean inefficiency; a great many of the handicapped are in fact more conscientious, single-minded, and efficient in the performance of their duties than are persons of normal capacity.

Within the limits of their resources, State governments have bestowed other marks of their favor upon the soldier. Writing in 1933, Talcott Powell collected information concerning these State benefits. In part, they are as follows: Eleven States granted poll-tax exemption. Twenty-six gave a limited tax exemption to veterans or their organizations or both. Seventeen had a fund for World War orphans. Twenty-eight supplied guardianship for orphans, thirty-three for veterans. Twenty-seven paid burial expenses. Seven gave assistance in purchasing farms and homes. Two gave free notary service in connection with veterans' benefits; fifteen gave other aid in prosecuting compensation cases; nineteen furnished a service officer to assist in making claims to the Veterans' Bureau. Nine supplied scholarships or other funds for educating veterans. Thirteen gave a free vending license. Seventeen at that time had civil service preference. Twenty maintained a state veterans' home. Three States legalized loans on adjusted service certificates for state banks. Two cared for graves and eleven furnished headstones or special markers; one furnished a firing squad for funerals. Twenty States had a state bonus. Indiana gave free hunting and fishing licenses to veterans. North Carolina provided that the veteran's body might not be dissected. West Virginia exempted the American Legion from the boxing tax. There were many other special provisions of the State laws, and each meeting of the State legislatures adds to the list.[10]

10 Talcott Powell, *Tattered Banners.* Harcourt Brace. 1933, appendix.

Thus we see that America has tried many experiments in its attempt to alleviate the miseries of ex-soldiers. The political power of the veterans, aided by the guilty conscience of the remainder of the population, has resulted in a proliferation of measures designed to benefit those who have fought our wars. But these often whimsical and fantastic expressions of good-will have generally not been very helpful to veterans; they usually came too late to help in any way that counted much. The past history of our attempts to help veterans is useful principally as showing us the kind of thing we should avoid. In the succeeding chapter we shall continue this theme with an analysis of some of our more spectacular failures.

Some Spectacular
Failures In
Helping Veterans

B Y the time we entered World War I, the United States had accumulated considerable experience with the veteran problem. Wilson was an historian and social scientist, and he was responsible for some well-conceived plans, but his careful planning did not prevent us from repeating many of the tragic errors of the past. In the years after the war, we failed to give adequate care to the disabled. There was scandalous mismanagement of veterans' affairs and graft of epic proportions. There was pauperizing relief and a rehabilitation program that failed. There was agitation for the bonus which arose directly from these failures. There were the thousands of soldiers and sailors who spent the post-war period in the Big House—also the result of our failures. Then came the pitiful bonus army which President Hoover ordered General Douglas MacArthur to disperse with tanks and tear gas. Let us review some of this recent history, in order to learn what not to do.

In 1918 nothing was too good for the soldiers. The sky was the limit—on promises. We were particularly proud of our concept of rehabilitation, which we thought of as applying only to the wounded. Our surgeons were going to perform miracles; they would make a man a new face or patch him up otherwise until he was better than ever. And there was much talk of those marvelous artificial limbs which, one was led to believe, were much better than the real ones and had the additional advantage of not being subject to disease and decay. We appropriated vast sums for hospitals, and never built them. We neglected a great many men who had obvious service-connected disabilities, and thus invited later frauds. We set the great mass of veterans adrift with the magnificent dismissal pay of sixty dollars. Sixty dollars, in those days, would buy a fairly good suit of clothes but left no margin for shoes, hat, overcoat, shirts, and other such accoutrements worn by the decently dressed civilian in 1919. Then we all voted for Harding and forgot about the veterans.

The Scandals of 1923

The veterans' organizations had retained an interest in their disabled comrades. As they had done before in our history, they were able to awaken the conscience of the nation on behalf of this neglected group. They kept up their fight. In the last days of 1919, Legion officials dramatically brought in some disabled veterans to speak before a group of Congressmen. An infantry corporal stood on his one leg and said that the morale of 1600 disabled veterans at Walter Reed Hospital was "lower than the morale of the German army ever was even when we had them on the run." A badly wounded private told of his inability to support his wife on the governmental allowance. A crippled tank corps sergeant, who had enlisted at sixteen, told of the shortcomings of the rehabilitation program. Immediately after this the Sweet Bill was passed, increasing the compensation of the disabled from $30 to $80 a month. But still the hospitals did not get built, and thousands of disabled continued to be left to their own meager resources. In 1921 the Veterans' Bureau was established, but Harding made one of his worst appointments in selecting its chief, and the graft, mismanagement, and neglect of the veterans continued.

In 1923 the public clamor was so great that a Congressional investigation was ordered. The administration of veterans' affairs had been in the hands of Colonel Charles R. Forbes. He was a curious character to have been chosen for such a large responsibility even in Harding's administration. A drummer boy in the Marines at the age of twelve, he was discharged at fourteen, and after some years he re-enlisted, this time in the Signal Corps. While serving at Fort Meyer, he deserted, was apprehended and briefly imprisoned for the first time at the age of twenty-two. The charges were dropped, and he was permitted to serve out his term of enlistment. During World War I he served with distinction, winning the Distinguished Service Medal for bravery beyond the call of duty. Colonel Forbes was not a great success in business, but was very much of a good fellow, the possessor of a curious charm which even his enemies admitted. Forbes became a friend of Harding, and did not hesitate to capitalize on that friendship. From time to time, however, he went too far even for the good-natured Harding, thus incurring the presidential displeasure.

Waste and graft in the Veterans' Bureau under Forbes were estimated at $225,000,000. The greatest sin of the Forbes administration was the failure to build hospitals and the graft connected with the purchase of hospital sites. The hospitals were badly and carelessly planned; on one occasion the absence of a kitchen was not discovered until the builders were ready to break ground for construction. In 1923 the hospitals were not yet completed; those finally available had cost from $4000 to $5000 *a bed!* Canada, with a much worse problem, had completed the construction of her hospitals by January, 1920, and had supplied facilities adequate in every respect at an average cost of $1500 a bed.

Forbes had operated recklessly in his purchases and disposal of surplus stores. He bought enough floor wax to take care of the needs of the Bureau for one hundred years, or "to polish a dance floor half the size of North Dakota," and then had most of it destroyed in order to cut down fire risks in storage. He bought $35,000 worth of a certain floor cleaner worth two cents a gallon at a price of ninety-eight cents a gallon. He bought, and never used, tremendous quantities of gold for dental fillings. He sold 85,000 sheets which cost $1.25 each for $.20 apiece, at a time when fresh purchases of sheets were still being delivered to the bureau. He attempted to dispose of large quantities of liquor and narcotics. One of the gems of German propaganda in the United States during World War I was the statement that garments made for the Red Cross by American women were sold in department stores at high prices. Forbes made that dream come true. He sold 98,000 pairs of Red Cross pajamas of good quality at thirty cents each. Forbes was alleged to have received a third of the profits on certain contracts. There were other "irregularities." One man was paid a salary of $4800 for working two hours a year. Railway passes were issued to persons who had never worked for the bureau, one for a European trip and two for Asiatic trips.[1]

1 The story of these scandals is told at length in U.S. Congress, Senate, Select Committee to Investigate the Veterans' Bureau. *Investigation of the Veterans' Bureau*, pursuant to S. Res. 466, 67th Cong.; 4th Sess., Senate Report 103, 68th

Forbes, of course, went to prison, after a legal fight and a trial in which his guilt was established in a moderately convincing manner. There had been neglect and mismanagement, and someone had to be punished, and therefore Forbes, who had meanwhile suffered a paralytic stroke, was committed to Leavenworth in March, 1926. The punishment of Forbes was, to be sure, a just and salutary action, but a diligent search of the contemporary record fails to reveal that any of the veterans who undoubtedly died of neglect in the Forbes administration were restored to life when the aging scoundrel limped through the prison gates—nor does it seem logically demonstrable that Forbes was the only person to blame for the neglect of veterans in the years following 1918. Forbes emerged from prison in November, 1927, declaring that he would yet vindicate the name of President Harding, and also prove that his cellmate, Dr. Cook, had actually discovered the North Pole. After that, he planned, with Dr. Cook, to discover the South Pole.

When General Hines took office, he attempted not only to improve the efficiency of service to veterans, but to remedy the pauperizing procedures which went hand in hand with inefficiency. He found, as so many have before and since, that in the human relations field the best service is the least expensive in the long run, and that neglect and inefficiency are the parents of demoralization. General Hines introduced various reforms designed to check the increasing pauperization of dependent veterans. But that was 1923, and much damage had already been done.

This five-year period of neglect of disabled veterans opened the door to many spurious claims then and later. The proper policy would have been to make an active and determined search for all disability cases in the years following 1918. This was not done, and in consequence a great many deserving cases remained undetected, while a number of fraudulent claims were pressed with vigor. Since the search for the disabled had not been conducted, there was no way in 1923 of doing justice to the disabled of war except by framing rules in such a way as to include with them many cases of disability not of service origin.

Cong., 1st Sess. For shorter statements see: Carl C. Dickey, "Plundering the Wounded Men," in *The World's Work*, June, 1924, and Stanley Frost, "Salvaging the Veterans' Bureau," in *The Outlook*, Oct. 3, 1923. See also *The Outlook*, Nov. 21, 1923, p. 477.

Investigations of disability rolls have accordingly shown that many persons receive compensation who are not in any real sense disabled. One man certified as totally and permanently disabled by flat feet won a prize by dancing continuously for thirty-six hours in a marathon dance. Another totally and permanently disabled veteran was found to be a regular player on a college football team. New York City's policemen and firemen pass very exacting physical examinations before appointment, but a number of them have been on the force while drawing army pensions for physical disability. There have been many such cases. These injustices are part of the price we pay for not seeking out and discovering the truly disabled in the years immediately following the war.

The Program of Vocational Rehabilitation

As we have already observed, one of the good ideas for dealing with the disabled veteran of World War I was to teach him a new trade or profession in which his disability would not be a handicap. This program, instituted in 1918, was continued with various administrative changes until June 30, 1928. Approximately 180,000 veterans were enrolled in training courses, and of these 118,355 were subsequently considered to be rehabilitated and employable by reason of their training. The cost of the program was $644,019,720.78.

The program of vocational rehabilitation started poorly, and never reached a high state of efficiency. In August, 1919, The New York Times attempted an evaluation of the program to date.[2] It estimated that 247,000 Americans had been disabled during the war, of whom seven-tenths would require vocational rehabilitation—an estimate which proved remarkably accurate. But up to June 28, 1919, The Federal Board of Vocational Education, with 1,635 employees, had managed to put only 3,923 veterans into training. The Times concluded that "The long delays to which the crippled and disabled men have been subjected, the entanglements of red tape, and the worry over money matters while they waited, in many instances with nothing to live on and no way to make a living, have seriously affected their morale. This is apparent even among those under hospital treatment."

2 The New York Times, Aug. 24, 1919.

In March and April of 1920, a Congressional committee, aided by the newspapers, subjected the program of vocational rehabilitation to further scrutiny. Many pitiful cases of neglect and mismanagement were revealed, and the suspicion of graft was certainly not excluded. A veteran with one arm, one leg, one eye, and one ear told the committee of his struggles to obtain vocational training. It was discovered that a soldier who had lost his sight in battle was receiving twenty-five cents a day as compensation. Crippled veterans were being exploited as a source of cheap labor, and they were frequently misplaced in training. A fly-by-night vocational school in Pittsburgh, operating under no supervision from the Board, was receiving more than $125,000 a year in return for alleged vocational training given to 300 veterans. It is worth noting that all this happened before Harding's administration.

In spite of this drum-fire of criticism, the Board continued to work with exasperating slowness. Up to August 15, 1921, three years after the end of the war, only 5,393 veterans had completed their training. A number of administrative reorganizations improved the program by decentralizing responsibility and speeding up action on applications. But the program never became more than moderately effective.

In 1923 Stanley Frost investigated the rehabilitation program and published his findings in *The Outlook*.[3] His progress report and analysis of five years after the war make interesting reading today. He notes that the work was started by a curiously mixed body of educational theorists and deserving Democrats, the Democrats being replaced in 1921 by equally deserving Republicans. Some of the difficulties of the program arose from the policy of entrusting its administration to political appointees. The Bureau had created some thirty schools, in which about 4,000 students were enrolled in 1923. Analysis of the salaries paid to the teachers leads one to believe that these were not first-rate schools. Most of the trainees had been farmed out to other schools, which ranged from first-rate universities to fly-by-night diploma mills. There was no adequate inspection of these schools, and there was reason to believe that some of them continued to exist only because of the political connections of their owners. About half of the trainees

[3] Stanley Frost, "Grab-Bag Training for Veterans," in *The Outlook*, Sept. 26, 1923.

were "in placement," under a sort of apprenticeship arrangement, which was a useful device but one in which the possibility of exploitation by the employer was present. Little attempt had been made to fit the training to the veteran's needs or abilities. Nor was there any coordination with the world of industry. Men were trained for overcrowded trades in which they could not hope to find employment. Several hundred sign-painters, for example, were trained when no employment was available. Crippled men were trained for trades which insurance regulations precluded them from practicing. The compensation drawn by some men during their training was more than they could have hoped to make at their trades, and therefore they prolonged their training and kept shifting their courses. Many veterans took "snap courses" as a way of loafing. A music course was considered excellent for this purpose, since it required only a couple of hours a week for lessons and the rest of the week was supposed to be devoted to practice at the student's option. There was little or no inspection or follow-up of the student's work. Frost gave special commendation to the College of the City of New York, where some 1300 veterans were being trained.

In another article Frost compared the veterans' program of the United States with that of Canada.[4] In Canada rehabilitation courses lasted seven months and cost $820 on the average; in the United States, twenty-seven months and cost $3,850. Nevertheless, Canada's results were superior.

It is interesting to bear in mind that Frost's report described conditions existing five years after the end of the war. And yet we may reasonably suppose that if vocational rehabilitation cannot be completed in five years it cannot be done at all.

The "Bonus Expeditionary Force" of 1932

The Bonus Army—"Bonus Expeditionary Force" it called itself— was a collection of pitiable misfits who descended on Washington, D.C., in 1932 and frightened many well-fed people into thinking the Communist revolution was just around the corner. But this was a mistaken notion; members of the bonus army were veterans and conservative. They just wanted their bonus, and went about

4 Stanley Frost, "Where Veterans Fell Among Friends," in *The Outlook*, Oct. 10, 1923.

getting it in a rather stupid way. Only after they had been dispersed by force did they develop revolutionary sentiments, and then their movement was incipiently fascistic rather than communistic in nature.

The theory of the Adjusted Compensation Act of 1924 was that the soldier had been treated worse, economically, than the civilian, and was thus entitled to a gratuity which would partially redress the balance. This was given in the form of an insurance policy which had no immediate cash value. At once there arose demands for the cash payment of the bonus. When, in 1927, it became possible for veterans to borrow on these certificates, the Veterans' Bureau found itself in the small-loan business in a big way. By June 30, 1932, certificates to the number of 2,584,582 had been pledged for an amount of $1,369,042,679. There had been repeated and ever-increasing loans to many veterans.

In 1932 the bonus was still unpaid, although Congress had recognized the veterans' moral claim to compensation by passing the adjusted compensation law. Needy veterans could no longer borrow on their certificates, since they had already pledged them to the limit. The demand for cash payment became clamorous. Then there arose one of the most curious mass phenomena of history, a migration of thousands of veterans to Washington to present in person their claim for the immediate cash payment of the bonus. Nobody seems to have planned or inspired the movement. It just started, and, like miniature golf, marathon dancing, and other manias, it spread.

The march appears to have begun with a party of veterans in need of the bonus who took off from Portland, Oregon, in old cars. By the time they reached Council Bluffs, Iowa, they were joined by many others. When they crossed the free bridge at St. Louis, they numbered at least 300 and included representatives from all parts of the West. Many of them were clad in tattered uniforms and carried cooking utensils. They had their own "military police," to keep order in the group and to prevent crimes against the civilian population. They commandeered a train at Caseyville, Illinois, and went to Indiana; the Indiana authorities obligingly furnished transportation to Ohio. In this manner, they went to Washington.

Meanwhile, other cells of this curious organism appeared elsewhere, and all assembled and coalesced in Washington. On June 4,

1932, a bonus-seeking army of 900 from Detroit, Toledo, and Cleveland tried to commandeer a freight train at Cleveland but was balked by the police. On June 6 other contingents were reported on their way to Washington. On June 7, upwards of 7,000 Bonus Army marchers paraded on Pennsylvania Avenue, while an estimated 100,000 spectators lined the sidewalks.

General Glassford, in charge of police in the District of Columbia, treated the B.E.F. with kindness. Himself a veteran, he felt that, however misguided, they were within their constitutional rights. At first he billeted them in vacant stores and government buildings, but they quickly overflowed these quarters and encamped in Anacostia Flats just outside Washington. Soon there were thousands of them. They built crude huts from such materials as could be obtained at the city dumps: egg-crates, paper, roofing, scraps of lumber, etc. They took burdock leaves and long grass and wove them through chicken wire for roofing material.

Soon there were 12,000 and then probably 20,000 impoverished veterans encamped near the Capitol and determined to stay there, as they put it, until 1945 if necessary. These men lived by charity. General Glassford was said to have contributed $773 from his own pocket. Other Washington citizens helped as well as they could. Soon the members of the B.E.F. were joined by their wives and children. Sanitary arrangements were extremely primitive, as in all the Hoovervilles of the time. There was great danger of an epidemic.

All investigators agreed that these men were really veterans. One writer estimated that about sixty per cent of them were married. When they left Washington and went through Pennsylvania, they were investigated for the Pennsylvania Department of Welfare by Helen Glenn Tyson and Prentice Murphy, two well-known social workers, who pronounced them migrants of a high type and not mere floaters. There may even have been some professional men among them. However, some weeks after the dispersal of the army, Attorney General Mitchell published a report showing that of a group of 4,723 who had applied to the Veterans' Bureau for help, 829 had been convicted of some criminal offense, and a large proportion for serious offenses, 138 for larceny, 66 for burglary, and so on.

The B.E.F. maintained good discipline in camp and in Washington. The official leader of the group was W. W. Waters, a thirty-four-year-old ex-canning factory superintendent of Portland, Oregon. Three times elected leader, he had been a sergeant and had an excellent war record. He administered the camp well, assigning newcomers to quarters and otherwise taking care of the needs of his army of homeless men. Waters was an ex-socialist, and had been out of work for more than a year.

The Bonus Army veterans professed to be not at all radical in political ideology. They maintained a constant hunt for Reds, whom they ejected into the outer darkness upon discovery, though many of them were almost ready to concede that the Reds had some good ideas. There was a camp newspaper, a weekly called the "B.E.F. News," about which there was some mystery. It was surprisingly well edited, and no one unfamiliar with professional journalistic techniques could have produced it.

A group of some 700, mainly from the Pacific Coast, became dissatisfied with Waters' mild methods, and advocated the use of stronger pressures. This group, led by Roy Robertson, a pathetic sufferer whose health was so poor that he often fainted, engaged in a continuous, twenty-four hour picketing of Capitol Hill. They proved difficult for the police to handle.

But the B.E.F. was not in any sense revolutionary. An unidentified writer quoted in *The New Republic*, August 10, 1932, described the temper of the camp as follows:

> Personally, I'm convinced that the whole temper of the bonus army is that of a Baptist camp meeting. Mr. Hoover is an evil man who is disobeying the commands of God in not giving them a bonus. Their reasoning proceeds thus: The flag is sacred; they fought for the flag; therefore some of the sacredness of the flag has been transmitted to them; this sacredness not only exists but is recognized by the "real" America which wants to give them a bonus; Mr. Hoover is frustrating the desire of the real America; consequently Mr. Hoover is trying to defile sacred things; consequently Mr. Hoover is an evil man who, in God's good time will receive his just deserts. Now you can't make a revolution out of that.

Revolutionary the Bonus Army was not, but its members retained the soldier's irreverence and his talent for sour humor. Among the marching songs of the organization were "President

Hoover, He's a bum," (sung no doubt to the tune of "Hallelujah, I'm a bum") and "My Bonus Lies Over the Ocean." Similar sentiments were expressed in slogans written on their huts and jalopies. One man placed two crusts of bread and a glass of water on a stand in front of his shack; over this he put a sign, "Hoover Diet." Another man exhibited two dried and bleached bones under the legend "Contributed by Senator Reed of Pennsylvania." Another veteran dug three graves in front of his hut, one each for Mellon, Dawes, and Hoover. But the members of the B.E.F. continued to curse bankers and communists with equal fervor.

Through June and most of July the B.E.F. maintained its numbers and its morale. An attempt was made to get the veterans out of the city by furnishing funds for the trip back home—the same proposition that had been made to the bonus seekers who infested London in the time of Queen Elizabeth. Waters and his group resisted this, but a few members of the army took the bribe. The sum of $76,712.02 was advanced to 5,160 veterans at this time. Some took the money and remained in the city; others went home to recruit more members for the army, speaking at this time of an army of 100,000.

Some unpleasant incidents arose as the idea of the B.E.F. began to lose its novelty. Someone, evidently without proper authority, called out the marines, and a clash was averted only by the presence of mind of a young officer and the discipline of that body. Then on July 28 officials of the Treasury Department attempted to clear the men out of some of the buildings. There was an encounter in which one of the bonus marchers was killed. Then came the order to General Douglas MacArthur to bring in the troops from Fort Meyer. He came in with infantry, cavalry, and five tanks. With military precision, and tear gas, and in accordance with the most up-to-date tactics, the Bonus Army was evicted from its shabby encampment. The shacks were burned. Very likely all this was done without unnecessary cruelty, but the effects of the incident were bad. Hoover had made a political blunder from which a certain shrewd man in New York profited greatly.

Somehow the rumor spread among the weary and homeless men that Johnstown, Pennsylvania, would receive them. Apparently Eddie McCloskey, the decidedly unorthodox mayor of that city, had in fact invited them to come there. About 5,000 of the marchers managed to reach Johnstown, in spite of efforts to direct them elsewhere, and encamped in a park near the city. The people of Johnstown, particularly those who paid the taxes, were greatly perturbed, but the camp was evacuated in a few days. Other members of the army came to New York City, where they lived for a time in a squalid Hooverville below Riverside Drive.

Commander Waters tried for a time to keep his movement going, and planned a Utopian camp in Maryland, then turned his efforts to the organization of the "Khaki Shirts." The khaki shirt movement undoubtedly had many of the elements of fascism. In founding it, Waters used language not unlike Hitler's, calling upon all good citizens to join the movement to take "the United States Government away from the moneyed powers, by legal means, and return it to the common people, whose government it should be."

After the dispersal, the B.E.F. assumed great political importance. The demand for cash payment of the bonus became more insistent because of public sympathy with the veterans. Members of the B.E.F. carried their message to all corners of the land. In New York City, Talcott Powell collected the following parody which expresses the sentiments of the group eloquently:

> Hoover is my shepherd, and I am in want. He maketh me to lie down on the park benches. He leadeth me beside the still factories. He restoreth my doubt in the Republican party. He leadeth me in the paths of destruction for his party's sake. Yea, though I walk through the valley of the shadow of starvation, I do fear evil for he is against me. His politics and the profiteers they frighten me. He preparest a reduction of wages before me in the presence of mine enemies. He anointest my income with taxes. My expenses runneth over. Surely poverty and unemployment will follow me all the days of this Hoover administration, and I will dwell in the poor house forever.[5]

The Bonus Expeditionary Force dramatized the failure of the nation to deal adequately with its veterans of World War I. If we had not neglected the veterans in the crucial five years after the war, if we had sought out the disabled, if we had helped the veterans to get on their feet and make a start in the world, if we had contrived to heal the veterans' attitudes, there would never have been a Bonus Army.

[5] Quoted by Talcott Powell, *Tattered Banners*. Harcourt Brace, 1933. Attributed by Powell to R. E. Jacobs, who was active in the B.E.F.

Entr'acte:
The Challenge
Of The Veterans
Of World War II

I N the midst of the battle of Chancellorsville, while the issue was yet in doubt, General Lee sat calmly in his saddle, and fell to talking about the future of the brave young men in the armies of the South. He wondered what they would do to improve themselves when they were done with war.

Lee had a special reason to be concerned about veterans. He knew what sometimes happened to heroes when their days of heroism were over. His father, the famous Light Horse Harry Lee, was the *beau sabreur* of the Revolution; he was a hero then, but he proved too unstable and inept for peace. Robert E. Lee was the son of a veteran who slowly deteriorated, committing follies and errors of judgment by the score, losing fortune and friends, even suffering imprisonment for debt, until the day came when the very young Robert saw the father, crippled, disfigured, and discredited, a ruined and a beaten man, leave the family he loved and the State he had governed to find his death in a foreign land. He was a fine soldier, this father; "a man born for war," as Sandburg said of another. He seemed "to have come out of his mother's womb a soldier," but he was a poor veteran. In the end, he could not even die in peace in his native land. Perhaps Robert E. Lee thought of some of these things in the days when he commanded armies and disposed of the destinies of men.

We, too, may well pause to ponder what will happen to our young men whom we have exposed to death and destruction. What will happen to these war-made men when they must take up once more the ways of peace? How can we help them to find the road back?

The veterans are already beginning to return. They will constitute about one-tenth of the population—a very dynamic and dangerous tenth. They are the one-tenth that the other nine-tenths of the nation has used to fight a war, the tenth whose lives, limbs, eyes, health, and sanity we have used up recklessly in attaining the ends of national policy. They are the principal social problem of the coming years. Like no other group, the veterans command our minds and hearts today. The kind man pities them. The just man feels guilty toward them. The informed man fears them.

Not To Plan Now, Is To Plan Disaster

We know from past experience that we must not be caught unprepared. The veterans will descend upon us with frightening suddenness, "Full of strange oaths and bearded like the pard, jealous in honor, sudden and quick in quarrel," jabbering the *patois* of a dozen different foreign lands; resentful and explosive in unexpected ways; men who know no trade but war, widely experienced with death but strangely naïve and unsophisticated; expecting jobs and good jobs too but lacking the skills or the stability to hold them; indignant over the good times and prosperity that civilians have enjoyed during the war; eager for life but unaware where or how to begin living; given to hectic gaiety and sullen depression; familiar with death, *connoisseurs* of death but illiterates of peace:— they will be aliens in the land that bore them. Not to plan for their return is in fact to plan disaster.

Some of the veterans will return with frightful wounds. Others will enjoy their pitiful share of the blessings of peace in institutions for the mentally deranged. Many more will be borderline mental cases who will never recover from the war. Some will beg and some will go to prison. Most will suffer in silence and will solve their own problems as best they can. All will be in need of some form of rehabilitation, the apparently normal along with the others.

Experience has also taught us that the public will soon tire of veterans. So long as the veterans are safely out of sight, so long as the obligation to the veterans remains a theoretical matter, it is possible for most of us to think kindly of them. But this sympathetic attitude can easily change to hostility when the flesh-and-

blood veterans return to our city streets, in need of everything and
with a strong tendency to make unreasonable demands in a highly
truculent manner.

It is better to decide upon a policy beforehand, and to set up
machinery and train personnel to carry out that policy, than to
trust to spontaneous outpourings of the milk of human kindness,
for history shows that the sources of this fluid often dry up at
critical moments and flow too abundantly at the wrong time where
veterans are concerned. Veterans are not very satisfactory as objects
of charity. It will be better for us, if we can, to arrange to put them
in a position where they will have no need of charity.

When one thinks concretely of the veterans-to-be, it is difficult
to realize that they will be the problematical element in our society. Before war came most of us did not consider these boys to be
problems. Our soldiers are just ordinary American boys, how can
war have changed them so much? We think of them as the boy
scouts of a few years back, a little older now, the boys who sold
Collier's and *The Saturday Evening Post* from door to door, who
mowed our lawns, went to the local high school, and occasionally
got into small scrapes as a result of moderate adventures in hell-
raising—typical middle-class Americans of the Andy Hardy type.

You say you have known these boys all their lives. But have you?
They were perfectly normal boys, you think. Yes, but they certainly
did not have what we should ordinarily consider a normal American boyhood. They were a blighted generation before they ever
studied war. These present soldiers were depression children. They
have never known peace. It is hard to predict what the impact of
war and the inroads of veteran psychology will do to such people.

During the years of depression these soldiers, most of them, lived
in families haunted by the specter of insecurity. Many of their
fathers lost their jobs, grew shabby, almost ceased to think of themselves as men. Many of their families were on relief. Meals were
sometimes scanty. Spending money was hard to get. Often the boys
were glad to go to the CCC for its square meals, warm clothes, and
the few dollars that went home to their families. Some of these boys
went on the road—one less mouth to feed at home. "Depression
stiffs," the hoboes called them. Some of them married and went on
relief, in accordance with the pleasant custom of the time.

Most of the present generation of soldiers have known poverty, hunger, and the fear of the gaunt, grey wolf. Nearly all have known what it is to be unemployed.

People in the comfortable, well-educated classes never quite realized what was happening to that generation of youngsters during the depression. A study made in the middle Thirties, published in a book, *Youth Tell Their Story*,[1] offered a great deal of information about the attitudes and characteristics of our World War II soldiers in the years before war came. The study was based on interviews with a carefully selected sample of 13,500 Maryland youths, and its findings are probably reasonably correct for the entire country. The youths of that period, together with their younger brothers, make up our present army.

Our Army: Men Who Did Not Believe in War

The world had not been kind to those young men, even before the shadow of war overcast their lives. In those days there was an ominous gap between the completion of one's schooling and the beginning of one's working career. From forty to forty-six per cent of the youths studied had not obtained full employment within a year after leaving school. At the time of the study, about thirty per cent of the youth in the labor market were unemployed.

Society gave little to these young men and expected much of them. Forty per cent had received no dental care in the year previous to the study, but about one in five was supporting or helping to support his parents. Others felt that help was needed but were unable to give it. Those who had jobs worked long hours for little pay, often in blind-alley jobs. Many of them started work before the age of eighteen. They had no guidance and no effective vocational training; there was little relationship between the jobs they held and the training they had received. A large percentage of the group considered economic security their most urgent personal problem.

Most of the youth group were dissatisfied with the places where they lived. Forty-six per cent of farm youth wanted to move. Three

[1] Howard M. Bell, *Youth Tell Their Story, A Study of the Conditions and Attitudes of Young People in Maryland between the Ages of 16 and 24*. American Council on Education, Washington, D.C., 1938.

out of four village youths would have moved if they had been able. Most of them wanted to settle in cities.

The majority of youth regarded war as needless and preventable; 60.7 per cent of all youth, males and females, so regarded it, and 54.7 of the males. If war should come, 35.5 of the young men expected to volunteer; 35.6 would go if drafted; 12.2 would go if invasion threatened; and 11.9 would refuse to go. The younger boys were more willing to go to war than the older ones. Of the sixteen-year-olds, 46.5 per cent expected to volunteer, while only 28.4 per cent of the twenty-four-year-olds would volunteer. Only 10.3 per cent of the sixteen-year-olds would refuse to go, while 15.1 per cent of the twenty-four-years-olds expected to refuse. There was a rough correlation between amount of education and opposition to war: the more educated, the more opposed to war.

Some of the typical attitudes expressed by the war-resisters were: "Better a live coward than a dead hero." "I'd cut off my finger so I couldn't shoot that gun." "I'd face a firing squad before I'd go out and shoot people." "I'd go in the bush till the war blew over." A young woman stated her attitude eloquently when she said, "I don't want no one-legged man."

If we suppose that the young men of this Maryland survey, with their younger brothers, constitute our present army, the following conclusions are justified:

(A) They are not enthusiastic about war. An army of ten million would include three and a half million patriots (volunteer), three and a half million realists (go if drafted), a million or more reluctant soldiers (go if invasion threatens), and a million to a million and a half one-time conscientious objectors to war. Five and a half million once regarded war as unnecessary and preventable.

(B) Among the many war-resisters, or former war-resisters, the rate of psychiatric rejection and psychoneurotic breakdown is probably very high.

(C) The woman friends of the soldiers are more opposed to war than the soldiers themselves. Their attitudes do not help the young men to accept the harsh realities of war, and they will probably not be too helpful to veterans in the post-war period. Here one thinks especially of the young woman who "didn't want no one-legged man."

After the war, many veterans will expect to move to cities. The problem of caring for them in cities will be great. Problems created by desire for occupational mobility will also be great.

This generation of soldiers had already been kicked around a great deal before the war, and had learned—even before entering the army—to look to the government for help.

What may we suppose that war has made of these young men who had never received a very generous share of the American standard of living, who had known and feared economic insecurity from the cradle upwards, who did not believe in war, who did not want to fight, and who have been told what they were fighting against but never yet just what they were fighting for? What will they expect us to do for them when they return? What political creeds will they accept and what leaders will they follow? In spite of everything, these young men have been docile soldiers. Will they be equally docile as veterans?

We cannot yet know the answers to these questions. The best that we can do is to prepare to do the veterans justice, and hope that they will be just.

Helping the Veteran to Adjust

to Peacetime Living

The Human
Materials
At Our Disposal

I N our discussion so far, we have spoken of a sort of veteran type, overlooking the many variations in the group of veterans. This was a necessary device of exposition, which we must now abandon for a time. In planning for the rehabilitation of veterans, we must allow for the infinite variability of personality. Rehabilitation procedure must be adapted to the needs of different age groups, to different levels of education and intelligence, to the married and unmarried, the rich and the poor, the lazy and energetic, and to a number of other variable characteristics. A uniform prescription will never do for a heterogeneous group of human beings.

Let us, therefore, for the moment, forget our veteran type and look at the variations within the type. While detailed information concerning the social characteristics of the men in the armed forces has not been made available, enough has been published to give a rough idea of the sort of problem we face when the veterans return.

The total number of men mobilized in the current war will probably be somewhere between twelve and fifteen million. At the time of writing, the size of the Army has been fixed at 7,700,000 officers and enlisted men, while the Navy, Marines, and Coast Guard will shortly reach a maximum of 3,600,000. It is estimated the inductions will continue at the rate of 75,000 to 150,000 a month in order to maintain this figure. More than a million men have already been discharged from service in this war, of whom about 100,000 are already receiving pensions.

How Old Are Our Veterans?—Age Groups

A recently published survey of soldiers' attitudes toward postwar education contains information that enables us to estimate the age distribution, level of education, and marital condition of the army, on the basis of a sample of 10,000 soldiers.[1] Computations based on this survey justify the following conclusions (the figures being approximate):

28 per cent of our soldiers are between 18-20 years of age
33 per cent of our soldiers are between 21-24 years of age
21 per cent of our soldiers are between 25-30 years of age
19 per cent of our soldiers are 30 years of age and over

———

101 per cent

It has been announced that the average age of the army in the early months of 1944 was twenty-seven. This age-level will probably increase slowly as the war goes on, but the continued induction of eighteen-year-olds will slow down the rate of increase considerably. If it becomes necessary to draft the older age groups, the average age will mount rapidly.

In planning for rehabilitation, it will be necessary to consider the needs of different age groups. The large group of boys under twenty-one will be likely to respond to treatment in a different manner from the two-fifths of the soldiers who are twenty-five or over. We may suppose that most of the soldiers in the 21-24 age group have had little economic experience outside of the army, while those below twenty-one have had practically none.

As to the educational level of the soldiers, the picture is rather discouraging. A little more than half of the soldiers have never finished high school. About a quarter have finished high school but no more. A small proportion, perhaps three per cent, have been graduated from college, while possibly a little more than a sixth have had some college training. Here our figures, based upon the survey, check reasonably well with the results of the earlier study, *Youth Tell Their Story*, which reported that of the out-of-school youth 39.1 per cent had completed eighth-grade education or less, 23.7 had had some high-school training, 26.5 had graduated from high school, and 10.7 had gone beyond high school.

1 "Soldiers' Attitudes Toward Post-War Education," in *Education for Victory*, Vol. 2, No. 17, March 3, 1944. The survey reported in this article was made by the Research Branch of the Morale Services Division of the Army Service Forces.

Do They Want to Go Back to School?

Not only the amount of schooling, but the attitude toward education varies widely among the soldiers. Seven per cent of the men believe that they will return to full-time school or college at the end of the war, whether or not they receive government aid. But many of the men included in this seven per cent are married, or had been out of school for more than a year before joining the army, or are more than twenty-five years old. Since each of these contingencies discourages school attendance, we *may suppose that not more than four per cent would actually return to school without government aid,* on the basis of present attitudes.

Another seventeen per cent expect to return to part-time school or college, for the most part to business or trade courses. The condition of the labor market will affect these decisions profoundly. About eighty per cent of the soldiers state that they will return to school if they can get no job at all and if government aid for schooling is available. As to the amount of government aid needed for schooling, sixty-two per cent of the soldiers would be satisfied with tuition, books, and fifty dollars a month, while thirty-eight per cent would require more. It should be noted that the soldiers probably have a very vague notion concerning what fifty dollars a month would purchase in the way of shelter, food, and clothing.

The conclusion of the authors of the survey seems to be that the attitude of the soldiers toward education is generally lukewarm and somewhat inconsistent. However, a large number of soldiers would be inclined to accept educational aid if satisfactory jobs are not available.

Along with these differences regarding education go the to-be-expected variations in intelligence. Intelligence scores of soldiers are probably distributed on a normal curve, with the lower ranges completely and the upper ranges partially excluded. The average soldier, with only a modest Intelligence Quotient and with high school education or less, is not an intellectual giant. Veterans in the lower intelligence and educational categories will be most likely to be problematical with regard to self-support, while the more intelligent and better educated will be likely to give trouble in other ways.

Are They Equipped to Earn Their Living?

As to the economic backgrounds of soldiers, there is the same variation. Bossard notes that more than half of the families of those inducted into military service in eastern urban areas are known to the social service exchanges in their area—a very instructive and disturbing fact.[2]

Some of the soldiers have trades. Various attempts have been made to estimate the number of members of trade unions in the armed services, and this figure has sometimes been placed, by union statisticians, as high as 2,500,000. Many difficulties are involved in such estimates, of which a principal one is the problem of defining a member of a trade union.

One fact stands out concerning the soldiers who had trades, or jobs, before the war: A high proportion of them were dissatisfied with their jobs and do not wish to return to them. A recent news-release of the OWI reveals that only one-fourth of the veterans discharged from hospitals during World War II have returned to their pre-service employment.

Some of the soldiers have professions, although this group is relatively small. There are probably between 40,000-50,000 doctors in the armed services and at least 100,000 former school-teachers. Other professions, such as law, have also a large representation. We may suppose that in the post-war period many of the teachers will not return to their profession, while most of the lawyers and doctors will attempt to resume practice, but may experience some difficulty in building up a business. Likewise, some veterans will be ready and able to set up their own businesses, and will need help in getting started.

A large number of soldiers had no economic experience before joining the army. Of this group, some have developed new skills applicable to civilian life, but more have not. Here much depends upon the soldier's rank and branch of the service. It is also necessary to consider the labor market. We shall, for example, have great numbers of skilled and perhaps too daring pilots, but there will be employment for only a small number in aviation, even if the coming years should be the "air age."

[2] James H. S. Bossard, "Family Problems in Wartime," in *Psychiatry Journal of the Biology and Pathology of Interpersonal Relations,* Feb. 1944.

Planning for Differences Among Veterans

On the basis of the survey cited above, we may suppose that a considerable proportion of the soldiers are married. Of this group, some will return to established families, and will have to face the sort of problems that war introduces into such families. Other soldiers have contracted war marriages, and these men must face the task of readjusting to civilian life and to the marriage relationship at one and the same time, while their wives must adjust to a husband and a veteran simultaneously. A great many parents of the present huge crop of G.I. babies must also adjust to the intimate responsibilities of parenthood.

It seems likely that the adjustment problems of the unmarried group will be less complex, if not less severe, than those of the married. But different policies must be employed in the guidance of the two groups.

While most of the soldiers will be relatively sound of body and mind, there will be a great many disabled. The physically disabled must learn to live with their disabilities; sometimes must learn new trades; must adjust their attitudes to their new condition in life. The great number certain to be discharged with hidden disabilities, such as tuberculosis or recurrent tropical disease, or latent or "delayed" psychoneurosis, will constitute a problem both of case work and of public health.

There will be a vast number of mentally disabled. Their readjustment will necessarily call into existence a whole new field of social work, and if this is not forthcoming, readjustment will not be accomplished. There will be an even greater number of borderline cases of mental illness, many of whom will refuse help and resist all attempts to treat them, preferring, as do other neurotics, to keep their neuroses and build their lives around them.

Programs of rehabilitation must provide for the different needs of the sound and the disabled, must differentiate between the physically and the mentally ill, and must recognize such divergent types as the psychotic, the neurotic, and the marginally psychoneurotic.

Just so will the attitudes of veterans vary, each constellation necessitating a differentiation of treatment. The prevailing emotional tone of many, no doubt, will be one of bitterness and resentment, but this will vary greatly in intensity and duration and will show itself in different forms, sometimes as a slow-burning anger and sometimes as explosive rage. There will be other variations of attitude; some veterans will bring back with them a driving compulsion to work hard to get established in the world, to make up for lost time; they will "work as if they were killing snakes." But others will be mentally set to be supported for the rest of their lives, "too lazy to say sooey if the hogs had them." Some veterans will be loud-mouthed and full of words, others taciturn and morose. There is also a time dimension to the variations in veteran psychology. For many, the period of acute maladjustment will quickly pass, while with others it will persist throughout life.

In planning for the return of the veterans, we must bear these differences of traits and conditions in mind. We cannot expect to apply the same methods to all. While providing for the needs of the entire group, we must see clearly the idiosyncrasies of the individual case, and must adapt our methods and procedures to the requirements of each particular flesh and blood ex-soldier. Every human being has his own unique individuality; he is, in some respects, unlike anyone else in the world. We must make sure that, in providing for the mass of men, we do not overlook the unique individual. Indeed, we must proceed upon the social-worker's principle that each veteran is a case unto himself.

Objectives And
Principles Of
A Veterans' Program

MANY worthy enterprises fail because the actors in them do not see with sufficient clarity what it is that they wish to do or do not understand how the means employed are related to the ends desired. Let us, therefore, at the risk of seeming to counsel perfection, state our objectives and principles as clearly as possible.

The one great objective of rehabilitation is to remedy the damage of war. We have already analyzed this damage and found it to consist of several distinct elements, each of which calls for a distinct task of rehabilitation procedure. The objectives of rehabilitation may therefore be stated as follows:

(1) To restore the veteran to the competitive position which he would have occupied if he had never been called for military service.

(2) To reinstate him in the communicative process of society, making him a civilian once more, with the knowledge, interests, habits, and sentiments of a civilian.

(3) To encourage and help him to overcome any handicaps, physical or mental, which he may have incurred as a result of service.

(4) To assist him to take his place once more in the political life of community, state, and nation.

(5) To help and encourage him to overcome attitudes of bitterness and antagonism, and to establish a normal and rewarding relation with family, church, and community.

In all the work of rehabilitation it would be wise to keep these purposes clearly in mind, and attempt to devise means to these ends, revising and improvising the means from time to time, but never changing or losing sight of the ends. If further analysis of the damage of war reveals other objectives of rehabilitation, they should be added to the list.

It should be emphasized that at present we have insufficient knowledge of the methods to employ in reaching these objectives, and lack the necessary means. We must feel our way toward them, improvising methods, constantly inventing new methods and abandoning them where they do not work, but being sure to make use of all the lessons and experiences of the past. The job of rehabilitation has never been done before in a society like ours; hence, we must feel our way. But we have accumulated a considerable body of past experience from which we should not neglect to draw the proper lessons.

Must Be Administered under a Flag of Truce

The work of rehabilitation must take place under a flag of truce. Those who work with veterans must be neutral in the embittered domestic struggles of the post-war world. No one must endanger the work of rehabilitation by introducing into it anything that pertains to factional dispute.

In American life, the work of many important institutions goes on in such an area of neutrality. Public schools must reach all the children of all the people, and all must pay for their support; we have learned, therefore, to exclude religious disputes and political factionalism as far as possible from the schools. Any violation of this truce—any attempt, for example, to use the schools to foster a new religion or to make a new social order—injures the work of the schools. Likewise, social work must carry on its ministrations without taking sides on many great controversies. Its practitioners have the privilege of helping human beings out of trouble and of alleviating human misery but are thereby estopped from any attempt to make a revolution.

So it will have to be with the work of rehabilitating the veteran. The needs of the veteran must come first. No one must be allowed to get control of the program who would use it for any other purpose, however worthy he may deem that purpose to be. The persons who do the job must be fanatics about veterans and about nothing else. They cannot take sides on other questions. They cannot make use of the rehabilitation program for veterans in furthering any other cause.

We may be sure that a struggle will take place over this issue. The veterans' bitterness is the great political force of the years to come. Many persons will attempt to direct it and to make use of it for their own ends,—to make themselves rich, or to destroy their enemies, or to topple the social system to the right or the left. Radicals will try to make revolutionaries of the veterans. Well-meaning do-gooders will try to make them pinko-liberal. Labor leaders will be eager to enlist them on their side. Reactionaries will try to reach the veteran with cleverly phrased propaganda. "Hate-groups" and "love-groups" of every shade and hue—from the Ku Klux Klan to the Prohibitionists—will try to utilize the resentment of the ex-soldiers for their social purposes. Every one of these persons has a cause; nearly all of them regard their cause as just and honorable. Every one would be happy to make use of the program of rehabilitating veterans in the interest of his own cause. None must succeed in capturing such a program, or there will be no such thing as rehabilitation.

Political and social neutrality in the rehabilitation of veterans is by no means impossible. We have invented a piece of social machinery well adapted to assuring such neutrality. That machine is the representative board. Let the work of rehabilitation be watched over at every stage by such a board, and it will be neutral. On the board should be representatives chosen in accordance with every principal cleavage in society: capital and labor, Negro and white, Catholic and Protestant, Jew and gentile, radical and reactionary. The board should, of course, be bipartisan, and should so far as possible represent different shades of political belief. Put representatives of all such groups on the board, let them watch over policy—not administer—and the veterans' program will be neutral.

Veterans: A Key in Post-War Planning

Needs of the veteran must be considered in post-war planning. The air is thick with post-war plans. Every interested party has its plan for the domestic economy and for international relations, a plan in which its own interests will not suffer. A few responsible citizens and a few sober scholars have serious and well-considered plans. They are in the minority, because every zany, crank, publicity-seeker, international crook, wise guy, or just plain fool also has a plan. When such thinkers go in for social planning, the wonder is, as Dr. Johnson might have put it, not that they do it well, but that they can do it at all.

Post-war plans must consider the special needs of the veteran, and for the most part they do not. In the post-war years, millions of veterans will be making the most difficult adjustments of their lives, finding occupations, building families, getting their belated start in the world. The probabilities are that these young men are going to be concentrated in cities; many will never return to farms and villages. Probably the young women will follow them to the cities. These young men and young women will be restless in their behavior, exigent in their demands. Some few will have plenty of money; most will be poor. They will be politically capable of ruling the country; they will have the votes and the motivation. Start your economic and social planning from there. The veterans are the group for which some sort of plan is most urgently necessary. Plan specifically for them and their needs.

Veterans can be reassimilated into society only through participating in social life. The objectives of rehabilitation include getting the soldier back into the communicative process and reincorporating him in the established patterns of family, community, church, and political life. The veteran must learn to participate in civilian life; *he must find satisfactions there,* form habits, readjust his emotions, acquire a stake in the moral order, learn to plan for himself and to discipline himself from within. All this he can only do by real group living. We cannot bring such things to pass by wrapping something in a package and handing it to the veteran. A set of lectures, however good, a series of pamphlets, however brilliantly written, or a nicely organized group of propaganda movies will never make the soldier a civilian again. The soldier must participate; he must join in, and of his own free will.

They Must Share in Planning for Themselves

The natural beginning of this participation is to *let the veteran have a share in planning his own future.* In the army, one has little opportunity to plan for himself. It is the part of virtue to submit, to do as one is told, to take what comes. The transition to self-initiated plans is difficult and could easily be impeded by an attempt to handle the reeducation and reemployment of veterans by mechanical, mass methods. Personal relationships must somehow appear in this work. The veteran's own wishes must be consulted. Like the child in the progressive school, the veteran must be compelled to do as he pleases whether he wants to or not.

Readjustment to the community demands natural, spontaneous participation in some phase of community life. To arrange for this kind of thing is one of the most difficult problems in the whole field of social engineering. Organization is necessary in order to give veterans—or any other group—an opportunity for spontaneous social life, but organization often kills spontaneity. Many settlement houses, churches, and colleges have failed in their attempts to organize a social life in such a manner and keep it attractive to their clientele. There are a few gifted persons who have the know-how of making such things run. A hint derived from a study of their methods is to give wide latitude to self-organized groups, and to be lavish in praise of such attempts but fertile in suggestions for which one never takes the credit. *The moral is that the veterans must organize their own pattern of participation, under such guidance as can be given without destroying their sense of spontaneous participation.*

Assimilation Through Veterans' Organizations

Group-Wise Assimilation. As the veteran comes to participate in community life, he is caught up in the ongoing communicative process, and he becomes a civilian. It is significant that this process tends to take place in *groups* of veterans, and that these groups, rather than single veterans, become assimilated to society (hence the term "group-wise").

As we have noted earlier, the veteran, for a considerable time after demobilization, must depend heavily upon the society of his comrades. His fellow veterans understand him and sympathize with his attitudes, but civilians do not understand and cannot sympathize. The veterans' attitudes isolate him from the fellowship of civilians, and he usually has at least a mild antagonism toward them. Toward other veterans he retains some of the fierce loyalty of fighting men, and the remnants of that old solidarity make his association with them meaningful.

Relatively isolated otherwise in civilian society, veterans seek one another out to form little clumps, nodules, and groups. These agglomerations of men are already a society, and in fact a civilian society. In these groups the ex-soldier learns once more the ways of discussion and overcomes his antipathy to the arts of persuasion. In the society of veterans, he submits once again to being convinced rather than commanded. He learns to mend his own rough ways, civilizes his language, expresses many of his resentments and thus renders them harmless, and in short becomes socialized once more.

Veterans' Organizations. Grouping of ex-soldiers arises spontaneously in answer to the social needs of demobilized veterans. Sooner or later such groups, some of them, become formalized by organization. The veterans' organizations so produced play a most important part in the reassimilation of the veteran in society.

The emergence of a formal organization of any such group rests upon a sort of compromise with the surrounding society. Society tolerates the group, permits it to meet, gives it status, and endows it with respectability. In return, the group subscribes to certain social principles and often changes the nature of its leadership in the direction of social acceptability.[1] Cellar clubs of adolescents began as socially rebellious groups, but when they achieved toleration they became harmless social clubs. As one phase of this metamorphosis, there was a change of leadership, which put a socially acceptable "front man" in charge of the organization. Similarly, dangerous and vicious gangs may become harmless when recognized and incorporated in society; in many such cases, the gang gives up something and society gives up something and the gang becomes a political machine.

A compromise between the veterans and the rest of society is implicit in the formation of the veterans' organization. Society gives to such a group recognition and a secure place in the social hierarchy. Society permits the group to organize and hold meetings, helps it to find a house to shelter its activities, respects its

---

[1] For this interpretation I am indebted to William Henderson, who was killed in 1942 while serving as a Lieutenant in the Air Force. Henderson derived the principle from a study of New York City's cellar clubs of adolescents, a study that he carried on in connection with his work for Greenwich House.

uniforms and attends its parades, gives to the group, when duly put on notice to do so, the reverence owing to men who have fought for their country. The veterans' organization receives a privileged status that permits it to raise money by bingo games, and boxing shows, and to hold meetings at which the members conduct a mild flirtation with sin.

In accordance with this contract, which like many another is "the more binding for being unspoken," the veterans also give up something. They give up, in so far as in them lies the power to do so, their bitterness against the society that sent them to war and requited their sacrifices so poorly. They accept certain social responsibilities as their special charge. There is a gradual metamorphosis in their status and responsibilities as the veterans progress from youth to age.

In its earliest period of life, the veterans' organization finds its chief interest in the attempt to secure adequate care for the disabled and for the dependents of their fallen comrades. There is a great tendency for the disabled to be neglected in the period immediately following a war, and the veterans' organization performs a great service in pressing for satisfaction of the needs of this group. The widows and orphans of the slain are also in need of help, and the veterans have an opportunity to find their own souls in helping them.

To some extent in the Grand Army of the Republic, and to a very great extent in the American Legion, these objectives were gradually extended to include wide social aims of a philanthropic nature. A concern for the children of veterans is easily expanded into a concern for all children. Besides, considerations of national defence necessitate proper care for all children, and so child welfare in the broadest sense becomes a proper objective of the American Legion. Every good cause is inextricably interwoven with certain other good causes, and this fact sooner or later involves the veterans' organization, in one way or another, in the struggle for social betterment.

There are many persons to whom this view of veterans' organizations may seem far from the facts. They remember the pension exactions of the Grand Army of the Republic, and they quarrel with the ideology of the American Legion. The Grand Army of the Republic, as it happened, fell into the hands of a group of politicians who used pensions as a means of mobilizing voting power. The pension system after the Civil War arose from the fact that a system of taxation, which certain interested parties wished to continue, poured into the treasury funds that somehow had to be expended, and the veterans were a suitable object of expenditure. If blame attached to anyone for this procedure, it was to the politicians far more than to the veterans. Pension agitation for the veterans of World War I has never been on the same scale. Veterans, however, would be more or less than human if in the exercise of their great political power they did not sometimes employ that power in their own interest.

At the end of the present war, the presence of two large groups of veterans will create a situation without parallel in our history. There is no doubt that veterans will dominate our political life for some time to come.

Scientific Screening for Disabilities

During the post-war period, every community should make an active search for cases of disability, and should give to the disabled such assistance as may be necessary to obtain prompt and just settlement of their claims. Such a policy will prove to be not merely humane, but also excellent business. In the long run, it will save money. It will be to the interest of local communities to help in making these claims, because in that way they will transfer certain obligations from local to federal budgets. It will be to the interest of the Federal government to have all legitimate claims presented promptly and settled fairly, because this will make it easier to reject fraudulent claims in after years.

The necessity for a search for disability cases could be avoided only by prolonging the demobilization process over a period of years, and releasing veterans only after a series of physical examinations equal in thoroughness to those given at the famed Mayo Clinic. Of course this is not possible, and we shall therefore turn loose a great number of men suffering from various service-connected disabilities. Military service produces great numbers of used-up men, and often the nature and extent of disability does not become clear until months or years after discharge.

If an active search for these cases is not made, thousands, perhaps hundreds of thousands, of those who have honorable and legitimate claims will be overlooked during the early years that are the golden period for recovery and rehabilitation. If we do not try to find such cases, thousands of tubercular veterans will go to the West in the hope of recovering their health by a change of climate. Thousands of others will be unable to make a living and they will beg. More thousands—at least 15,000 if we follow the yardstick of World War I—will carry service-connected disabilities to prison with them.

If we do not search out the legitimately disabled, many of them will never press their claims. They will die, proudly keeping their secrets, and then perhaps their widows and orphans will become public charges. They will pawn their Purple Hearts to get money to buy food for their children; the pawnshop windows will be full of medals and a man will be able to buy any medal he wants for a dollar or so. Others will feel that it is more honorable to rob than to beg, and they will rob. We repeat: To care for these people is not merely humane; it is good business.

The fakers, the chisellers, the fraudulent wounded who flourish after every war will never hesitate to press their claims. Neglect of veterans never affects them. They will camp on the doorstep of the army surgeon until he satisfies their demands. They will get the benefits for which others are too proud to apply. Years after the war, when the public conscience has been awakened, the period of neglect of the veterans will come to an end, but the fact that there was such a period will be very useful to the fraudulently disabled, as happened in the wake of World War I. We shall have to presume that all disabilities of a certain date are service-connected, and in order to compensate the legitimately disabled we shall have to compensate also a great many frauds.

Pauperization and Unlovely Traits of Veterans

Timely and adequate help for the disabled will take away most of the pathos that enables a veteran to make his living by begging and thus to become pauperized. If there is no "Brother, can you spare a dime?" period after the war, there will be fewer paupers.

Many good people believe that help to veterans should be limited in amount, because adequate care will be pauperizing. This is a misconception. Help can be given in such a way as to pauperize, especially if it is the wrong kind of help and is administered without proper attention to the nature and needs of the individual. But, for the most part, the policy that pauperizes is the one that fails to provide help, that neglects the needs of the veteran and thus forces him to depend upon the charity of passers-by. Adequate care, properly administered, prevents pauperization. It also is good business.

One kind of disability in particular calls for the ministrations of the most skilled social workers in the country, if we are to avoid being saddled with terrific costs for the care of demoralized and pauperized veterans. *The hundreds of thousands of psychoneurotics will require intelligent treatment in order to save a great proportion of them from becoming public charges.* Pensions, or mere compensation, will never do for this group. Pensions, in many cases, will give them a social gain from neurosis, which will make recovery impossible.

Unlovely Traits of Veterans. We may suppose that at some time in the operation of the national program for helping veterans some thousands of non-professional persons will be called upon to help. Such persons are due for some surprises.

Charitable work is very rewarding when Lady Bountiful comes into the poor widow's home with a Christmas basket, and finds the widow is a lovely, gentle woman who works hard, manages well, keeps her home clean, brings up her children with loving care and excellent judgment, and does the best she can with her limited economic resources. For the very best results, everyone must be extremely grateful for the joy that Lady Bountiful brings into those drab lives. It does not often turn out in just that way.

A certain number of the veterans in need of help will be grateful, cooperative, and intelligent. Their cases will probably be handled reasonably well and their affairs will almost certainly prosper. We need give no more thought to this —small—group.

But there will be a great many of the veterans, as of all such groups, who are stubborn, wilful, and wrongheaded, many who are ignorant, stupid, dirty, cantankerous, extravagant, and ungrateful. Some will be immoral or criminal, and will contribute to their own misery by their own bad judgment and misbehavior.

It will be well for the amateur social worker to bear in mind that it is *precisely because of their own difficult qualities that many of these persons are in need of help.* They are ignorant and stupid and cantankerous; that is what is wrong with them. Their attitudes are very bad, of course; they are sick and that is the nature of their illness. They won't help themselves, and can't because they won't. But we cannot on that account cast them into outer darkness. That is the point where treatment must begin—with their attitudes. There is no great virtue in just taking care of the deserving poor. Everybody does that. The undeserving poor need help much more, and there are more of them. And the strange thing is a bad man gets just as hungry as a good man.

Learning to accept such unlovely persons and to deal with them is the beginning of wisdom in human relations. One cannot manage them, or make their decisions for them; they must learn to make their own decisions. They must find their own way out, and the worker can help only a little. It goes without saying that such persons will not often be grateful for what is done for them. That is part of their maladjustment. It takes a rather strong man to support the crushing burden of gratitude.

Professional social workers have perfected their skills and disciplines for dealing with delicate problems and unstable personalities. There is at present an alarming shortage of properly trained social workers, with every prospect that we shall carry this shortage into the post-war period. Nevertheless, we should plan to turn over as much as possible of the work with difficult cases to persons trained for such work. And certainly we should begin at once to train a small new army of social workers—to help us win, if that is possible, the battle of the peace.

What the Local Community Can Do: A Program

WHILE much of the work of rehabilitating veterans can be accomplished by Federal and State agencies, its most important phases can be carried on only by local communities. Local communities must search out many cases of disability and assist them in pressing their claims. Local communities must find a job for the returning veteran, later for the occupationally rehabilitated veteran, and must help him to work out a pattern of family and community relationships. They must break down the veteran's barriers and get in communication with him. They must get the veteran into politics and make him into a citizen once more. They must teach the veteran to work for community goals.

In short, *the real work of rehabilitation must be done in the local community.* There are two points that can never be stressed too much: That every veteran is in need of some sort of rehabilitation, and that the job must be done in the local community. It is the job of the local community to make the veteran a civilian again, to train him to think, feel, and act like a civilian once more.

Normally, one would expect to find local communities strongly organized and ready to tackle such a task at the end of a war. This is not true at the present time, except for rural areas and some smaller cities, that part of the war program having been feloniously mismanaged in Washington. Where community organization has actually taken place during this war, few thanks are due to the central administration. Nevertheless, if the job of rehabilitation is to be done, local communities must organize for it. Each community must prepare to receive back into the fold approximately a tenth of its population, and a very dynamic and dangerous tenth.

Community organization, as the phrase is usually employed,

means the organization of the resources of a community in order to deal with some problem or to accomplish some community purpose. It means, as good people think of it, the organization of men of good will for worthy purposes. But any mobilization and concentration of community energies on a particular project is community organization, whether the purpose is to put over a drive for a community chest, to build a new high school, to buy equipment for the fire department, or to carry the community for the Ku Klux Klan. Thus a great many of the best community organizers in the country are persons who have never heard of the term.

The usual practice in community organization is to depend heavily upon the leaders of institutions and agencies and upon persons who in the past have shown themselves concerned with community welfare. Included in this group would be educators, preachers, social workers, merchants, industrialists, lawyers, etc. Service clubs, such as Rotary and Kiwanis, have played an increasingly important part in community organization through the years. While these groups should certainly not be neglected in organizing communities for the return of the veteran, it is likely that the most dynamic leadership will come from the veterans' organizations.

Techniques of Organizing Local Communities

The work of community organization may be done by either amateurs or professionals with almost equal effectiveness. The amateur, being a member of the community, has a detailed knowledge of community alignments, which the professional often lacks, and may, because of his secure status in the community, use rough-and-ready methods that professionals must avoid. If through lack of skill he makes mistakes, as he almost certainly will, the amateur community organizer is able to overcome these errors by persistence and by his command of the realities of local politics. Against the amateur should be recorded the probability that his understanding of the purposes for which the community is to be organized is less sure and extensive than that of the trained professional. Even more serious is the amateur's lack of realization of the interconnectedness of good causes, and his tendency to do damage in other fields while promoting the cause that is dear to his own heart.

Where a professional organizes the community he is usually acting as the representative of a national or State agency and is trying to bring the local community into line with the program of the agency. After World War I the Red Cross did much of the work of organizing communities to take care of veterans and other postwar problems. The methods employed by one extraordinary organizer are described in the chapter on Dale County in Walter Pettit's *Case Studies in Community Organization.*[1] One of the worker's devices, a common one, was to get local backing for her projects by sending out many of her letters over the signature of local citizens. Some of her other principles were:

(1) To avoid any expression of opinion with reference to factional disputes in the county.

(2) To attempt to create the impression that the Red Cross is non-sectarian, non-political, and non-factional.

(3) Not to attempt to convince people by talking of social work in the abstract, but to put before them actual, concrete cases and thus to educate them.

(4) To educate the members of the committee by conferences and by taking them on visits.

(5) To use as many volunteers as possible, but not to solicit volunteers until there is a definite need for them.

(6) To call meetings only with a definite purpose.

This same worker, whose story the interested reader should study, was particularly skillful in her handling of groups and organizations of veterans. She stressed the practice of making an active search for cases of disability among veterans.

There are other "secrets of the trade" of community organization that the writer is loath to give away in print, especially in a book intended to reach a general audience. Perhaps the professionals will forgive him for revealing their chief secret, which is: One must not expect praise for such activity, however selfless and devoted his work may be; he must give all the praise to others for their minor contributions. That is how he gets others to work for him. If the work goes well, that must be triumph enough for the person who engineers the job, and he must publicly give all the credit to others. Such selflessness is rare. So are good community organizers.

Another hint seems justified on this subject, although it is not at

1 Walter Pettit, *Case Studies in Community Organization.* Century, 1928.

all orthodox doctrine. In setting up a board, or agency, to mobilize community resources on behalf of veterans, it would be well not to rely wholly upon good men, upon do-gooders, but to include a certain number of hard and practical men who are accustomed to getting things done, even though these men have the reputation of being liars and swearers and are in general tough customers. The trouble with do-gooders is that in their universe the means employed are chronically inadequate to bring about the ends envisaged. They often fail, therefore, when confronted with such tough, practical problems as that of preventing race riots or arranging for the return of the veteran to society.

It is generally regarded as the best practice in all sorts of welfare work to use existing agencies wherever possible. There is a great temptation for a person who is much impressed by some new problem to attempt to set up a new agency, disregarding the contributions that can be made to the situation by existing agencies. It is wiser to refer many kinds of problems to agencies already established, thus making full use of their skill and experience, and to construct new machinery only when this is unavoidable.

Current experience with the veteran problem demonstrates once more the validity of another of the commonplaces of welfare work: That all such work must be organized and coordinated in such a way as to avoid duplication and competition of agencies and to make the full use of all agencies and community resources. Ten thousand men, runs the old saw, cannot throw a cannon ball much further than one man, because ten thousand men cannot get hold of it. So with the veteran problem; a dozen agencies, duplicating services, competing for clients, and feuding over jurisdiction cannot do very much more than a single agency working alone and unimpeded. But if someone organizes and coordinates the work of a dozen agencies and assigns to each its proper sphere of operation, their effectiveness will greatly increase. There must be, then, central planning and coordination in the attack upon the veteran problem.

A Basic Minimum Program for the Community

Specifically, community organization for the returning veterans should provide at least the following things:

(1) Machinery for getting the names of all veterans, whether local

boys or migrants, as soon as possible after their release from the army. Draft boards can supply the names of the local inductees. Some other way must be found to establish contact with the migrants. There will undoubtedly be large numbers of these migrants in the urban areas.

(2) A preliminary interview to give the veteran a welcome to his home, to discover his needs, and to arrange for

(3) Referral to:

> (a) Employment agencies for those ready, willing, able, and sufficiently skilled to accept immediate job placement. These agencies should systematically assess the job possibilities of the local community.
>
> (b) Persons trained in evaluating and pressing claims for disability. Veterans' organizations are most likely to be of help in this respect, as they have had years of experience with just this sort of thing.
>
> (c) Guidance workers competent to give the younger veterans advice concerning choice of vocation, plans for vocational training, etc.

(4) Adaptation of welfare- and case-working agencies to the needs of the veterans' group. This would include not merely family welfare agencies and the relief organization, but in many cases, organizations which give legal aid. Welfare workers should prepare to give special attention to the problems of psychoneurotic cases among veterans.

(5) Adaptation of the school system to veterans whose schooling can be provided in the local community.

(6) Provision of medical and social work facilities for an active search for cases of disability among returning veterans.

(7) Provision of small-loan services for needy veterans and larger loans for veterans wishing to start business or buy homes or farms.

An Example: New York's Veteran Service Center

An ideal organization of community services for veterans is the Veterans' Service Center established in New York City by Mrs. Anna M. Rosenberg under the auspices of the Selective Service and the War Manpower Commission. Intended as a demonstration of what communities can do to help veterans, the Veterans' Service

Center proved its usefulness by giving aid to more than 4,000 veterans in its first month of existence.

Usually such an agency would seek to be principally a clearing house helping ex-soldiers by referring them to the proper agencies. Like any other large city, New York has such a wealth of social agencies that a veteran seeking aid would not know which one he should consult with his particular problem. Intelligent referral of cases calls for such specialized knowledge and skill as to justify the existence of a veterans' center.

However, the New York Veterans' Service Center has been able to handle many cases by means of its own resources, which provide such services as an employment bureau, vocational guidance, physical examinations, and the help of a case worker in coping with personal problems. The value of such a coordinated battery of services is very great, which is demonstrated by the large number of veterans who elect to take advantage of two or more services. The effect of this coordination of services upon the veteran's morale is considerable. If a veteran, for example, needs a physical check-up, vocational guidance, help in finding employment, and assistance with personal problems, it would ordinarily be necessary for him to turn to several agencies to get these services, and he might feel before he was through that he was "getting the run-around," but the Veterans' Service Center is organized to give all these services without delay, perhaps on a single day. Since the Service Center is in the hands of skilled social workers, it is possible to make the differentiation between the services which the veteran requests and those which he really needs. A cheerful, informally furnished waiting room adds much to the atmosphere of the Center.

New York City has, of course, far more facilities for helping veterans than are possessed by smaller cities. However, as the workers at the Center point out, the objectives of the smaller community are the same as those of New York, and the needs of the veteran are the same, wherever he may be located. It is planned to extend this experiment to a number of other cities, making use of the New York City experience.

The veterans' programs of even the smaller communities should thus include a wide mobilization of community resources to meet the needs of veterans. The focus of these activities might well be furnished by a veterans' service center, similar to that of New York

City, in which representatives of various agencies would be accessible. This center should carry on its own testing and placement program, perhaps in cooperation with industry but in some cases independently. Various other aids should be furnished by the center or by other social agencies interested in veterans. Group work and recreation, if the community can afford it, will pay off handsomely in the long run. The least that any community can do is to provide a meeting place or "hangout" for returning veterans. For all these services, trained personnel will be scarce, and authorities in charge of training programs should give the matter immediate attention.[2]

As the veterans return, thousands of heartless rackets will arise to separate them from their money. No one can say what these will be. Crooks without imagination will resort to such trustworthy dodges as the fur neck piece, the badger game, and the myth of the Spanish prisoner, and human ingenuity will devise a multitude of new swindles. No doubt the loan sharks are already whetting their teeth for the returning veterans. Protection of the veterans from these people is a major responsibility of the community.

If communities are not properly organized for returning veterans, the results will undoubtedly be bad. The veterans will be turned over, as soldiers have so often been in time of war, to the lowest elements of the population. Possibly the "good people" of the community will not want to have anything to do with veterans. If so, the veterans will not lack for company. The gamblers, prostitutes, saloon-keepers, and loan sharks will meet them at the train, ready to welcome the "little fishes in with gently smiling jaws."

In planning and organizing community facilities, we should avoid placing them on a temporary, emergency basis. The work of adjusting the veterans to society will necessarily last for several years. Machinery established for dealing with veterans should be a permanent part of the community structure. The lesson of World War I is that organized community effort tends to decline rapidly if not actually to disintegrate in the post-war period.

If, however, there is adequate and continuing interest in the matter, the rehabilitation of veterans may furnish an excellent

[2] For an excellent discussion of this problem, with concrete and practical suggestions, see Morse A. Cartwright, *Marching Home, Educational and Social Adjustment after the War*. Bureau of Publications, Teachers College, Columbia University, 1944.

focus of community life. But first it must be brought home to the community, and as vividly as possible, that rehabilitation is not something that can be done in some wonderful hospital far away from the sight of the public, but something that must take place in the local community, in every community, before everybody's eyes every single day, if the job is to be done.

The Economic Aspects Of Rehabilitation

FINDING a satisfactory job for the veteran is vital to his readjustment in society. A job will not, as some believe, solve all the veteran's problems, but without a job none of them can be solved. Self-support, in American society, is essential to self-respect; holding a job is one of the central disciplines that give backbone to our lives. The job itself is the source of many of our social contacts. It is therefore necessary to find jobs for all veterans who are able and willing to work.

But if we are to find jobs for all the veterans the economic machine must be functioning at full capacity; there must be jobs enough for all. Here the veteran's fate is interwoven with that of the millions of war workers who will have to turn to other tasks when they cease producing the instruments of death. There must be jobs for the war workers too. If we get jobs for the veterans, and none for the war workers, the labor market will be so badly disorganized that the veterans will not fare well, and the war workers and their families will suffer privation. If nevertheless by legislation, political pressure, and executive fiat we appropriate all the available jobs for the veterans, and leave other potential workers idle, all that we shall accomplish will be that the veterans will work and pay taxes to support the rest of the population—a consummation which one would hardly suppose that the veterans would desire.

An adequate handling of the veteran problem, therefore, requires full, or nearly full employment, for which, on the basis of America's past record, the prospect is not exactly bright. At the peak of prosperity, 1929, several millions were unemployed. Through the Thirties we were unable to operate the economic system without producing surpluses that fatally glutted the market; we could not get supply and demand adjusted then, and it will certainly be harder to bring them into line with each other now that we have enormously expanded our productive capacity, increased the supply of labor and the productivity of labor, and unbalanced our economy far more than ever before. Possibly we shall be able to make our economic system work. If not—chaos, for the veteran as well as for everybody else.

It is no part of the task of the present work to set forth one more plan for the management of the economic system in the post-war years. Some of our ablest economists have given this matter their attention. Any one of several existent plans would almost certainly work better than no plan at all. What is needed is to put some plan into effect. The balance of forces in American political life being what it is, it is likely to prove difficult to take this last step of actually putting into effect any plan that imposes an adequate set of controls on industry.

Ideally the demobilization of soldiers should be geared in to post-war economic planning. Soldiers should be released in accordance with industrial needs and only when jobs are waiting for them. This means that the time-honored practice of discharging soldiers by military units should be abandoned. The imperatives of politics being what they are, it seems hardly probable that the demobilization will actually take place in this ideal manner.

First Step: Nation-wide Job Survey

While conceding that the economic fate of the veterans is inextricably intertwined with that of the rest of society, we propose to concern ourselves in the present work with the easily practicable things that can and should be done for the veterans. Among these would be a nation-wide job survey, or inventory, that would determine the places in the economic system where the labor of the veterans could best be utilized. Such a survey should start with the assumption that the reemployment of the veterans furnishes us with an opportunity to redistribute our manpower in accordance with considerations of both efficiency and welfare.

Such a survey might well lead to some very important conclusions concerning the policies to be followed in placing veterans in jobs after the war. For example, an intelligent redistribution of manpower might involve the decision to place a quarter of a million veterans in the profession of school teaching. The percentage of men in teaching has been declining since the Civil War. In 1870 about 41 per cent of the teachers of the United States were men. In 1920 the percentage of men was 14.1; by 1934 it had risen again to 19.1. The present war has almost certainly reduced the proportion of men far below the 1920 figure. There is a very serious shortage of trained teachers, a deficiency, according to recent estimates, of at least 150,000. There is a rapid turnover in the profession even in normal times. It would be easy for the teaching profession to absorb 250,000 veterans, and the work of the schools would benefit thereby, because men are necessary in the schools. They are indispensable for the control and education of boys—and they do not leave teaching to get married.

Smaller numbers of veterans could be profitably utilized in institutions for juvenile delinquents, which need young and vigorous men for their staffs. Police work, which is rapidly maturing into a profession, should prove attractive to considerable numbers of veterans. The field of social work could furnish employment to some thousands, the related field of recreation to thousands more. Obviously, a large number of veterans will have to be employed, over a period of years, in administering the veteran program itself.

A survey would doubtless reveal many other wide-open spots in the economic order where veterans could profitably be employed. State and local surveys would likewise disclose the needs of segments of the national community, and would furnish a background for intelligent placement. It is worth remembering that large numbers of veterans will very probably gravitate to cities, where the market for their services may not be very active. In this connection we should note that careful city planning for utility and beauty could provide good jobs for millions of veterans—a matter receiving consideration in the Moses plan for post-war New York City. According to a recent survey, about two-thirds of all American cities of 10,000 or more are planning large-scale projects for the post-war period, total projected expenditures amounting roughly to four and a half billion dollars.[1]

[1] Reported by Emmet Crozier in The New York Herald Tribune, May 7, 1944.

A List of Economic Aids for Veterans

Assistance to be extended to veterans should include the following services:

(1) Demobilization pay and unemployment compensation. Dismissal pay should be adequate to defray immediate expenses and to support the veteran while he is seeking a job. If he has trouble in finding a job, then he should have unemployment compensation for a period of time.

(2) Guidance in the choice of an occupation. This guidance, if it is to be effective for veterans, must involve more than giving a few tests and handing out pious advice. Vocational guidance for veterans will be a difficult job, inseparable from personal counselling and from the comprehensive task of helping the veteran to find his place in society. There are certain to be many cases of great disparity between the kind of job the veteran wants and the kind he can get; the task of adjusting the veteran to his actual status in society will call for a great deal of skill. Conflicts are also certain to arise between the veterans and certain entrenched occupational groups, notably members of professions and labor unions. One part of the guidance program must be to work with such groups and to persuade them to open their ranks to a reasonable number of veterans. Self-interest would certainly dictate that labor unions, for example, should do this.

(3) Help in preparation for jobs. After the veteran has chosen a vocation intelligently, he may still need help in fitting himself for it. There is every indication that such assistance will be provided. One problem involved is that of making sure that instruction given to veterans is of high quality. It is also important to make sure that veterans who accept such help are serious students willing and able to submit themselves to the disciplines of the teaching-learning process.

It would certainly be most desirable for the vocational guidance and planning of training programs to be in the hands of persons trained, and well trained, for this kind of work. This is the type of activity in which a little knowledge is often a dangerous thing, but it is also a field in which a great many shysters have operated in the past. Such considerations are crucial for the disabled veterans, who will require expert and careful attention if their needs are to be met. We assume, of course, that the sound rehabilitation program planned for the disabled veterans of World War I will be continued after the current war, with, it is to be hoped, better administration this time.

(4) Help in job-finding. This is a routine activity that should be closely correlated with the guidance and training program.

(5) Business loans. Some veterans will be capable of starting their own businesses, if given some help in raising capital. Some State governments already provide for such loans, the State of New Jersey having recently passed a very generous law. Such loans may also properly be extended to cover the purchase of a home or a farm. This seems a legitimate field of operation for the State governments, and far more constructive than the usual bonus legislation. Such loans, if properly extended, are certain to have a very stabilizing effect upon veterans.

(6) Small personal loans. Being an impecunious and not very provident group, and a young group that will shortly have heavy family responsibilities, the veterans will often be in need of small loans. Arrangements should be made to supply these loans, under proper safeguards, at the lowest practicable rate of interest.

(7) In planning and administering these services, we should remember that our obligation to the disabled veteran is greater than to any other. But all these services should also be extended, if they are needed, to the dependents of deceased or disabled veterans.

Industry should be prepared to take over the burden of scientific job placement and intelligent management of job relationships. Interviews and tests should be given to determine the attitudes, aptitudes, and capacities of veterans. Studies should be made—are already being made by some companies—to determine the kinds of work that can be done by persons suffering from various kinds and degrees of disability. The development of foreman-training in job relationships is indicated as a necessary step in dealing with the attitudes of veterans.

Both industrialists and labor unions are in fact thinking along these lines. Both groups realize that the veterans will constitute their greatest problem for the coming years. The following statement illustrates the attitude of one of the largest of the labor unions, the United Automobile Workers:

The program of our union for men in the armed forces

(which is incorporated in our "Post War Plan") calls for the following: Guarantee of jobs through a peace time economy of full employment; through the enforcement of seniority provisions in contracts; and through extension of inadequate protection of the Selective Service Law to give legal protection to all members of the armed forces and merchant marine so that they will be guaranteed the right to return to their former jobs with accumulated seniority.

We call for what might be termed a new Homestead Act which would be a government financed program for settling returned veterans who care to go on farm lands, through individual and community projects.

One of the big problems we feel has to be dealt with is provision for adequate bonus which we prefer to call a separation allowance, up to $2500 to help discharged veterans get back on their feet, rest, investigate new occupational opportunities, possibly initiate new ventures in life. To further facilitate this, we ask for free education, including training for any trade or profession. . . .

In spite of all the propaganda attempting to show a split between the soldiers and the people who are doing the war work in the factories, it would surprise you to know how frequently we hear from members who are looking to their union to give them protection in the post-war period. There is no question that many of the returning soldiers have some feeling of security through the knowledge of being members in good standing of well established trade unions who have been able to negotiate contracts which provide security for them when they return. . . . [2]

Realistic study of the problem of the economic adjustment of the veteran brings us squarely up against the problem of personal adjustment. It is not enough to get a job for the veteran; unless he can be adjusted to society he will not keep the job. The task of helping the veteran in meeting his problems of personal relationships is thus inescapable. We shall deal with it in the following chapter.

[2] From a personal communication by William H. Levitt, Director, International Education Department, U.A.W.-C.I.O., under date of June 5, 1944.

Helping The Veteran
In His Personal
Relationships

THE task of helping the veteran in his personal relationships is one to tax the skill of the well-trained and talented social worker. As much as circumstances permit, we must rely upon the social workers to do this job. There are, however, many cases that amateurs must handle on their own, with no chance to call in the doctors of human relationships, and there are aspects of all cases which must be handled by the veteran's family, friends, and community. Every employer, every wife or mother of a veteran, many teachers and preachers should therefore become as expert as they can in veteran psychology. In considerable part, it is the aim of this book to help such persons to attain an understanding of the veteran.

Are Veterans Strangers in Their Own Homes?

Veterans are certain to return to an extraordinarily complex set of marriage and family relationships. Helping people to straighten out such relationships is a job for the trained experts, and one in which the amateur will do better not to meddle if he can help it. One might perhaps without irreverence suggest a little supplement to a famous text which causes it to read: "Love thy neighbor as thyself, and let his family relationships severely alone." Perhaps the best way to be a really bad neighbor is to bestow such advice gratis.

Among the cases that the social workers are even now being called upon to adjust are many arising from the veteran's relations with his children. While he has been away, the children have developed rapidly, and the veteran himself has changed. A recently reported case illustrates the type of difficulty which may arise.[1]

1 Reported by the Catholic Charities, in The New York World-Telegram, April 26, 1944.

The father, discharged after four years of service in the Navy, returned home to find his nineteen-year-old daughter a grown-up young woman. When he left home she was an adolescent of fifteen, slaving over home work, engrossed in childish concerns—strictly a nine o'clock girl. On his return he found her an independent woman, a war-worker earning forty dollars a week, with tastes in amusement corresponding to her age and income level. The father was horrified to find that his little girl sometimes stayed out as late as two o'clock in the morning, and he felt that her mother had allowed her to go to the dogs. Attempting to exert his authority as a father, he met argument and resistance from both wife and daughter. In desperation he went to the social worker, who heard him out patiently and sympathetically, and tried to convince him that he was wrong, explaining that he had missed many stages of his daughter's development, that these stages would have passed almost imperceptibly if he had remained at home during the last few years, and that now he must accept his daughter as a grown-up young lady of nineteen.

No doubt this case had a more or less happy ending, but there are many others for which the prognosis is less favorable. Suppose, for example, that the veteran returns to his home to find that his wife has a child that could not possibly be his. And what of those cases in which the veteran has been compelled to continue his allotments to a wife whom he knows or believes to be unfaithful? Or consider the case reported earlier in this book, in which the wife has remained technically faithful but is in love with another man. Since human nature is what it is, such cases are certain to occur with some frequency, but no one has as yet discovered any really satisfactory solutions for them.

Then there are the problems of those war marriages, many of them utterly preposterous, which the young people have contracted because death was whispering in their ears. Celebrated on a moment's notice by persons who hardly knew each other and had no conception of the meaning of their vows, many of these marriages were highly immoral in nature, more immoral, in the view of many church authorities, than the cohabitation which they were supposed to legitimize. When the veterans return, they and their "wives" must decide what to do about their marriages.

Are War Marriages Actually Worth Saving?

With regard to such marriages, Bossard raises a really fundamental question: Are they worth saving? [2] The answer inheres in the question. In a great many cases they are not; we may as well reconcile ourselves to that fact, and accept a thumping increase in the divorce rate as one of the costs of war. The hastily married couples, on the basis of such guidance and help as they can get and such wisdom as they can summon for the occasion, must decide whether to try to build a life together, with home and children and mortgages, or to liquidate their "marriages" in the divorce courts. Either solution is certain to be costly. Adjustment to married life under such circumstances is certain to be difficult, and divorce is never emotionally inexpensive. If such a union has been blessed with a G.I. baby, as so many have, the difficulties of either alternative are of course multiplied.

Many soldiers will also bring back brides from foreign lands. It will require the deepest mutual affection to overcome the cultural disparity between these men and women whom war has strangely yoked together. The women will be living in a foreign land, cut off from family and friends, perhaps unable to speak our language. Life adjustment will be hard for them at best. The men may find that their exotic brides look different to them in America, perhaps comparing unfavorably with the native product. A certain proportion of these marriages will be interracial, in which case their problems will be much greater. Of these marriages, too, we must ask: Are they worth saving?

Outside the field of family relationships, other aspects of the veteran's behavior may call for the ministrations of the social worker. Even now the newspapers contain frequent stories of crimes committed by shell-shocked or psychoneurotic veterans, and these cases are certain to multiply when demobilization turns loose some millions whose personalities have been warped by their experiences. It is clear that the veteran who has been diagnosed as psychoneu-

2 James H. S. Bossard, "Family Problems in Wartime," in *Psychiatry: Journal of the Biology and Pathology of Inter-Personal Relations*, Feb. 1944. In a recent article Hart and Bowne estimate that in the peak year following demobilization the divorce rate will be roughly 38 divorces for every 100 marriages. (Hornell Hart and Henrietta Bowne, "Divorce, Depression, and War," in *Social Forces*, December 1943.)

rotic is not altogether responsible for his actions, but what of the veteran whose condition, though equally severe, does not happen to have been diagnosed? Law enforcement officers will have need of all their humanity, as well as of the wisdom of the experts, in order to deal with such cases.

A Wide Variety of Other Personal Problems

Still other kinds of cases will require the help of trained social workers. A good many veterans will have tuberculosis or other diseases requiring continued hospitalization. Welfare agencies must assist in discovering them and in making plans for their families. In other cases, veterans will be unable or unwilling to work at the jobs they can get, and they and their families will come to the attention of the relief agencies in that manner, because they are indigent. But here also the real problem will be that of reconstructing the veteran's attitudes and his system of personal relationships.

Such cases as we have mentioned will call for the services of a small army of social workers to devote themselves exclusively to the problems of veterans and their families. Amateurs, no matter how well intentioned, cannot handle such cases; in fact, they are certain to do harm, more harm than good; about as certain as if, never having been near a College of Medicine, they went around indiscriminately performing appendectomies with butcher knives. It requires great skill to minister to a mind diseased, and great discipline, too; and unfortunately the number of persons trained in such skills and such disciplines is very limited. We should begin at once to train a large number of social workers for the express purpose of dealing with these problems of the post-war world.

As a further step, we must attempt to accustom the people in the middle economic groups to accept assistance in their own personal problems. The rich, in urban areas, are already accustomed to help from the psychoanalysts, while the poor receive it from the welfare agencies; but people of the middle economic group cannot afford psychoanalysis and hesitate to apply to the family societies. The solution is a family clinic that charges a modest fee for professional advice. Such clinics already exist, and some of them are said to be quite successful.

After we have turned over as many as possible of our cases to the professionals, there will still be many aspects of such cases in which amateurs will necessarily be involved: hence, widespread public understanding of the veteran problem will be highly desirable. Employers will do well to make a study of veteran psychology in order to prepare themselves for the peculiar attitudes that they are certain to encounter in the next few years, and other persons must study the problem for other reasons.

A type of case rather frequently reported to the writer illustrates the need for community understanding of veterans. A man recently discharged from the services is employed as a teacher; he is effective, and does his job well, but he proves to have an ungovernable temper, and his language is sometimes unfit for the classroom. Obviously it is the task of the principal to work with such a man, and of the community to give him a reasonable period of time to recover his balance.

Likewise the wife or mother of a veteran will not be able to delegate her function to a social worker, nor will she wish to do so. If she can gain an understanding of his condition, she may be able to help him along the road to recovery. She must try to learn, as well as she can, being a woman and a civilian, what it feels like to be a veteran, and she must thoroughly realize that the boy who comes back is not the boy who went away. She must give him time to find his bearings again, to rest and recover; she must make him feel secure again, must tolerate his outbursts, and forbear to lecture him for his eccentricities and strange habits. Above all she must give him lavish—and undemanding—affection, for part of his emotional maladjustment arises from his love-starved condition. But this love she gives him must expect no immediate return from the man whose sickness is his soul. A great part of the problem is to reestablish the free flow of communication and of emotional give and take.

In particular, parents of a veteran must recognize that they no longer have the right to supervise his behavior or to censor either his habits or his morals. Even in normal times differences of opinion on morality are a chief source of conflict between the generations; the unmarried boy often seems wild to his parents, but when that boy has been a soldier he is apt to seem inconceivably depraved. Perhaps a veteran who has learned to depend upon tobacco returns to the home of parents who believe that anyone who smokes has taken a long step on the road to hell. The parents must choose between the attempt, which is almost certain to be ineffectual, to get him to stop smoking, and the opportunity to restore a pleasant and mutually satisfying relationship with their son. If they comment on the smoking, preach to him, pray with him, scold him, he will still not stop smoking but he will rebel against his parents and probably leave home. The same is true of other vices that parents may find even harder to accept. A boy may be only nineteen, but if he has been in a war he will never again accept very much moral supervision from his parents or anyone else.

The Disabled at Home: Stoicism or Realism?

The case of the disabled veteran who must return to wife or mother in a crippled condition presents inescapable problems whose singular pathos cannot escape the person who gives even passing notice to the matter. Certainly every wife or mother of a mangled man would like to know what she can do to help him through his terrible period of readjustment. The present tendency seems to be to advise her to receive him casually, without emotion. This doubtless has its good points, but it is certainly dangerous.

An administrative officer at Halloran General Hospital, who himself had suffered and overcome a disability, recently stated a set of rules of behavior for the families of disabled veterans. They follow:

> Be casual. An initial expression of sympathy is to be expected, but don't dwell on it.
> Get all the false feeling of frustration—yours and his—out of the way immediately.
> Be hardboiled, to his face at least. If the man understands the reason for this attitude, he will regard it as a service.
> Be on the alert to discourage any tendency toward an invalid complex. Encourage him to go on and be the useful citizen he would have been if he had not been hurt.
> Recognize the fact that whatever differences exist are purely physical, that they in no way make him a different person.[3]

3 Reported by Frances Mendelson in The New York Herald Tribune, April 30, 1944.

These rules are in accord with the current tradition. They are based upon sound psychological understanding of the harm that can be done to a disabled veteran by an over-solicitous family, but they have their point of danger in that they overlook the very great possibility of carrying this casualness, this bravery, too far. Both the disabled veteran and his family must react adequately to his handicap. They must face it and not try to pretend that it does not exist. They must mourn for his loss and win emancipation from their grief at the cost of pain. If a person tries to put such things out of his mind, they fester in the unconscious and produce neurotic symptoms. It is precisely from such ways of meeting situations, such often admirable courage, such militant ignoring, that neurosis arises; for the neurotic is only a person who has carried some virtue to such an extreme that it has become a vice.

If one dared to give it, a sounder pattern of advice to the wife or mother of the disabled veteran would be:

> If your son comes home disabled or disfigured, cry! That is the natural and human thing to do. Let him cry too. Let everybody cry. Cry until you get it out of your systems. Then when you have had your cry, and he has admitted and expressed his own heartache, try to pick up the pieces of your lives and put them together again. Admit the disability. Get used to it. Then help your son to build up the best possible life with what he has. This will rule out all possibility of pampering or encouraging invalidism. But do not start being hard-boiled until you have been sympathetic.

The disabled veteran who is too brave, so that he refuses to recognize his disability, runs the risk of building up inner tension that will sooner or later put him in a mental hospital. The wife or mother who tries to overlook a disability can easily spoil a relationship by imposing upon herself and the veteran a mental strain greater than either can bear. The wife of a disfigured man stated her courageous but mistaken policy in these words: "If a man is disfigured, don't ever mention that fact to him. Imagine how it would hurt him! And above all, concentrate on what is left, not what is gone." Her psychology was short-sighted. By excluding such a fact, obvious to them both and very much in the minds of both, from their conversation, she will end by making the disfigurement—the horrible never-to-be-mentioned thing that both think about all the time—far more important to both of them than it would otherwise be. The workable solution would be: Accept the disfigurement. Talk about it until you have finished. Grieve over it until you both feel better. Refer to it when necessary, and never let it get to the point where it cannot be referred to. Then it will slowly recede from the center of the field of consciousness and you may both forget it in a healthy manner, as you forget things that you take for granted and toward which you have no emotion.

It is absolutely necessary that the disabled veteran and his family should mourn in order to free their minds from his handicap. As long as the disability or disfigurement is not faced, it will dominate consciousness. The disabled veteran must say to himself, "I am crippled. I have lost an arm. Nothing can ever bring it back. It is a great loss," and then he must give suitable expression to his sorrow. Only then, perhaps after months of the psychic pain of grief, can he go on to other things with a mind free and void of tenseness. There is no recovery without an intermediate state of unhappiness. Nothing can cure grief but grief itself.

For the disabled veteran who mourns but not too long—as for the widow who weeps but not forever—the prognosis is good. He will recover, to accept his disability and to lead a calm and useful life. But if he does not mourn, if he does not get his sorrow out of his system by expressing it, if he does not learn to face the changed reality, his emotional life will be lastingly dominated by his disability. This is the risk we run by counselling casualness and bravery. Courage the disabled veteran must have in any case, and his wife or mother must have courage also, but perhaps, for the sake of their mental hygiene, they should not show it until they have purged themselves with weeping.

Helping the Veteran
By Sending Him
Back to School

P RESENT-DAY soldiers are, as we have seen, lukewarm about going back to school, and yet education has certain advantages over every other method of rehabilitation. These advantages are so great that it seems the part of wisdom to attempt to overcome the veterans' indifference to education and to rely upon the schools as a principal agency for restoring them to their place in society.

Better than any other kind of experience, schooling can restore the veteran to the communicative system of society. That is what education is: communication. And even if it works poorly it communicates more than a man is likely to acquire by any other method, more, that is, of the kind of thing that we should like to have our veterans learn. If it is at all effective, education opens up new worlds of thought and involves the student in a wider system of communication than he has ever before experienced.

An educational environment will be good for veterans because it will give them a chance to recover their emotional balance. The school environment can be adapted to the veteran's needs, allowing him to take the kind of courses he requires in the combination he desires, permitting him a light or a heavy schedule, encouraging him to express and to develop his own unique individuality. A work environment can never be so adapted; a man in industry must submit to the discipline of the job, accepting it or rebelling against it. The pressures, furthermore, of an educational environment are not harsh, and the penalties for failure not crushing. School-teachers, for all their faults, understand that their job is to foster the growth of personality, while employers, rightly enough, usually refuse to accept any such responsibility. A school, therefore, with its infinite adaptability, is a nearly ideal place for a veteran who is travelling the steep road back to civilian society.

If a veteran suffers a disadvantage in competition because
military service, a properly planned educational program wi
able him to overcome that handicap. Thus it may come about
some veterans will be able to take up occupations from which
expense of a long training period would have excluded them
normal times.

If after the war it is necessary to provide employment for some
millions by make-work devices, an educational program would be
an almost ideal outlet for surplus labor—non-competitive, as regards its relation to private industry, requiring little investment of
capital, capable of being curtailed without loss when the economy
may require it, and the best way of conserving for a future time
the productivity of temporarily unusable labor. Schooling, furthermore, would return the laborers to the economic world in small
assimilable driblets, and would thus not glut the market.

The Great Potentialities of Veteran Education

Better than any other rehabilitation program, education can
work on the veteran's attitudes, helping him slowly to overcome
the bitterness and resentment that may otherwise interfere with
his adjustment throughout life. It often comes about that the
teacher's dry didacticism, his objectivity and disinterestedness, his
repetitiousness, are more persuasive than any eloquence. The
teacher traditionally presents facts and leaves the individual free
to make up his own mind, but by so doing he often commands the
minds of others more effectively than can the demagogue. Furthermore, the better the student's mind, the more it is subject to the
type of influence that the teacher exerts.

Lastly, education and retraining are the only possible solution for
many disabled veterans. If a man has received an injury that inca-
pacitates him for one occupation, train him for another in which
this disability will not be a handicap. Such a solution is in every
way superior to the previous device of pensioning him off and thus
depriving him of the psychic rewards of work, productivity, and a
career.

There are certain obstacles in the way of using education as
a rehabilitative device for veterans. Veterans are, as we have seen,
lukewarm in their attitude toward education. This is a poser. But

we should note that the survey previously quoted deals with the attitudes of soldiers still in the service and that there is at least an even chance that these men will change their opinions when they become veterans. Another obstacle is that the schools and colleges have suffered serious deterioration as a result of the damage done by war. College faculties have been raided by many agencies, while the supply of recruits has been cut off. This situation can probably be best met by training veterans who have already had some advanced work to become teachers of other veterans.

It seems reasonable to hope that in spite of their present lukewarm attitude, large numbers of veterans can in fact be reached through education. Benjamin Fine, education editor of the New York Times, recently reported on his survey of the opinions and attitudes of more than 1,000 veterans of the present war who had already returned to college. He found that many were working with great earnestness on their studies, but he stated that the schools should teach "what the veterans want, not what the schools or the Government think they should be taught." [1] We should add that even if we could reach no more than five per cent of the veterans through education this would be very much worth doing, because a great proportion of the leaders of the veteran group would be certain to be included in the educable five per cent.

As to the method of supplying educational opportunities to veterans, school authorities seem agreed that the educational program for veterans should not operate by means of contracts that would put education under the control of the Federal government. A great number of scholarships to be awarded to veterans best qualified and most in need would serve the purpose much better; such scholarships should, of course, cover both tuition and living expenses. Loans have been advocated for this purpose, but they entail the great disadvantage of forcing young men to begin their occupational life heavily in debt. The history of loans to veterans indicates that many such loans would never be repaid, and that they would constitute a political football for a generation.

[1] The New York Times, May 7, 1944. In a later and more extensive report, Fine summarized his findings as follows: "Former service men who have returned to the college and university campus are more serious-minded than they were as civilian students, are more interested in technical and vocational courses leading to immediate jobs than they are in the humanities, do not want to be segregated into special schools or departments, and are finding it rather difficult to readjust their lives from the excitement of the battlefront to the peace and quiet of the classroom." (The New York Times, June 4, 1944.)

It would be most unwise to establish separate institutions for the education of veterans. It would be difficult to staff such institutions, or to supervise them in order to make sure that they do work of standard quality. It would open the door to political corruption. Worst of all, it would defeat the main purpose of veteran education, which is to restore the veteran to communication with the rest of society. The best practice would be to make full use of the educational assets and traditions of existing institutions. We may feel sure that the faculties and administrators of these institutions will display great adaptability in dealing with the needs of veterans.

A few hints as to methods to be used in educating the veteran may not be amiss. The approach should be that of adult education. Regardless of his age or educational level, the veteran is always an adult in certain respects.[2] He must participate more than the school-child in planning and carrying through his education, and he must be free from personal supervision. Education, furthermore, must follow his tastes and interests.

Special Methods for Teaching Student-Veterans

It would certainly be a good idea to start the veteran's education with the veteran and his own attitudes. Let him study himself, then learn to see himself in the perspective of the veteran problem in general. Encourage him to express his grievances, go into details, elaborate on them; then formulate reasonable plans for the rest of his life, and plan in such a way that his life will not be marred by his own lasting bitterness. Encourage the veteran to work out methods for dealing with the veteran problem in society. Encourage him to discuss and argue until he recaptures the mastery of words. This sort of discussion could be conducted on any level

[2] Fine recounts the following incidents: "Upon being interviewed by the dean, one boy said, 'I am too old to sit in the classroom; I feel out of place.' He had just returned from grueling campaigns at Tarawa and Guadalcanal. 'How old are you?' he was asked. 'I'll be twenty-one next December,' came the reply. A similar instance took place at Syracuse University. A veteran came to his adviser and said, 'One thing that disturbs me is that I am in with a lot of boys who are so much younger that I am.' An investigation showed that of the thirteen boys in the house, four were 19—the same age as the returned veteran who had seen action in the South Pacific—three were under 19 and six were older than he. But he felt more mature than his elders. Emotionally he was more than 19." The New York Times, June 4, 1944.

of education or intelligence, and should be a part of the socialization of every veteran.

This method seems so promising that it ought also to be employed among veterans who do not return to school. Its basic psychology is simple but effective; it consists of inducing the veteran to gain perspective on his own problems by looking at them in a generalized way and viewing them from the standpoint of society. As soon as the veteran has learned to see the veteran problem as a problem, and his own behavior and attitudes as a part of that problem, he has taken an important step in assimilating himself to and restoring communication with the rest of society. This method of working on the veteran's attitudes through discussion could be employed by any group or community which can supply competent leadership for such discussion groups.

While the veteran's education must allow great freedom, it must also involve discipline. Though it may seem strange that a man should still be in need of learning discipline after a period of military service, it is nevertheless true. The discipline of military life, unfortunately but necessarily, is largely external, in contrast to the self-direction and self-control which civilian life demands. Discipline of the veteran must aim at restoring his dominion over himself. In psychoanalytic language, it must rebuild the Super-Ego.

It goes without saying that in educating veterans we must make use of the tests and the apparatus of guidance which the last few years have brought forth in such profusion. The education of veterans is sure to be something of a mass job, so that any possible short-cuts of technique for fitting square pegs into square holes should receive full use. But such mass techniques should be supplemented by case methods as well. The group of veterans, crippled by subjection to an impersonal machine, can be brought back into society only by means of human contacts.

Schools that assume the responsibility of educating veterans will do well to increase their facilities for hygienic and psychiatric guidance. If facilities permit, every veteran returning to school or college should receive a physical examination and a psychiatric interview at the time of enrollment. Since the need for guidance will be great, it would also be wise to instruct the teachers of the veterans, in veteran psychology and psychiatry.

The most urgent educational task is the retraining of disabled veterans. The policy of reeducating the disabled veteran in some trade or profession in which the disability will not be a handicap was adopted during World War I. Though the idea was sound, the administration of the program was bad. We are now in a position to profit from the mistakes and experiments of the past. We should employ the most advanced testing procedures in order to guide veterans into occupations for which they are fitted by skills and attitudes. We should select schools for trainees with great care, and make sure that they give competent instruction. We should follow up the trainees, strive to keep them at their studies by the various persuasions and inducements known to teachers and to deans of men. The program should be integrated with the needs of industry, rules of labor unions, and state laws in order to make sure that men will in fact be able to practice their trades after they have completed their training. In all this work we should attempt to improve the veteran's attitudes as well as to give him skills. We should teach him to live as well as to make a living.

As to the curriculum, it seems to be generally agreed that returning veterans will wish to stress training in the practical arts; at least that is their present temper. No doubt the veterans are right in this preference, but we should attempt, in many cases, to dissuade them from making their training too narrowly and immediately practical. If a boy is college material, he should go to college for four years and not to a trade school for six months—if we can persuade him to do so, and if the girl he wants to marry is not too clamorous in her demands.

In planning the education of the veteran, we should not forget that the so-called humanities, the humanistic studies, literature and the arts (in which should certainly be included the social sciences which are a modern form of the humanities), have a special importance for him, whether he knows it or not. More than other subjects, these "impractical" studies, which interpret man's life and acquaint the student with the thoughts and written dreams of men, can help the veteran to overcome the effects of his long-time isolation from society. Better than any other studies, the humanities can work upon the veteran's unwholesome attitudes and help him to become a citizen in a world of peace once more.

What We Can Do
For the Veteran Now:
A Summary

W E have surveyed the veteran problem and assessed the possibilities of dealing with it by various methods. It is now time to summarize some of our results and set down such concrete suggestions as seem to be justified by our study. It should be emphasized that these are highly tentative suggestions. We make no claim that these ideas are original or that they will suffice to dispose of the problem once and for all. We record them in the hope that they may prove helpful in the process of learning how to take care of our veterans.

Essentials of a Veterans' Program

It is clear that, if we are to handle the problem of the returning veteran, we must make a radical change in our thinking. We must stop thinking about "veterans' benefits," and begin thinking about a veterans' program. The difference is essential.

A veterans' program is a set of coordinated activities designed to restore the veteran to his place in society. Obviously, such a program is what we need.

Veterans' benefits, on the other hand, are gratuities or concessions to the veteran. They are based upon the idea that the veteran has been unjustly treated and the nation owes him something. They are granted, in a haphazard, senseless way, because veterans are useless and needy and men's hearts are warm, or merely because veterans are politically powerful. It would be better for the world, and for the veteran, if the concept of veterans' benefits had never been invented.

A veterans' program, to be worthy of the name, would be prompt and timely, and it would give adequate aid, once and for all; unfortunately, veterans' benefits do none of these things. A program aims at rehabilitation and the complete restoration of the veteran to normal life. When its work is accomplished, a veterans' program will come to an end; but veterans' benefits, as we know, have a way of going on forever. Furthermore, if there were an adequate veterans' program, there would be no need of, and no excuse for, veterans' benefits.

When we evaluate the hodge-podge of veterans' benefits that we have, in the light of the veterans' program that we ought to have, we see that many of these benefits are useless or worse than useless. Pensions, with a few exceptions, are valueless as a solution of the veteran problem, and sometimes, because of their pauperizing effect, they are a positive hindrance. Bonuses and gratuities, except for dismissal pay, are equally useless. Tax exemptions are likewise of little value. Mere concessions or privileges do not help the veteran very much.

If, then, we attempt to frame a veterans' program that will be adequate to restore the veteran to society, how shall we go about it? Various agencies must contribute, each in its own way:

The Federal government must, of course, play a crucial rôle. It must, in the first place, so manage the national economy, with the cooperation of business leaders, as to assure full employment, a matter outside the scope of this book but essential in solving the veteran problem. It must give every veteran adequate dismissal pay, and assistance in finding a job, as well as support during the period of job-seeking and economic readjustment. Further, it must supply guidance during this period of crucial decisions. The Federal government must assume financial responsibility for the discovery, care, and rehabilitation of the disabled, as well as the support and possibly the retraining of their dependents. It must also develop methods and procedures for dealing with some hundreds of thousands of psychological cripples.

The Federal government must supply financial backing for an extensive program of reeducation, so designed as to reach as large a number of veterans as possible, but must not set up separate educational institutions for veterans or seek to dominate existing institutions. Justice dictates that veterans who do not obtain education or trade training at government expense should receive something roughly equivalent in some not easily expendable form, such as a paid-up life insurance policy with a limited borrowing capacity. The Federal government should also assist veterans through loans to purchase homes or farms, and to establish businesses or professional practices. The program of governmental life insurance should be continued, as it is certain to be, because of its encouragement to thrift. Veterans' preference in civil service is not only politically inevitable, but also, within limits, a useful device for veteran rehabilitation.

The field of operation of State governments in a veterans' program is much more limited. They should abstain from bonuses and from permanent tax exemptions, on the theory that the veteran will receive ample justice without such concessions. They should conduct a search for cases of disability among demobilized veterans, and give aid in pressing claims. They should cooperate in the task of veteran education through the State-supported educational institutions, but should resist the temptation to establish separate institutions for veterans. They should supervise the organization of local communities for returning veterans, and arrange for State-wide organization of veteran social work. The field of small loans to veterans might also be a proper sphere of operation for State governments.

As previously stated, local communities must bear much of the responsibility for veteran rehabilitation, depending upon Federal financial support where necessary. *Each community should organize now* to help veterans find jobs, plan educational careers, choose vocations, press claims for disabilities, and provide small loan services. The local community must also adapt its educational agencies to the needs of veterans. It should also, where possible, provide help and guidance for the many veterans' organizations certain to spring up after the war.

Case-working agencies must prepare to assume heavy burdens in helping veterans in their personal relationships, and to develop new skills for dealing with a very difficult set of clients. Social workers must also play a prominent part in the task of post-war community organization, to help veterans and to deal with the generally chaotic conditions of the post-war world.

Veterans' organizations should prepare to receive dynamic new elements into their membership and to meet the competition of new and lively organizations among the veterans of World War II.

A principal contribution of veterans' organizations in the next few years will be to see that aid given to veterans is timely, adequate, and properly administered. The time when the veteran needs help is in the years immediately following a war, and this is the time when he is usually neglected. It is up to the veterans' organizations to supply the necessary pressure to assure that this does not happen.

It is quite clear that we do not as yet know how to do all the things which are here set down as desirable. In many important matters, we must learn by experience or depend upon further study and research to show us the way. How this research might best be planned, set in motion, and coordinated is discussed in the following chapter, the epilogue.

The Cost of Saving the Men Who Fought for Us

The costs of our post-war program for veterans are certain to be great. A recent business letter estimates the monetary costs of veterans' care in the post-war years at from three to five billion dollars a year, adding that a "Veterans' Deal" is coming to replace the New Deal in those years. Included in this estimate are such items as hospital care ($217,000,000), pensions, adjusted compensation, (at a minimum of one billion and a maximum of three and a half billion dollars), unemployment compensation, and education ($600,000,000). Expenditures of state and municipal governments, which are certain to be heavy, are not included in this estimate.

Such estimates are useful only in giving us a conception of the size of our problem. They are not based upon an attempt to plan a really adequate veterans' program, but merely upon existing or proposed legislation, which is at best a structure of contradictions. An adequate rehabilitation program might cost more in the early years than proposed measures on behalf of veterans, but in the end rehabilitation would certainly save money as well as lives.

Rehabilitation is preferable to legislative patchwork in our treatment of veterans, but we do not know how much it will cost. For various reasons, it is impossible to estimate with any accuracy the money costs of an adequate program for veterans. We shall not know how large our problem of disability is until some years after the end of the fighting; service-connected psychoneurotic breakdowns will continue to occur for many years after the end of the war. Nor do we as yet know enough about the art of rehabilitation to be able to say just what specific benefits should be extended to veterans or what the veterans themselves will elect to take. Like doctors who do not too well understand some pathological condition of the human body, we must try out different remedies and treatments and use the medicines to which the patients seem to respond; the most useful medicines, to continue the figure, may be cheap, or they may be expensive, but we must not count the cost.

The cost of the veterans' program will also depend in part upon general economic conditions. If the removal of wartime controls produces a runaway inflation, that will affect the problem. If we are unable to solve satisfactorily the problem of post-war employment for veterans and war workers, that will make the readjustment of the veterans immensely more difficult and will call for increased expenditures.

In any case, while we should avoid emotionalism and excess in our provisions for veterans, we should not permit the expense of a program to be the decisive consideration. A father whose child is mortally ill should not bargain with the doctor or the hospital concerning the price of the treatments which may save the child's life. Our obligation to the veteran is equally overwhelming and in one way even stronger because we have sent these young men out to fight as an incident of national policy; we have elected to sacrifice this group in the supposed interest of the remainder of the nation. Every war produces a ruined generation. If we choose to go to war we must be willing to take the responsibility of compensating its victims. The obligation is clear, unavoidable, and almost limitless. *Whatever the price of rehabilitating our veterans, we must be prepared to pay it.*

Along this line, it is well to reflect that if the war should continue until 1950, we should defray the costs of that extended conflict without any question. If war costs $100,000,000,000 a year, we do not try to avoid payment of that astronomical sum. But if we are asked to spend the price of one year of war in restoring our veterans to their place in society, many persons would consider this claim exorbitant. *And yet it would be a wonderful bargain for us as a nation if we could really rehabilitate the veterans of the present war, and solve the veteran problem, at a cost not exceeding the cost of a single year of war.*

However clear our obligation to the veterans is in morality and ethics, we may suppose that there will be great opposition to paying the bill. Nations like to have wars. They do not like to pay for them. They especially dislike paying the men who have done the fighting, or taking adequate care of them, once the war has been won. From the time of the Carthaginians down to the present, history is full of swindled and neglected soldiers. The United States has been lavish in its expenditures on account of veterans, but it has never been generous or even fair to its veterans. It has never dealt justly with the veterans of a major war in the years immediately following a war, and once those years have passed little that is constructive can be done with any group of veterans. Apparently our national psychology reacts sharply to the emotional spree of a war: we feel guilty and ashamed and disillusioned, we feel so guilty toward the veterans that we do not permit ourselves to think about them.

After the war, people will no doubt say that an adequate veteran program would bankrupt the country. They will be wrong. A program which will restore the veterans to productivity will be cheap at almost any price. To illustrate this point, let us take some entirely hypothetical figures. Suppose that the present war leaves us 3,000,000 disabled and handicapped veterans. We could pension them off at a hundred dollars a month, and that would cost $3,600,000,000 a year. At the end of ten years, we should have spent thirty-six billions of dollars, and the men would still be disabled. Let us suppose, however, that we rehabilitate these men at the fantastically high cost of $10,000 a man. That would mean an expenditure of thirty billion dollars, but in a very few years the veterans would have contributed a vastly greater sum to the national income. Rehabilitation would still be a good investment if it cost $25,000 a man.

The same arguments hold for other than disabled veterans. Millions of men, without having any actual disability, will be less useful than they might have been if they had never gone to war. Their trouble, in many cases, is in their attitudes that unfit them for civilian society. If we can devise a program that will enable the veterans to overcome these attitudes, the veterans themselves will repay the costs of the program many times over in the years to come.

We have deliberately put the case in cold-blooded, economic terms. If we think in terms of human life rather than in terms of dollars, the case is immensely stronger. Whatever we may do to prevent it, the present war will produce many millions of blasted lives—has already done so, in fact. Anything which we can do to reduce this damage will prove to be a good social investment.

The cost of solving the veteran problem will undoubtedly be high. The cost of not solving it will be immensely higher. If we neglect our veterans, we shall pay for our heartlessness in a thousand different ways. Not one of us will be able to escape the impact on our own personal lives of the mass misery of millions of maladjusted veterans. Like disease, this misery will permeate the air we breathe and it will reach us in mysterious ways; no one will escape it. If their needs are unsatisfied, the veterans of this war may become an extremely dangerous political group. If we do not rehabilitate our veterans, we shall certainly have to pay immense sums for pensions, bonuses, and other useless handouts from which no one will derive any benefit. If, in the years immediately after the war, we do not give the veterans what they need and have a right to have, they will in later years force us to pay a heavy price for our thrift.

Epilogue: Rehabilitation
A New Social
Art to be Learned

I N order to deal with the veteran problem, we must create a new art, the art of rehabilitation. This art does not yet exist.

For the present, we must rely to some extent on trial and error, but that does not mean that we are as helpless as the rat in the maze or the cat in the box. We are not condemned to unguided empiricism. We know enough about the problem to make intelligent trials; we know in what general direction the solution lies. And we ought to be able to discover our errors quickly and to analyze them in such a way as to learn the proper lessons from them.

Contributions to the art of rehabilitation can and should come from many fields. Probably social workers have more to contribute than anyone else. They have perfected skills and disciplines for handling people. They have their wonderfully flexible arts of case work. They are beginning to learn how to handle groups. They have had some years of experience with veterans' relief, and know a great deal about veterans.

Important contributions may also be expected from other fields. Psychiatrists and psychoanalysts can supply many important clues to the understanding of the veteran. Psychologists can organize and summarize the results of tests and experiments in order to give us a picture of the group with which we have to deal. Historians, economists, political scientists, and sociologists will have something to say about the problem. Educational specialists have already produced workable plans for the reeducation of the veteran; we may depend upon the educators to be quick to learn and ready to subject their results to study and evaluation. Industry is also learning to deal with veterans, and the larger companies are organizing their learning in communicable form. Veterans' organizations have already accumulated a vast body of knowledge concerning veterans and their officers have developed certain skills to a high degree.

We already know something about the veteran problem, but it is not enough that this knowledge should exist; it must also be put together, it must be disseminated widely, and it must be applied. It is not enough for the psychiatrist to know that the shell-shocked veteran has a tendency toward explosive aggression; *everybody must know it in order to understand how to live with and treat such a man.* Other sorts of facts are known to specialists but not to any large proportion of even the highly literate public. The historian knows the history of pensions and of pension drives, perhaps knows also that deserving veterans are often neglected after a war. The social worker knows that it is wise and humane to make a search for cases of disability, and the story of the veterans' attitude of disillusion as recorded in the literature is known to many persons. As long as these facts are kept in solitary confinement in the minds of a few learned men, they can be of little use.

But put such facts as these together with a thousand others, puzzle out their significance, then shout this knowledge from the house-tops, and we shall begin to solve the veteran problem. Scholarship is not enough. We must synthesize and popularize if our knowledge is to be of any use. This book is intended to be a contribution, meager though it is, to this process of synthesis and popularization.

To put the matter in another way, we must understand the veteran before we can rehabilitate him. To understand the veteran, we must learn all that we can about him—his attitudes and habits, his behavior in past times—but we must couple this externalistic knowledge with that other sort of knowledge which can only come from inner sources, from the imagination. For the simplest and oldest method of psychology is still the best: It is to imagine what it would be like to be somebody else. We must understand the veteran by imagining what it would be like to be in his skin, borrow his eyes to see with, his heart to feel, his mind to recall the present and to think about the future. The tools with which to work in rehabilitating the veteran are in our selves, and the most useful of them is the sympathetic imagination.

When we have drawn on all available sources for what they can tell us about rehabilitation, when we have learned all that we can and imagined more, we shall still have to experiment, we shall still be forced to feel our way by trial and error. The important thing in this experimentation is to keep our objective clearly in mind and to evaluate every experiment strictly in terms of progress toward that end. The objective is to return the veteran "undamaged" to society. We must never lose sight of that goal or confuse it with any other good thing; nor must we ever accept the part of it for the whole. We must be flexible in methods, inflexible in goals.

Perhaps the most important step is to recognize at once that the veteran problem is one of the most important—if not the most critical—of our time. All devices of communication should be called upon to give publicity to the problem. Newspapers should devote columns to it. Radio speeches and the sermons of preachers should spread knowledge concerning it. There should be many college courses on the subject of veterans, some intended to give general understanding of the problem, others for the training of practitioners, yet others for the veterans themselves.

Particularly to be desired would be some great center of veteran research in which cooperative studies of the veteran problem could be carried on and the results of other researches synthesized and coordinated. In such a center doctors and psychiatrists could invent new methods to heal the minds and bodies of veterans, social workers could work out the best practices for veterans' relief and try to put the psychoneurotic veteran back on his feet, historians could inquire into the fate of veterans in the past, and economists, psychologists, sociologists, criminologists, and experts in government could carry on their appropriate researches. Such a center should be equipped with laboratories, extensive libraries, and all the apparatus of research. It should also have funds to subsidize researches to be carried on elsewhere; it should be responsible for encouraging veteran research in all fields and for recording its results. It should have a planning bureau to translate its results into action, a division of propaganda to disseminate its findings to the public.

For many years to come we shall spend several billion dollars annually on veterans. If the bill for the care of veterans is, say, five billion a year, then one ten-thousandth of that sum would suffice for the most elaborate kind of veteran research; one one-hundred-thousandth for the financing of more research than has ever been devoted to the problem in the past. Such research would pay for itself, perhaps literally, a million times over. The discovery of even a moderately effective method for dealing with the social, not sheerly medical, rehabilitation of the psychoneurotic veteran alone would be worth billions, many, many billions over the next three decades. If we had spent a million dollars on research in the years following World War I, or even, perhaps a hundred thousand, it would be worth billions today in money, and its value in human lives would be incalculable. But we spent almost nothing. *Billions for veterans' care, but not one cent to find out how to spend the billions intelligently!*

It would be possible to solve the veteran problem, but before it is solved, many men must study it over a period of years, and others must evaluate their results. We must build up a body of social knowledge centering around this great problem, a science of "Veteranology," analogous to criminology, which draws upon all fields of knowledge for help in solving its peculiar problems. This science of "Veteranology" must underlie the art of rehabilitation, at the same time contributing to it and emerging from it. Both the science and the art are for the future to discover.

THE END

Index

Index